UNDERSTANDING
AMERICAN GOVERNMENT
AND POLITICS

ST. DOMINIC'S SIXTH FORM COLLEGE

MANCHESTER
UNIVERSITY PRESS

UNDERSTANDING POLITICS

Series editor **DUNCAN WATTS**

Following the review of the national curriculum for 16–19 year olds, UK examining boards have introduced new specifications for first use in 2001 and 2002. A level courses will henceforth be divided into A/S level for the first year of sixth form studies, and the more difficult A2 level thereafter. The **Understanding Politics** series comprehensively covers the politics syllabuses of all the major examination boards, featuring a dedicated A/S level textbook and three books aimed at A2 students. The books are written in an accessible, user-friendly and jargon-free manner and will be essential to students sitting these examinations.

Understanding American government and politics

A guide for A2 politics students

DUNCAN WATTS

Manchester University Press

Manchester and New York

distributed exclusively in the USA by Palgrave

Copyright © Duncan Watts 2002

The right of Duncan Watts to be identified as the author of this work has been asserted by him in accordance with the Copyright, Design and Patents Act 1988.

Published by Manchester University Press
Oxford Road, Manchester M13 9NR, UK
and Room 400, 175 Fifth Avenue, New York, NY 10010, USA

Distributed exclusively in the USA by
Palgrave, 175 Fifth Avenue, New York,
NY 10010, USA

Distribued exclusively in Canada by
UBC Press, University of British Columbia, 2029 West Mall,
Vancouver, BC, Canada V6T 1Z2

British Library Cataloguing-in-Publication Data
A catalogue record for this book is available from the British Library

Library of Congress Cataloging-in-Publication Data applied for

ISBN 0 7190 6269 1   *hardback*
      0 7190 6074 5   *paperback*

First published 2002

10 09 08 07 06 05 04 03 02   10 9 8 7 6 5 4 3 2

Typeset by Northern Phototypesetting Co. Ltd, Bolton
Printed in Great Britain
by Bookcraft (Bath) Ltd, Midsomer Norton

Contents

10 Conclusion: the condition of American democracy 255

Comparative boxes: Britain and the United States

Acknowledgement

Manchester University Press and the Politics Association wish to thank Professor the Lord Norton of Louth for reading this text and for his helpful observations. Any errors are, of course, the responsibility of the author and/or publisher.

THE POLITICS ASSOCIATION

is a registered educational charity, committed to the diffusion of political knowledge and understanding. It produces a wide range of resources on government and politics, and on citizenship. Members receive the journal, *Talking Politics*, three times a year.

Further details can be obtained from the Politics Association, Old Hall Lane, Manchester, M13 0XT, Tel./Fax.: 0161 256 3906; email: politic@enablis.co.uk

US presidents and their parties

	President	Party	Term
1	George Washington (1732–99)	Federalist	1789–97
2	John Adams (1735–1826)	Federalist	1797–1801
3	Thomas Jefferson (1743–1826)	Democratic-Republican	1801–09
4	James Madison (1751–1836)	Democratic-Republican	1809–17
5	James Monroe (1758–1831)	Democratic-Republican	1817–25
6	John Quincy Adams (1767–1848)	Democratic-Republican	1825–29
7	Andrew Jackson (1767–1845)	Democrat	1829–37
8	Martin Van Buren (1782–1862)	Democrat	1837–41
9	William Henry Harrison (1773–1841)	Whig	1841
10	John Tyler (1790–1862)	Whig	1841–45
11	James K. Polk (1795–1849)	Democrat	1845–49
12	Zachary Taylor (1784–1850)	Whig	1849–50
13	Millard Fillmore (1800–74)	Whig	1850–53
14	Franklin Pierce (1804–69)	Democrat	1853–57
15	James Buchanan (1791–1868)	Democrat	1857–61
16	Abraham Lincoln (1809–65)	Republican	1861–65
17	Andrew Johnson (1808–75)	Union	1865–69
18	Ulysses S. Grant (1822–85)	Republican	1869–77
19	Rutherford B. Hayes (1822–93)	Republican	1877–81
20	James A. Garfield (1831–81)	Republican	1881
21	Chester A. Arthur (1830–86)	Republican	1881–85
22	Grover Cleveland (1837–08)	Democrat	1885–89

President	Party	Term
23 Benjamin Harrison (1833–1901)	Republican	1889–93
24 Grover Cleveland (1837–1908)	Democrat	1893–97
25 William McKinley (1843–1901)	Republican	1897–01
26 Theodore Roosevelt (1858–1919)	Republican	1901–09
27 William Howard Taft (1857–1930)	Republican	1909–13
28 Woodrow Wilson (1856–1924)	Democrat	1913–21
29 Warren G. Harding (1865–1923)	Republican	1921–23
30 Calvin Coolidge (1871–1933)	Republican	1923–29
31 Herbert Hoover (1874–1964)	Republican	1929–33
32 Franklin Delano Roosevelt (1882–1945)	Democrat	1933–45
33 Harry S. Truman (1884–1972)	Democrat	1945–53
34 Dwight D. Eisenhower (1890–1969)	Republican	1953–61
35 John F. Kennedy (1917–63)	Democrat	1961–63
36 Lyndon B. Johnson (1908–73)	Democrat	1963–69
37 Richard M. Nixon (1913–94)	Republican	1969–74
38 Gerald R. Ford (b. 1913)	Republican	1974–77
39 Jimmy Carter (b. 1924)	Democrat	1977–81
40 Ronald Reagan (b. 1911)	Republican	1981–89
41 George H. W. Bush (b. 1924)	Republican	1989–93
42 William Jefferson Clinton (b. 1946)	Democrat	1993–2001
43 George Walton Bush (b. 1946)	Republican	2001–

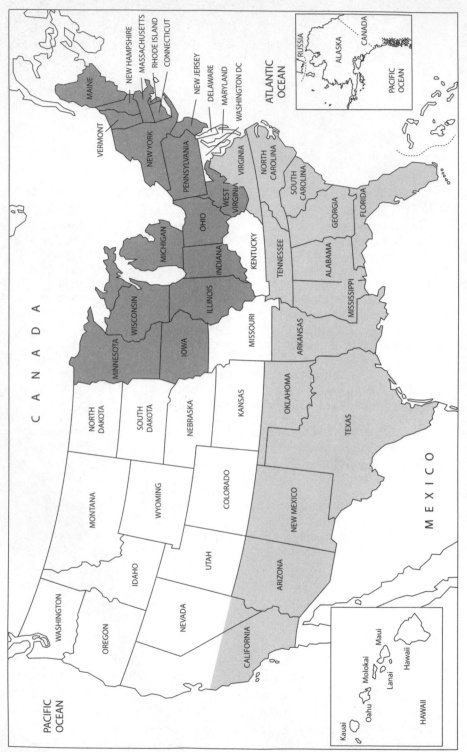

Map of the US: the sun-belt ▨ and the frost-belt ▨

Introduction: the setting of American politics   **1**

A knowledge of the social and economic environment of any country is important in achieving an understanding of its government and politics. Many students will know little of American human and economic geography. So here we are concerned with finding out more about the influences on American politics, and the factors which influence attitudes and events today.

In this section, we are concerned with examining those features of the United States, ranging from its size and landscape to its population and religion, which have a bearing on its political activity. Given its vast extent, it is inevitably a country of great diversity, and differences in race, gender, religion and social class have an impact on the way in which voters behave.

Geographically, the United States is a huge land mass, exceeding that of all but three nations in the world: Canada, China and Russia. It borders Canada in the North and Mexico in the South, and on its west and east coast lie two oceans, the Pacific and the Atlantic, respectively. It is a land endowed with considerable resources, ranging from coal to precious metals, and it is also rich in farmland. Nature has been generous and enabled America to develop as a country remarkably self-sufficiently. Areas have their own regional economic concerns, and political attitudes reflect these regional differences. Some parts of the country are well suited to ranching and agriculture, others to mining or manufacturing. The political perspectives of the automobile worker in Detroit are far removed from those of the farmers of Kansas, for example.

Geographical isolation

The country is not only vast, but it is also geographically rather isolated. Having only two immediate neighbours, it faces little threat of invasion or conquest. Moreover, as it is cut off from other continents, it has been able to keep itself aloof from many struggles in Asia, Europe and elsewhere, unless they are conflicts where key American interests are perceived to be involved. Between the two world wars, the country adopted an isolationist stance, whereas after World War II it assumed a global role including the leadership of the free, Western world. At times, as in Vietnam, it has chosen to involve itself in conflict, and during the era of the Cold War its military machine was much involved in overseas struggle. Sometimes, it has been more reluctant to meddle in other countries' affairs, and this has enabled it to develop its own distinctive political traditions and concentrate on its own internal development.

Isolationist voices have always periodically reared their head, particularly from politicians more remote from the European scene (such as in the Midwest). After the experience of Vietnam and with the Cold War over, there is again a greater wish for America to 'play in its own backyard'. Many Americans display a sense of anxiety when presidents take them into commitments, such as those in Somalia and Bosnia, from which little credit is likely to emerge.

Sectional differences

Of all the sectional differences within the US, the most obvious is that which separates the American South from the rest of the nation. Traditionally, the South has been more rural and agricultural and the North more industrial, but the issue which was at the root of the distinction between them was slavery. Lincoln and the Republicans were opposed to slavery, and it was over this issue that the eleven southern states broke away to form the Confederacy in 1860–61. Their secession led to the Civil War, fought between the forces of the Union and those of the Confederalists.

The secession made the Democrats the party of the South, and after the Civil War was over the distinction of North and South remained. These differences were strengthened by the policies pursued during the era of Reconstruction, by differing economic interests, and above all by the continuing racial problem. Today, a further difference can be ascribed to military establishments, for most of the military facilities are based in the South which tends to mean that on matters of national defence the South takes a more conservative viewpoint.

In religion, the South remains distinctive. There are strong Protestant leanings in the 'Bible Belt' and religious **fundamentalism** is widespread. Above all, however, it is the treatment of the American blacks (Afro-Americans) which has

fundamentalism
The interpretation of every word of the Bible as being literally true.

proved to be the key issue over the last century. Although black slaves were freed after the Civil War, they were still the victims of segregation, intimidation and discrimination; they were long denied basic rights, such as the franchise (rights to vote). Since the 1960s, things have greatly changed. In 1960, in a southern state such as Mississippi, only one in twenty blacks were registered to vote. Today, many more blacks than whites remain unregistered, but that is true all over the country and it is not specifically a southern issue. With the advent of more civil rights and the spread of educational opportunity, the South has become less backward even if it still lags behind the rest of the nation in educational achievement and per capita income.

The South has changed significantly over the last generation. It is no longer true to speak of the 'solid South', as the Democrats used to do. It is now less cohesive as a society, and certainly less committed to the Democratic cause. In recent presidential elections, the Republicans have outperformed the Democrats, and in 2000 Al Gore was able to make little headway; in state and local elections, however, the Democrats continue to do well. White voters seem to have been disenchanted with Democratic presidential aspirants, but the voting rights won by blacks have been a reinforcement of the Democratic position, especially at local level.

Compared to the South, no other region has such a cohesive identity, but there are nevertheless other sectional differences. The West has tended to be more isolationist (as it is further from Western Europe), as well as more committed to the alleged virtues of rugged individualism and less federal intervention. Such a sense of self-sufficiency made this obvious territory for Ronald Reagan in the 1980s, for he was identified with the attitudes and values of the West.

California is a state with a special importance, not least because of its 54 representatives in Congress. No candidate for the presidency has much chance of success unless he or she can win its vote in the Electoral College – Nixon, Reagan and Clinton, among others, all carried the state. In 1992, it was suffering badly from recession which helped to tilt it away from the Republican incumbent and towards the Democrats.

The population and where it lives

The diverse American population has grown by leaps and bounds as the figures below indicate. In 2002, there are more than 280 million people living in the US, and projections suggest that within fifty years that the figure will increase by more than 100 million. Not only is the population growing, it is also ageing. The median age of the population is in the mid-thirties, the highest it has ever been. The number of elderly Americans (counted as being those over 65) is now approaching 12 per cent of the total. This is politically significant for politicians because the political outlook and concerns of this aging population are likely to be a factor in determining election results and shaping public policy in future decades.

The growth in population

Year	Population
1900	76,212,168
1930	123,202,660
1960	179,323,175
1990	248,709,873

The population is not growing at an even rate across the country. The population of the West (particularly California and Nevada) is increasing most rapidly, followed by the South. By contrast, the Northeast and Midwest are barely increasing in size, as many inhabitants migrate to the South and West. More Americans today are seeking the warmth and other attractions of the so-called sun-belt (the bottom 40 per cent of the country), and deserting the frost-belt, those states in the Northeast (see map on p. xii). States such as Florida have an appeal to retired peoples but also to those tempted by the job opportunities in an area of new industries and substantial economic growth. As a result of this trend, documented by the census in 1990, the Northeast lost 15 seats in Congress, whereas the South/Southwest gained 17.

That same census revealed that nine of the largest cities had lost inhabitants in the previous decade, a continuation of an established pattern of suburbanisation which has characterised the last few decades. For many years, America was a predominantly rural society, but in the late nineteenth and early twentieth century, there was a movement of population from rural to urban parts as workers sought jobs in the expanding towns and cities. More recently, the trend has been away from urban centres and out to suburban areas, as new housing developments have grown up and new connecting roads have been built. In Los Angeles, four times as many people live in the metropolitan outskirts as actually in the city itself. Members of the better-off white community of some city centres have been keen to move out, so that their offspring can attend an all-white school and avoid the prospect of being 'bussed' to an integrated one. The population that remains in city centres now tends to comprise poorer whites, blacks and assorted racial minority groups. This is fertile territory for the Democratic Party. The suburbs (although they vary greatly in wealth and quality of life) tend to be places where the predominantly white people enjoy higher income levels, and vote Republican.

Fourteen of the cities that have a population exceeding 100,000 now have a black majority, places ranging from Atlanta in Georgia to Detroit in Michigan, from Gary in Indiana to Washington DC. Apart from the Afro-American population, there are many other racial minorities in this land of immigrants, ranging from Asians to Hispanics (persons of Spanish-speaking descent, who can technically be of any race) and Jews.

Main groups in the population of the United States
(rounded to nearest million)

Year	White	Black	Hispanic	Total
1970	178,000,000	23,000,000	n/a	201,000,000
1980	180,000,000	27,000,000	15,000,000	222,000,000
1990	187,000,000	31,000,000	22,000,000	240,000,000
2000	212,000,000	36,000,000	35,000,000	283,000,000

Figures adapted from those provided by US Census Bureau.

Racial groups

As the table indicates, some 75 per cent of Americans are white and 13 per cent are black. The 36 million people who make up the latter category have for much of the last one hundred years sought to improve their position in American society. Freed as a result of the Civil War, **the black** (mostly Afro-American in origin) **population** was long denied full participation and recognition. Its struggle to advance its position and achieve civil rights has been an important feature of postwar politics, and the freedom rides and sit-ins, the marches and boycotts, posed problems for white Americans as they finally had to concede a greater measure of equal treatment than they had ever contemplated before.

Until the twentieth century, most blacks lived in the South, and 45 per cent still do so; the population of some states is more than a quarter black. However, early in the twentieth century many left that area to seek a better lifestyle in the large cities of the West, Midwest and Northeast. Washington DC has the highest proportion of blacks (66 per cent of the population), but many other cities have a large Afro-American population, much of which is often to be found in poorer quarters. In places as far apart as Los Angeles and Detroit, riots have from time to time broken out in the ghettos (densely populated slum areas, inhabited by a deprived minority group) as a result of deprivation and discrimination.

Issues of racial division and race relations have bedevilled America for much of its short history, and although blacks have achieved greater rights and political power they tend to be worse off, with an average income substantially below that of the white population, and one-third of the black population lives below the poverty-line. It is a matter of political contention as to whether the black population should be helped by policies such as **affirmative action**, which provide certain groups with greater opportunities to achieve a range of positions long denied them.

> **affirmative action**
> Policies and actions designed to compensate for the effects of past discrimination, by giving preferences to specified ethnic and gender groups.

One of the fastest-growing groups in the United States is the Hispanic population, which grew by 53 per cent between 1980 and 1990. There are currently some 35m (12 per cent) **Hispanics**, and the number is expected to exceed the number of blacks by 2005. Indeed, since a significant minority of black Americans are also Hispanics, it is possible that the historic primacy of primarily English-speaking blacks is already at an end. Hispanics tend to be undercounted in surveys, a situation made more possible by the number of illegal immigrants ever year. Mostly better-off than Afro-Americans, very many live in California (7.7 million), and nearly two-thirds of the Cuban element live in Florida. A majority of Miami residents are Hispanic, but in cities from Dallas to Houston, Los Angeles to New York, they are also well represented.

Hispanics or 'Latinos' (as some Hispanics prefer to be called) hardly form a coherent group, and come from diverse places. Most of them have a Mexican origin, but there are also many Puerto Ricans who have left their overcrowded island for the mainland with the hope of improving their position in life. Those from Cuba are a significant group. They or their parents and grandparents fled from Castro's communist revolution in 1959. They tend to be more professional and middle class, and do not share many of the social and political attitudes of the Mexican-Americans and Puerto Ricans.

Inspired by the example of black activism, Hispanics have drawn more closely together, but the diversity of their origins has prevented them from becoming a solid national grouping. Their median age is significantly younger than that of most Americans, they tend to be poorer than whites and many have not qualified as citizens. Their campaigning has been done via local groups which fight for better conditions rather than through large nationwide associations. But they are becoming more organised and many are now acquiring citizenship. As they stand on the verge of being America's largest minority group, it is likely that issues of concern to their various sub-groups will gain greater prominence on the nation's political agenda. They may be still seriously under-represented in American institutions, but there have been recent signs of an emerging Latino-led radicalism, particularly among those who carry out many of the lowest paid and dirtiest jobs in the US. In the words of one writer:[1]

> The long history of political marginality is finally coming to an end. Latinos, all political pundits agree, are the sleeping dragon of US politics.

Of the **Asian Americans**, many originally settled in California and the Western states having journeyed from China and Japan. More recent immigrants have come from the Philippines, South Korea and South-East Asia (especially Cambodia and Vietnam), but the area of settlement remains broadly the same:

California and Hawaii, as well as the capital, Washington DC. There are nearly 7 million Asian Americans, a number of whom arrived in the 1970s and 1980s. In the past, the Chinese and especially the Japanese were the victims of regular discrimination, and in 1942 many of the latter were interned in camps because of their 'doubtful' allegiance. Since then, much of the anti-Asian prejudice has disappeared and most Asian groups have advanced in American society, though there are occasional outbreaks of hostile feeling.

The **Native American population** was originally called 'Indian' by the explorers and colonists who found it. By prior usage, the land belonged to the Native Americans, but these tribal peoples were gradually displaced as the settlers move westwards and the buffalo herds on which they depended were wiped out. They were eventually granted certain reserved areas, and many of the present Native Americans still live in or near these reservations, in Arizona, New Mexico and Utah. In a sense, it is wrong to group these Native Americans together, for they include representatives of many tribes whose cultures and lifestyles were once very different. Only about 1.5 million remain, and generally they experience inferior standards of living, the reservations being enclaves of social disadvantage. Native Americans are much more likely to live in poverty; they also earn less and achieve less via the educational system.

Some left their reservations because of the low quality of life there, and inhabit towns and cities such as Chicago and Los Angeles. However, those who have left have in many cases yet to become integrated in American society, and lack the occupational skills and cultural background to sustain themselves. They are prone to a variety of social problems, ranging from alcoholism and family disintegration to, at worst, suicide. Only recently have activist Native Americans begun to organise and press for changes in their quality of life.

Other than the Native Americans, all Americans are immigrants. The poor and oppressed from different parts of the world gathered in the country, so that it has developed as a land of diversity. In theory, all of those who entered the United States could benefit from the American Dream, by which every enter-prising person could improve his or her position in a land of opportunity.

Not all groups have benefited equally from this possible social mobility, but individuals of any race and background have been able to change their lifestyle and prospects, and via education, occupation and intermarriage have altered their status. America is often seen as a 'melting-pot', and groups from different backgrounds and of differing cultures have been able to mix with members of other groups, and have become assimilated into the American way of life.

The religious mix

Given the diversity of races represented in the United States, it is inevitable that many varieties of religious belief are to be found. There is no national or 'established' church for the whole country, though there were until the 1830s established state churches. Religious belief and practice is important in American family life and in the political process. God is alluded to in many public speeches, and religion is taken seriously. Americans profess to regard their beliefs and denominational allegiances seriously, and almost half of the population attend a church service at least every week.

There are many different religious denominations (well over 1200) but in most surveys over half of Americans place themselves within the Protestant fold. Most Protestant denominations have European roots. Among adherents, the largest group belong to the Baptist Church, which itself has many splinter offshoots; the Methodists, Lutherans, Presbyterians and Episcopalians are also well represented. Roman Catholics comprise more than a quarter of the population, so that they are larger than any single Protestant group. There are some 6 million Jews, as well as many other smaller sects. In recent years, there has been a growth in Islamic belief and Buddhism, among both Native Americans and the immigrant population.

This is the national picture, but the number of members of each particular sect varies widely from state to state. Baptists are very strong in Alabama, Georgia and Mississippi, and comprise more than half of the population in those states. The South has a strong Protestant majority. There are clusters of very firm allegiance in other areas, so that whereas Catholics are well represented in Connecticut, Massachusetts and Rhode Island, the Mormons (numerically small in the country as a whole) dominate the religious life of Utah, with 70 per cent membership. In New York State, as one would expect, there are members of any sect and none; in New York City, 14 per cent of the population is Jewish.

Religious affiliations, based on the 1990 census

Religion	%
Protestants	55
Roman Catholic	30
Jews	3
Eastern Orthodox	2
Others	3
Non-religious	7

Politically, religion can be a powerful catalyst of social change, and in the Civil Rights Movement of the 1950s and 1960s there were many prominent church ministers, notably Martin Luther King. Jesse Jackson was a younger member of the crusade for social justice and equal rights, and remains influential in the Democratic Party. On the political Right, the Christian Coalition is an increasingly significant force in the Republican Party. On issues such as abortion and school prayer its contribution to discussion and action has had a considerable effect on politicians and voters. A candidate's religion can be a factor in determining his prospects, though the choice of Senator John F. Kennedy showed that a Catholic could be chosen despite some initial reservations. On an issue such as abortion, the stand adopted may influence the prospects of election in certain states.

Broadly-speaking, Jews (although they tend to be prosperous and better educated than members of other minority groups) are more likely to be Democrats than Republicans, as are Catholics and members of minority denominations. The fact that the Democrats were willing to choose Catholics in 1928 and 1960 as presidential candidates, meant that many of that religious leaning were well disposed towards the party. It is perceived as being more accessible to them; they are welcome to join. Protestants, especially outside the South, incline strongly towards the Republicans, which is seen as the natural home for White Anglo Saxon Protestants – often referred to as WASPS.

Education, social class and economic inequality

America is much less preoccupied with social class than is Western Europe, and the Marxian division of bourgeoisie and proletariat has never been much applied to American society. Sociologists often talk of socio-economic status (SES) as a convenient tool by which to analyse the population, and this SES measurement is decided on the basis of education, income and occupation. The usual difficulty about any such categorisation applies, namely that people whose income places them in one stratum have a higher status than some who earn more than they do.

Whereas 'subjective social class' refers to the position in society in which a person places himself or herself, 'objective social class' depends on the position assigned by a social scientist. Many people assume that they are middle class, as befits a land in which people believe that they can achieve whatever they want if they seize their opportunities. In fact there are many people whose occupation and income place them lower down the social scale. Such persons may also wish to distance themselves from organised labour in the trade union movement, which has an unfavourable connotation to many Americans. Overall, the emphasis on class-based analysis fits the American experience less comfortably than in other countries, for the ethos of individualism and enterprise does not sit easily alongside any notion of class solidarity.

About one-third of Americans have stayed on and attended some kind of college, and education is valued in the United States as both a desirable thing in itself and as a necessary precondition for a successful economy in which skills and training assume ever-greater importance. However, the learning experience is not evenly shared, for among blacks and Hispanics there has traditionally been a much greater likelihood that they will not complete their high-school course. Most younger blacks do finish their high-school education, but relatively few go on to college; Hispanics are less likely to stay with their courses than blacks, and their drop-out rate is high even in the early years. Such differences in achievement have an impact on job prospects and earnings levels, and on the likelihood of political participation in adulthood.

In the early years of the Republic, agriculture was by far the most common occupation, but in the twentieth century America became the leading industrial country in the world. The invention of new machines and of techniques of mass production along with the super-abundance of natural resources paved the way for economic success as an industrial nation. Today, commentators often describe the country as being in a post-industrial phase, in which success and rewards depend more on skill and training than on the old industrial structure in which labour and management were often in conflict.

White-collar work has grown rapidly as more and more people enter the professions and management of some kind, whereas the numbers employed in manufacturing have diminished and those in farming have been dramatically reduced. In 1800, 83 per cent of the labour force was employed in agriculture; today the figure is below 3 per cent. Many people work in government, and education and defence are areas in which 3.5 and 3 million people work, respectively. Blacks are more often engaged in the service industries or, if more educated, in clerical work; Hispanics often work as labourers, operators and on the farms.

Income levels vary enormously as one would expect in a land in which enterprise and initiative are encouraged. The top 5 per cent of Americans earn 19 per cent of the income; the poorest 20 per cent earn only 4 per cent; 10 per cent of Americans live in poverty, as defined by the official poverty line of an income of $13,921 for a family of four (1990). Those who earn lower incomes are much more likely to be blacks and Hispanics than whites, and are much less likely to participate in politics, although they are the people who most depend on government help via federal and state welfare programmes.

A sense of unity, despite diversity: common values

We have seen that the United States is a land of great diversity, yet there are, nonetheless, forces which bring Americans together and give them a sense of common identity. Part of this sense of national unity can be explained by the pursuit of the American Dream by which, in a land of opportunity, all may prosper – if they are sufficiently enterprising. The Dream is often referred to in American literature and has been a theme of many a Hollywood film. Former President Clinton spoke of it as the 'dream that we were all raised on'. It was one based on a simple and powerful idea: that 'if you work hard and play by the rules you should be given a chance to go as far as your God-given ability will take you'. Americans are valued as individuals, according to what they make of their chances in life.

Adversity has also helped to bring them together. War and the threat of war often serve to bind a nation, and in World War II Americans of all types could recognise the service and patriotism of others from a different background. So too in September 2001 and thereafter, the terrorist attacks on the World Trade Center, which destroyed the well-known image of the New York skyline and killed nearly 4000 people of diverse backgrounds, also had the effect of uniting New Yorkers and their fellow Americans. They were determined both to hunt down those who perpetrated the outrage and to show the world that the spirit of the city could not be crushed.

Finally, shared values, a common culture, the prevalence of the mass media and intermarriage serve to blur the differences between different groups, for we have seen that in the melting-pot of modern America all national groups are to some extent assimilated into the mainstream of American life. They come to accept and embrace American values, and to share a common attachment for democratic ideals and processes.

CONCLUSION

The United States is a land of great diversity, even if there are factors which bind the nation together. Some enthuse over the positive benefits of multi-culturalism and multi-ethnicity, seeing it as an indication of vigour and energy. But diversity also creates special problems in a democracy, for it is associated with wide differences of opinion which can make it difficult to reach agreed solutions to political problems. Administering America presents a strong challenge to the governing institutions and those who run them. As de Tocqueville observed more than 150 years ago:

> A confused clamour is heard on every side and a thousand simultaneous voices demand the immediate satisfaction of their social wants.[2]

De Tocqueville's words carry considerably more weight today. The distin-guished historian and one-time adviser to President Kennedy, Arthur

Schlesinger, has written of 'the fragmentation of the national community into a quarrelsome spatter of enclaves, ghettos, tribes'.[3] Others too fear fragmentation, the possibility of what alarmists refer to as a Balkanisation of the United States which could ultimately undermine the forces which pull it together.

REFERENCES

1 Mike Davis, *Magical Urbanism: Latinos Reinvent the US City*, Verso, 2001.
2 Alexis de Tocqueville, *Democracy in America*, Vintage, originally 1835, edited 1954.
3 Arthur Schlesinger Jr, *The Disuniting of America: Reflections on a Multicultural Society*, WW Norton, 1992.

USEFUL WEB SITES

www.americansc.org.uk   The American Studies Resources Centre. A useful starting point for the discussion of all aspects of American government and politics, with links to many other sites.

www.census.gov   Bureau of the Census. Statistics on the US and its citizens.

The Constitution and the protection of rights

2

Constitutions are important in all countries for they set out the principles, rules and conventions according to which people should be governed. They normally outline the powers of the various parts of the governing body and the relationship which exists between them. Almost always, as in the case of the United States, they are written documents. Usually, they contain a declaration of rights, providing for civil and political liberties. However, the mere existence of a constitution and some written statement of freedoms is no guarantee that these will be respected.

In this chapter, we examine firstly the drafting of the Constitution, the type of person involved in its creation and its contents, before proceeding to some assessment. We then move on, in the second section, to examine how effectively the Constitution and in particular the Bill of Rights have protected liberties and rights, particularly those of women and black Americans.

POINTS TO CONSIDER

➤ How did the Articles of Confederation and the 1787 Constitution differ from each other?

➤ What role did the idea of a bill of rights play in discussions on the new Constitution?

➤ How easy is it to amend the American Constitution?

➤ How effectively has the US Constitution adapted to changing circumstances?

➤ To what extent have black Americans and other minorities benefited from the protection afforded by the Bill of Rights?

➤ Do you think that affirmative action is an appropriate remedy for discrimination? Would you apply such action to women as well as to black Americans?

➤ How well are liberties and rights protected in the United States?

➤ In what respects have Britain and the United States differed in their attitudes to constitutions and the protection of rights?

THE CONSTITUTION IN THEORY

In the Declaration of Independence (1776), drafted by Thomas Jefferson, he produced a classic justification for breaking the British connection. To Jefferson and those around him, the only legitimate basis for government was the consent of the governed, a revolutionary sentiment at the time and an ingredient missing from the relationship between Britain and the colonists:

> We hold these Truths to be self-evident, that all Men are created equal, that they are endowed by their Creator with certain inalienable Rights, that among these are Life, Liberty and Pursuit of Happiness. That to secure these Rights, Governments are instituted among Men, driving their just Powers from the Consent of the Governed, that whenever any Form of Government becomes destructive of these Ends, it is the Right of the People to alter or to abolish it, and to constitute new Government ...

The colonies – or the United States as they called themselves – drafted a compact which bound them together as a nation whilst hostilities were still raging. This agreement was known as the Articles of **Confederation** and Perpetual Union. It was adopted by a Congress of the States in 1777, and signed in July 1778. Not until March 1781 did these Articles become binding, when Maryland finally ratified them.

confederation

A political system in which there is a loose alliance of self-governing states, with a weak central government to bind them together.

The Articles provided for a loose association, and established a confederal government which had only modest powers. On many key issues – including defence, finance and trade – it was at the mercy of decisions made by the state legislatures. This proved to be unsatisfactory, and George Washington recognised the weakness of the union which hung by only 'a rope of sand'. The new nation was near to chaos, for it lacked political and economic strength. The Confederation was inadequate for the task of governing such a diverse area, and there was no stability in the arrangements which had been agreed.

In particular, Congress, the main institution in the Confederation, had insufficient power to fulfil its duty, 'the management of the general interest of the United States', for it was too beholden to the 13 states and lacked any means of enforcing its views. It was especially difficult for Congress to gain acceptance for a common foreign policy, for any agreements made might not be enforced by other states. Disillusion with the existing governing arrangements was rife. This was the background to the drawing up of the American Constitution.

The Philadelphia Convention, 1787

In 1787, the legislative body of the Republic, the Continental Congress, put out a call to all the states inviting them to send delegates to Philadelphia on 25 May 1787. The meeting was to be held in Independence Hall, where the Declaration of Independence had been adopted 11 years earlier. The delegates met to consider 'the situation of the United States, to devise such further Provisions as shall appear to them necessary to render the Constitution of the federal Government adequate to the emergency of the Union'. They were authorised to amend the Articles, but in the event they cast them aside and proceeded to draw up a charter for a more centralised form of government. It was this Constitution that was completed on 17 September 1787, and formally adopted on 4 March 1789.

Inevitably, there were disappointments with the outcome of the deliberations, and some delegates departed before the signing ceremony (of the 39 who did sign few were completely satisfied with what had been accomplished). The settlement had to be a compromise, given the obvious differences between large and small states, and those between who wanted and those who baulked at an extension of federal power. Benjamin Franklin articulated the viewpoint of those who had doubts but still gave their acquiescence: 'There are several parts of this Constitution which I do not at present approve, but I am not sure I shall never approve them'. Acceptance was justified because 'I expect no better and because I am not sure that it is not the best'.

It was in theory desirable for every state to ratify (give formal approval to) the new document, but the convention delegates realised that this would be difficult to achieve quickly. They boldly declared that the proposed Constitution should become effective when nine had given their approval. Delaware was the first to sign, followed by Pennsylvania and New Jersey, and then by Georgia and Connecticut where comfortable majorities were achieved. There was a fiercely contested struggle in Massachusetts over the absence of any Bill of Rights, but in early 1788 it too narrowly endorsed the document. In June 1788, the ratification by Maryland, New Hampshire and South Carolina meant that nine states had given their support, enough to see the document accepted.

The nature of the Constitution

The US Constitution is written and explicit. The document is relatively short and straightforward. It sets out the basic structure and functions of the various branches of government – executive, legislative and judicial – and the relationship between them. The Constitution is designated as the 'supreme law of the land', and this was taken to mean that in any conflict with state constitutions or state laws, the federal Constitution and federal laws take precedence. Over the succeeding two centuries, decisions by the Supreme Court have confirmed and reinforced this idea of constitutional supremacy.

The Constitution is the framework against which all political activity occurs, and laid down within it are the answers to key questions of governmental organisation. It explains the method of election for the federal executive and legislature, and the system of appointment to federal offices (including the Supreme Court). It itemises the powers of the central government, and denies certain powers to the states while giving them others. It provides certain civil, legal and political rights for the citizens which may not be taken away. It sets out the procedure for its own amendment.

The Constitution sets out the general political ideas, but its first three articles describe the three branches of the national government: legislative, executive and judicial, each with its own duties and responsibilities. The powers of the President are outlined, as are the topics on which the legislative branch can make laws and as is the structure of the federal courts. Since its introduction, the Constitution has changed in a number of respects, but its underlying principles remain unaltered. These are:

- The three branches of government are separate and distinct, and the powers given to each of them are carefully balanced by the powers granted to the other two. Each branch therefore acts as a check upon the potential excesses of the other (see the Separation of Powers, p. 18).
- The Constitution, and the laws passed under its provisions, and any treaties entered into by the President which have the approval of the Senate, take precedence over all other laws, executive acts and regulations.
- All free men are equal before the law and are equally entitled to its protection (but not slaves and women, until the passage of the Fourteenth Amendment). Similarly, all states are equal, none being entitled to special treatment from the federal government.
- Each state must acknowledge the laws passed by other states.
- State government must be republican in form, with final authority resting in the hands of the people.
- The people must have the right to change their form of government by legal means defined in the Constitution itself.

Final authority rests with the people, who can change the fundamental law should they so wish, by amending or replacing the Constitution. They express their views through the ballot box.

The Founding Fathers who devised the Constitution had several clear-cut objectives in mind, and these were set down in the 52-word Preamble to the principal document. They may be summarised as:

- 'to form a more perfect Union';
- 'to establish justice';
- 'to insure domestic tranquillity';
- 'to provide for the common defence';
- 'to promote the general welfare';
- 'to secure the blessings of liberty to ourselves and our posterity'.

Amending the Constitution

The framers of the Constitution recognised the need to make provision for amendment of the document, should this become necessary. As the nation developed and circumstances altered, change would become necessary, but it must not be so easy that it opened up the possibility of ill-conceived changes nor so unduly difficult that any proposal could be blocked by a minority of the nation. The answer was a dual process. Congress was given the right to initiate an amendment, by a two-thirds majority vote in each chamber. Or the legislatures of two-thirds of the states could request Congress to summon a national convention to discuss and draft amendments. Whichever procedure was adopted, there must be approval from three-quarters of the states before any amendment entered into force.

This was the direct procedure for amending the constitution. It can also be changed by judicial interpretation, for in a landmark ruling, *Marbury v Madison* (1803), the Supreme Court established the doctrine of judicial review, which is the power of the Court to interpret acts of Congress and decide on their constitutionality or otherwise. This doctrine enables the Court to offer its verdict on the meaning of various sections of the Constitution as they apply in changing economic, social and political circumstances, over a period of time. In other words, without any substantive changes in the Constitution itself, the thrust of constitutional law can be changed.

In the same way, congressional legislation can also broaden and change the scope of the Constitution, as also can rules and regulations of the various agencies of the federal government. Everything depends upon whether such legislation and rules conform to the intentions of those who devised the Constitution.

More than 5000 amendments have been suggested, but fewer than 40 have been submitted to the states. Twenty-seven alterations to the Constitution have been made so far, and it is likely to be further revised in the future. Most of these changes were made in the very early period after it was adopted: the first ten were made in the first two years.

Subsequent amendments have covered a wider range of topics, among them the method of electing the President, the outlawing of slavery, the right of

Congress to levy income tax and the direct election of US senators. Most recently:

- **The 25th Amendment (1967)** provided for filling the office of Vice-President when it becomes vacant in mid-term. The President must make a nomination which requires majority approval in both chambers. (The procedure was to be used shortly afterwards, in 1973, when President Nixon required a new

---

CHECKING POWER: CHECKS AND BALANCES IN THE AMERICAN SYSTEM

The federal system

The framers of the Constitution wanted a stronger and more effective national government than they had experienced previously. But they were aware of the dangers of excessive central control. They needed to balance the efficiency and good order that might come from central control against the liberties of the subject which might be threatened by an all-powerful administration in Washington DC. The answer was to establish a federal system, in which certain powers would be allotted to the national government and others reserved for the individual states. (See Chapter 3 for a full discussion of federalism in theory and practice.)

The separation of powers

All political systems need to have machinery to perform three basic tasks, which are the three arms of government – the Executive, to make decisions and put laws into effect; the Legislature, to create and pass laws; and the Judiciary, to adjudicate in cases of dispute or to determine whether the law has been broken.

Montesquieu (1689-1755), a French philosopher who wrote *De l'Esprit des lois*, argued that each arm needs to be separate, so that no one person can take control of all three functions of government. His influence is to be found in the work of the Founding Fathers, who drew up the US Constitution, for they instituted a number of checks and balances to prevent any danger of a powerful individual or group from dominating the whole structure by concentrating power in too few hands. In the 47th *Federalist Paper*, Madison quotes Montesquieu to that effect:

> There can be no liberty where the legislative and executive powers are united in the same person or body of magistrates, or if the power of judging be not separated from the legislative and executive powers.

Each branch of the American government can act as a brake on the other two, and in the case of the President and the two houses of Congress a further check is introduced by virtue of the fact that they each serve for different terms of office and are elected by different constituencies. In the words of Grant:[1]

Vice-President on the resignation of Spiro T. Agnew, and again the following year when on the elevation of that Vice-President – Ford – to the presidency, a new second-in-command was needed.)

- **The 26th Amendment (1971)** lowered the voting age to 18.

- **The 27th Amendment (1992)** concerned congressional salaries; no pay-rise under consideration can come about until an election has intervened.

Negativity is the chief characteristic of the separation of powers doctrine as it is concerned with producing limitations and constraints on government rather than looking at the positive use to be made of such authority.

Having separated the three branches of government, the delegates of the Philadelphia Convention allowed a certain amount of participation in, and checking of, the activities of one branch by the others. Thus, key presidential appointments have to be confirmed by a majority of the Senate, all legislation the President wishes to see enacted has to pass through Congress, and the Supreme Court can declare The President's actions and policies (and those of Congress) to be 'unconstitutional' (though this latter idea was not made explicit in the Constitution). The President has the opportunity to reshape the Supreme Court by making nominations in the event of vacancies, and can veto bills passed by Congress which are considered to be unnecessary or undesirable.

Other checks and balances

As we have seen, many checks and balances are written into the Constitution – although some have developed subsequently. Two examples of more recent checks are:

1 Political parties

The President and members of Congress belong to political parties, and therefore there are bonds between those who share the same affiliation. This may help the President pass his or her legislative programme through Congress, for if Congress has a majority of members who share the President's political allegiance then there are likely to be common legislative goals.

2 Congressional committees

Although neither the President or the cabinet secretaries may belong to Congress, executive branch officers may be questioned in committee about their work and responsibilities. Like parties, committees do not feature in the American Constitution.

Over the years, the system of checks and balances can be seen to have been effective in several ways: presidents have vetoed more than 2500 acts of Congress; Congress has overridden more than 100 of these; the Supreme Court has ruled more than 40 federal laws 'unconstitutional'; the House has impeached several federal officials; and the Senate has refused to confirm several nominations.

This amendment emerged in an unusual manner. A student at Texas University was working on a paper dealing with the proposed Equal Rights Amendment, and came across an amendment which was suggested as part of the original Bill of Rights. Six of the original thirteen states had ratified it, and later on another three had done so. The student launched a ratification movement, and found six more states which were willing to do so. Anti-Congress sentiment increased in the late 1980s and early 1990s, and in this atmosphere the movement for ratification gained ground, and finally – in May 1992 – Michigan became the 38th state to give its approval. This showed that even when 200 years had elapsed it was still possible for a proposed amendment to be put into effect.

Assessment of the Constitution

Without flexibility of the type we have seen, it is unlikely that the arrangements made more than 200 years ago would have survived, in a country which has changed dramatically. The diversity of the nation has increased, the country has spread westward across the entire continent, a stream of migrants has been absorbed, the population has soared, new resources have been exploited and all sorts of differing interests have developed, be they those of the east-coast ship owners who favoured free trade, the mid-west manufacturers who wanted protection for their goods from foreign competition, farmers who wanted low freight charges or railroad operators who wanted high ones: Texas ranchers and Oregon lumbermen all have their own priorities and concerns. Yet the essential unity of the nation has grown stronger. That this has happened is in no small part because of the success of the working arrangements drawn up in 1787, which had enough built-in flexibility to cater for changing circumstances.

The Constitution in retrospect

Americans pride themselves on having the world's oldest written constitution, and many still marvel at the wisdom of the Founding Fathers in devising a document that has stood the test of time and been capable of adaptation to changing conditions and circumstances.

Disadvantages and advantages of the Constitution

Not all writers have supported the various provisions of the Constitution. It has been found deficient by some critics who have been exasperated with the diffusion of power which was basic to its operation. The young Woodrow Wilson, then a Professor of Government but a future President, wrote his analysis, *Congressional Government*, in 1890, and therefore before the extension of federal and presidential power occurred in the 1930s. He argued that the American arrangements made it difficult to achieve coherence in policy-making or responsible government. In his view, there were too many people involved in the evolution of policy and there was too little likelihood of progress being achieved.

Wilson lamented the absence of strong parties, and particularly disliked the low quality of Congressional debate which – largely because of party discipline – in his view lacked coherence. Too much discussion took place in obscure committees, headed by entrenched and autocratic senior members, a point not effectively addressed until the 1970s. He much preferred the British system of government, with its clear allocation of power and responsibility.

A common point of criticism is the failure of the Constitution to permit quick and decisive action, except in times of crisis. One can understand why an American President might envy a British Prime Minister whose ability to achieve his programme within a parliamentary session is so much greater. But this was how the Founding Fathers wanted it. They were not looking for speedy action, and preferred to create machinery which would function at a slower pace, once all interests had had a chance to expound their viewpoints and to influence the outcome of the debate on any issue. This is what characterises the American approach, the fact that particular groups can frustrate the pace of advance where they think that change would damage their interests.

A contemporary of Wilson's, the British Liberal statesman William Gladstone, saw things differently. He described the American Constitution 'as the most wonderful work ever struck off at a given time by the brain and purpose of man'. For all of its alleged defects, many writers and commentators might still agree with him over a century later. The Constitution has now survived for over 200 years, and proved its endurability over years of extensive and often rapid economic and social change. It may have been amended 27 times but, after all, ten of these modifications were made at the beginning of its existence, and in any case the amendments and their subject matter suggest that there has been no fundamental alteration in its character.

In other words, the Constitution remains much as it was originally written. The whole **New Deal** was carried through with no attempt to amend the Constitution, and leaders who wish to innovate use the wording of the Constitution rather than seek to get it changed. Political fashion and

New Deal
The programme introduced by President Roosevelt in the 1930s to combat the depressed condition of the US. Several 'alphabet laws' (named after their initials) were passed to achieve the '3Rs' of relief, recovery and reform. The package greatly extended the role and authority of the federal government.

practices have made the system viable in the twenty-first century, and presidents now rely on the Supreme Court to interpret their actions favourably.

It may well be that if the framers of the Constitution were alive today, they might be surprised at the way in which its practical operation has evolved, for it has provided the political framework for a society immeasurably different from the one they knew. For instance:

- The Founding Fathers had fears about democracy and felt that the principle needed to be controlled, but subsequently the American system has become markedly more democratic. Politicians quickly saw merit in accepting the guidance of the electorate and the importance of the popular will has become much greater than was ever intended.
- The balance of power has tipped in favour of the federal government at the expense of the states, most evidently since 1933 when President Roosevelt began his New Deal programme to lift the country out of serious economic depression.

The constitution in Britain and the United States: a comparison

Most constitutions are written down and embodied in a formal document. Britain does not have such a statement describing the framework and functions of the organs of government and declaring the principles governing the operation of such institutions. Yet it obviously has institutions and rules determining their creation and operation, and the British constitution consists of these – found as they are in a variety of sources, mostly written down somewhere. It is more accurate to speak of Britain not having a codified constitution in which all the main provisions are brought together in a single authoritative document.

Written constitutions are normally produced following a period of internal dissension and upheaval, as in the US after the War of Independence. The US has the oldest written constitution in the world, but Britain has the oldest constitution of any kind. Britain has been relatively free from internal turmoil and has not been successfully invaded since 1066. It has not been found necessary to create a constitutional document to signify a break with the past and wish to chart a new course. Britain has a remarkably long and unbroken constitutional history.

There are advantages in having a written constitution, notably:
- they provide a clear statement of the position as to what is and what is not constitutional;
- they have an educational value, helping to curb the behaviour of those in government office;
- it is easier for the courts to interpret what is constitutional behaviour where a document lays down clear limitations on institutions and individuals;
- they are difficult to amend or tamper with, because the procedure for so doing is normally difficult.

Many Americans are thought to be much clearer of their constitutional position than people in Britain. Children are brought up to revere the work of the Founding Fathers and as they grow up they have a clear idea of how their system of government works. Their constitution

- The presidency has become more powerful, and although it was envisaged as being remote and above the political fray it has in fact become the most identifiable institution and an essential part of the political battleground. However rigid a written constitution may appear to be, in the American case it is as flexible as most citizens wish it to be.

What has remained, as the Fathers envisaged, is the built-in conflict between the various institutions. They wanted no part of the machinery to acquire excessive power at the expense of the others, and created a system in which it was difficult to get all parts moving in the same direction and at the same speed. They were happy at the prospect of disputation between the federal government and the states, and between the institutions of the federal government. In this, their wishes have remained intact.

is easily available and being short (seven articles, ten pages) it is readily accessible. The British lack this simplicity and ease of access. Anyone asked to find the British constitution would be hard-pressed knowing where to look for it. Yet there are disadvantages in having a written, codified constitution:

- Constitutions do not necessarily provide a clear protection for people's rights. American experience proves this, for the original document recognised slavery and the 15th Amendment passed in 1870 provides that:

  The right of citizens to vote shall not be denied or abridged by the US or by any states on account of race, colour or previous condition of servitude... Congress shall have the power to enforce this by appropriate legislation.

  Yet in many states blacks were excluded on grounds of illiteracy from exercising their democratic right to vote until the 1960s.

- Constitutions can be inflexible and rigid, incapable of being easily adapted to the needs of the day. Whereas the British constitution is adaptable and has evolved according to circumstances, a formal document can be difficult to amend, and therefore may act as a barrier to much-needed social change. Several US presidents have been attracted to the idea of gun control as a means of combating crime, but they have run into fierce opposition from the National Rifle Association (see p. 237), which reminds people of the statement in Article 2 of the Bill of Rights (see p. 24). The Supreme Court was similarly able to restrict some of the New Deal on the grounds that it was a breach of the Constitution, restricting states' rights and giving too much power to the President.

- Constitutions can be hard to change. In America, the fate of the Equal Rights Amendment (see p. 35) illustrates the difficulty in gaining adequate support.

In Britain, there was until recently no widespread demand for or interest in devising a written constitution, although there are now some groups such as Charter 88 which campaign for one. The present variety seems to work generally well, having survived several hundred years and provided the British people with a stable history and protection for their freedoms.

THE CONSTITUTION IN ACTION:
THE PROTECTION OF RIGHTS

Much of the early opposition to the Constitution itself was not centred on resistance to increased federal power at the expense of the states, but more on anxiety that the rights of individuals were insufficiently protected. There was widespread agreement that a set of constitutional amendments must be drafted to provide specific guarantees of individual rights, although this would not happen until after a government under the new Constitution had been established.

THE BILL OF RIGHTS

The first ten amendments to the Constitution were added as a block by the Congress in September 1789, and ratified by 11 states by the end of 1791.

The first ten amendments to the Constitution and their purpose

Protections afforded fundamental rights and freedoms
- Amendment 1: Freedom of religion, speech, press, and assembly; the right to petition the government.

Protections against arbitrary military action
- Amendment 2: The right to bear arms and maintain state militias (National Guard).
- Amendment 3: Troops may not be quartered in homes in peacetime.

Protection against arbitrary police and court action
- Amendment 4: There can be no unreasonable searches or seizures.
- Amendment 5: Grand jury indictment is required to prosecute a person for a serious crime. No 'double jeopardy' – a person cannot be tried twice for the same offence. It is prohibited to force a person to testify against himself or herself. There can be no loss of life, liberty or property without due process.
- Amendment 6: The right to speedy, public, impartial trial with defence counsel, and the right to cross-examine witnesses.
- Amendment 7: Jury trials in civil suits where the value exceeds 20 dollars.
- Amendment 8: No excessive bail or fines; no cruel and unusual punishments.

Protections of states' rights and unnamed rights of the people
- Amendment 9: Unlisted rights are not necessarily denied.
- Amendment 10: Powers not delegated to the United States or denied to states are reserved for the states or for the people.

The Bill of Rights was ratified in 1791, but its application was broadened significantly by the 14th Amendment to the Constitution, which was ratified in 1868. A key phrase in the 14th Amendment – 'nor shall any state deprive any person of life, liberty, or property, without due process of law' – has been interpreted by the Supreme Court as forbidding the states from violating most of the rights and freedoms protected by the Bill of Rights.

The contents of the Bill of Rights

James Madison did much of the drafting of the ten amendments. He was unconvinced about the adequacy of the existing protection and wanted to see clear constitutional guarantees of the liberties of the people. Those which he laid down in 1791 included a list of civil, religious and legal rights which remain intact today, in the same form in which they were originally set out. The first four set out individual rights, the next four deal with the system of justice, and the last two are broader statements of constitutional intention.

The new document applied to the federal government only, for many Americans were unworried about possible tyranny in their own states. It was the central government of which they were suspicious, although this fear has proved largely unfounded and many infringements of liberty have occurred at state and local level.

The 14th Amendment, adopted in 1868, includes a 'due process' clause, and this does apply to the states. It lays down that no person can be deprived of life, liberty and property without the due process of law, and this was seen as meaning that states were bound by the Bill of Rights in the same way that the national government was. For many years, the Supreme Court did not so rule, but in 1925, in a landmark judgement in *Gitlow v New York*, it was decided that:

> For present purposes, we may and do assume that freedom of speech and of the press – which are protected by the First Amendment from abridgement by Congress – are among the fundamental personal rights and liberties protected by the due process clause of the Fourteenth Amendment from impairment by the States.

The ruling was of profound importance, and once it had been accepted that freedom of speech and of the press were protected at state and local level by the First Amendment, so it was inevitable that other provisions of that same Amendment would be enforceable in the same way. Those rights laid down in 1791 – including rights of religion, assembly and petition – are now applicable to all levels of government.

Although the First Amendment has been accepted as binding, this is not true of all of the other nine. A minority on the Supreme Court wished to proceed from the 1925 decision to make all freedoms protected by the Bill of Rights binding on the states. In other words, this would mean that the Bill of Rights would be incorporated fully into the 14th Amendment.

This has not been the predominant opinion, and the majority have taken the view that some provisions of the Bill of Rights should be included, in other words selective incorporation. Gradually the number of those original amendments which have come within the scope of the 14th Amendment has been extended, and today only the second, third, seventh and tenth do not apply at state and local level – along with the Grand Jury requirements of the fifth. Other liberties not in the Bill of Rights also receive protection today – among these are the right of association, the right of privacy, the right to be presumed innocent and the right to travel freely.

Once much of the Bill of Rights was interpreted as being applicable at all levels, judges in state courts began to place more emphasis upon its provisions than upon those set out in state constitutions. More recently, however, there has been a more conservative leaning among the Supreme Court justices, and this has led to a greater interest in the protection offered by state guarantees. Justice Brennan became concerned about the way in which the Court was narrowly interpreting the scope of the Bill of Rights, and back in 1977 he urged judges in state supreme courts to take up the challenge, noting that:

> **State constitutions … are a font of individual liberties, their protection often extending beyond those required by the Supreme Court's interpretation of federal law.**

The Bill of Rights in practice: the effectiveness of the protection of liberties and rights

First Amendment freedoms

The key freedoms to protect citizens from an abuse of governmental power are to be found in the First Amendment, which is why they are commonly referred to as 'First Amendment' freedoms. These are the essential **civil liberties** which allow democracy to work, for they concern the right of people to communicate freely with each other and with the government. They allow

civil liberties
Areas of social life such as freedom of speech, religion and the press, in which the Constitution restricts or prohibits governmental intrusion on the free choice of individuals.

the public, the press, lobbyists and Congressmen* to 'go public' and organise an attempt to change government policy. It was Justice Oliver Wendell Holmes who argued that in a democratic society there is as much need for competition among ideas as there is in an economic marketplace for competition among producers. It is through free discussion that ideas can be tested, allowing all options to be explained and erroneous ones to be challenged.

Legal rights – the rights of the accused

The 5th and 14th Amendments prevent national and state governments from depriving citizens of their lives, liberty or property without due process of law.

---

* In using the term 'Congressmen', we are referring to members of Congress of both sexes.

Due process, a phrase used in the 14th Amendment, provides the guarantee of fairness in rulings and actions of government officials, especially those in the courtroom. In criminal trials, the right of due process includes:

- the right to free counsel if you cannot afford a lawyer, and to have a legal representative present at any police questioning;
- the right to reasonable bail after being charged;
- the right to a speedy trial;
- the right to confront and cross examine any who accuses or testifies against you, and to remain silent;
- the right to an impartial judge and a jury selected without racial bias;
- the right of appeal to a higher court if legal errors are committed by a judge;
- protection from double jeopardy ('nor shall any person be subject for the same offence to be twice put in jeopardy of life and limb').

In the landmark case of *Miranda v Arizona* (1966), the Supreme Court outlined a set of procedures to be followed by the police before any individual can be questioned. Once an investigation is underway with the focus on one individual, he or she must receive the following warning:

> You have the right to remain silent.
> Anything you say may be used against you in a court of law.
> You have the right to be represented by an attorney of your choice.
> If you cannot afford an attorney, a public defender will be provided for you if you wish.

These Miranda rules apply when a person has been taken into custody or otherwise significantly deprived of freedom of movement by the police. Although some exceptions have been created, in essence they still govern all police interrogations. Courts have often thrown out confessions obtained where the rules have not been followed.

Civil rights

We have so far concentrated on the protection of individuals from state action. We turn now from civil liberties to the ways in which national government can positively protect the rights of minorities from the unfair actions of state and local governments, individuals and groups. **Civil rights** issues are often less clear-cut than the freedoms so far covered, for often they involve a conflict between different disadvantaged sections of the community.

civil rights
Areas of social life in which the Constitution requires government to ensure equal treatment of individuals – e.g. by granting all of them the right to vote.

Questions of civil rights concern discrimination on such grounds as disability, gender, race, religion or sexual orientation. Any individual (or group) who feels unfairly treated may seek to get the situation changed by turning to his or her elected representative for assistance, or else to the courts. In many areas state and national governments have stepped in to ban discriminatory practices, as when in 1948 the Supreme Court declared that racial restrictions attached to the sale of property to 'Caucasians only' were unconstitutional.

The treatment of ethnic minorities

In the 14th Amendment, there is a guarantee of equal protection of the laws, yet for many years this never offered much protection for American blacks. Today, they enjoy far more rights than they did in the years following World War II. Much has been done to tackle inner-city deprivation, ban institutional discrimination and provide greater opportunities for those who long felt exploited. Racial disharmony and tension is less overt than it was a generation ago. Yet much remains to be done if American blacks are to gain their full acceptance as equals. In many cases, they are still the victims of inequalities, and in areas such as employment and housing they are seriously disadvantaged. Jobs are frequently in sectors of the economy where wages are low, and discriminatory practices in housing still exist.

In some ways, the racial situation has now moved on. Whereas for years the focus of minority politics was the black versus white issue, the discussion is now more often of multi-racial rather than bi-racial issues. The position of Hispanics, Asians and other minorities has assumed greater political significance, and sometimes multi-racialism has heightened group competition. The legitimate claims of one group have been pitted against the equally legitimate claims of another. Of course, there are other disadvantaged groups such as women and the disabled who make a claim upon the nation's attention.

Other minority groups

Since the 1970s, women have campaigned for greater equality, and have sought to influence the various administrations on issues such as equal pay and conditions of employment in general. Significant progress has been made in some areas. But campaigning groups have been uneasy about the trend in several recent affirmative action decisions and the inroads into the position on abortion.

With regards to the entitlements of the disabled, the United States made a major commitment to achieving equal rights in 1990. The passage of the Disability Act has already produced important changes in employment practices, and helps to ensure that improved facilities are available in commercial centres and places of public accommodation.

Civil rights for American blacks

The treatment of black Americans

Until the late nineteenth century, black Americans were kept in their place primarily by custom and economic conditions rather than as a result of legislation. But around the turn of the twentieth century, several laws were enacted which allowed persecution and separation to exist. It became illegal in many states for black and white people to travel together, or to share other public facilities such as hospitals and swimming baths. The statutes were often known as the **Jim Crow laws**, a name derived from a runaway slave who

> **Jim Crow laws**
> The generic name for all laws and practices which enforced segregation of the races in the American South, from the late nineteenth to the mid-twentieth century.

composed a song and dance in which the name was used. It was taken up by white comics and came into general use as a label for all black Americans. As a result, blacks were excluded from the electorate and from most worthwhile job opportunities.

According to the Constitution, the 'equal protection' clause of the 14th Amendment decreed that no state could 'deny to any person within its jurisdiction the equal protection of the laws'. Yet this requirement was easily evaded, because the *Plessy v Ferguson* ruling (1896) of the Supreme Court determined that racial segregation was not discrimination if 'equal accommodations' were provided for members of both races. In fact, there never was such equality, and for many years black Americans experienced inferior conditions, and – denied the vote – had no effective means of protest. There were a few challenges in the Supreme Court, but these never produced significant changes. The lot of the majority of black Americans was to suffer three indignities: **segregation**, discrimination and intimidation. The

> **segregation**
> The practice of creating separate facilities within the same society for the use of a minority group.

latter came in the form of terror from the Ku Klux Klan and other secret societies, and beatings and lynchings were commonplace.

At the turn of the century, 90 per cent of blacks lived in the South and the vast majority of them were employed in agriculture. But between the wars there was a drift to the North as they and their offspring looked for work in the developing towns and cities where they hoped to make a better life for themselves and their families. Again, their social status was still low, and life was hard and many were poverty-stricken. It was American involvement in World War II which created jobs for people of all colour and race. Once the fighting was over, returning black soldiers wanted a better deal for their families than they had known before. In the North, the number of blacks was growing, so that in Washington there was a black majority by 1961. They were becoming frustrated with their rate of advance. There were among them some articulate and able leaders who began to make an impact in their chosen field – business, education, the church, the law and the arts. The majority of black people had no such good fortune, and resentment was becoming more overt.

Postwar progress on civil rights

A major step forward had already come about by then, for in 1954 the Supreme Court reversed the 1896 'separate but equal' judgement, and laid down that separate facilities were 'inherently unequal'. The case was *Brown v Topeka Board of Education*, and it was concerned with the issue of desegregation. At that stage, there were still 17 states which segregated schools in accordance with their own laws. The Court said that segregated schools were illegal, for 'segregation is itself discrimination'. It had to be ended with 'all deliberate speed'. This judgement of the Warren Court shocked conservative America which disliked such judicial liberalism. Although several states implemented it speedily, there were others where the dominant whites were determined to retain their privileged position. Governors in the Deep South sought to use the law to evade the ruling, but over the coming years the Supreme Court struck down many attempts to frustrate its will.

In 1957, President Eisenhower had to send in federal troops to Little Rock, Arkansas, to ensure that black children were allowed to enter the white school. The President saw the attitude of the Governor as a challenge to federal authority, and it was probably his determination to insist on central power as much as his determination to enforce civil rights which influenced his action. Over the following years, segregation gradually disappeared, and in 1969 the Supreme Court decreed that 'all deliberate speed' must in be interpreted as immediately. Dual schools were brought to an end.

Much of the progress in the 1960s came about as a result of the campaigning of the Civil Rights Movement. In particular, the National Association for the Advancement of Colored People (NAACP) had achieved a significant victory in 1955, when a bus boycott by blacks in Montgomery ended in the company relenting and ceasing to reserve seats for white people. This episode led to the emergence of Dr Martin Luther King as a leader in the crusade for racial justice.

There were many protests and demonstrations in the early 1960s, and Dr King won over much white liberal opinion with his 'dream' of racial equality. President Kennedy was sympathetic on the issue of civil rights, but after his assassination it was Lyndon Johnson who introduced the Great Society legislation which included many measures to end racial injustice – among them, the Voting Rights Act of 1965 and the Civil Rights Acts of 1964 and 1968 which tackled discrimination in jobs and housing. The integrationist phase of the civil rights movement reached its peak in the 1960s.

The rise of black power

Much was being done to improve the rights of blacks and to remove some of the worst forms of discrimination, but many of them still found that their conditions in areas such as education, employment and housing were markedly worse than those of white Americans. Many felt powerless, and unrest in the underclass of black Americans was beginning to gather pace. Dr King preached passive resistance and non-violent direct action, but younger, more militant leaders of black opinion wanted to see a different approach. They questioned the desirability of integration, the strategy of non-violence and the presence of white liberals in the leadership of the cause. Local activists in the northern cities often adopted the rhetoric of the radicals and were active in the racial violence of the 'long hot summers' of 1965–67. The protest and rioting showed just how much discontent there was in the ghettos.

The assassination of King (April 1968) confirmed for many blacks the belief that society was so rotten that peaceful change would not work. Some leaders were more confrontationalist, among them Stokely Carmichael who felt that the whites would never surrender their supremacy. Whereas King talked the language of integration, Carmichael was committed to separatism. He and other 'Black Power' activists called on blacks to reject white society; they urged the use of the term 'blacks' rather than 'negroes', a term with overtones of past humiliations. They wanted to see black children taught pride in their black culture, so that a generation would grow up willing to challenge those who suppressed them. A more militant group was the Black Panther organisation, which believed in armed revolution – an open war with white society.

Within the black leadership, there were many divisions. Many of the older generation still believed in the methods of Martin Luther King; others believed that the pace of advance was too slow if they relied on seeking to secure white goodwill. Some of the spokesmen were unimpressive, and over personality and tactics there was discord. Nevertheless, the emphasis upon 'black power for black people' helped to make many black Americans more proud of their race and their individuality. They were gaining a personal dignity which many had never had before.

Progress since the 1960s

After the burst of activity in the 1960s, the rate of progress has been patchy. There have been legislative and other advances, but in many areas of life much remains to be done:
- In housing, it has proved difficult to end discrimination, for white residents and estate agents in some districts combine to ensure that 'undesirable' elements are kept out.
- In employment, blacks still suffer twice as much unemployment as whites, and access to jobs can be limited by factors such as poor educational

attainment and covert or indirect discrimination. Some blacks have 'made it' and done well, and act as a role model for others, but the majority who work do so in low-paid positions.

- Poverty is still a serious problem, for whilst there are some examples of successful black Americans, one in three live in poverty, and many are very deprived.

Affirmative action

Affirmative action programmes are those which are intended to correct the effects of individual and societal discrimination in the past. They provide special benefits to those in the community such as blacks, women and other disadvantaged who have traditionally been the victims of discrimination. Usually, these programmes involve a special effort to recruit and promote members of these groups.

Although segregation and discrimination had been made illegal, many supporters of equal rights saw this as insufficient. Neutral treatment would do little or nothing to equip women and racial minorities (primarily Afro-Americans, Hispanics and native Americans) with genuine opportunities, and they would still be denied the chance to participate fully in American life. In particular, blacks had suffered so much in the past that the continuing weight of disadvantage meant that they would never have equal openings in areas such as access to education, skilled employment or winning government contracts. This, then, was a well-intentioned – and not unsuccessful – attempt to give modest preferences to those long denied their full citizenship and a fair chance in life. In the process, it might have other benefits, such as improving the nation's economic and social life (enriching it by bringing in a diversity of talents and experience) and removing a cause of disaffection and thereby promoting order and stability. It might also help create a black middle class.

Special federal money was available to help promote racial or gender balance. The 1964 Civil Rights Act laid down regulations prohibiting any discrimination against women. Subsequent schemes have enabled women to assume positions which once were not open to them and to progress to the top in their chosen field of scholarship or employment. Since the late 1960s, many such programmes have been adopted by national, state and local governments, by public institutions such as state colleges and universities, and by some private employers and organisations.

The affirmative action policy has been highly controversial. Its opponents believe that it is a form of reverse discrimination: replacing one form of discrimination with another. They feel that appointment, progress and promotion should be organised on the basis of merit rather than any other consideration. In particular, they dislike the quotas which are often written into programmes; these establish a target number of women or members of a minority group who must be employed. When there is work for everyone, the quota might seem more acceptable. When employment is in short supply, or when a few particular jobs are much sought-after, there tends to be a backlash against the concept. Similar controversy is stirred over educational provision. Achieving the target of a certain number of minority representatives in universities involves allowing some to be enrolled who are less academically qualified than others who were being rejected.

Northern whites began to be upset by the policies designed to promote opportunities for black people, such as **busing** and affirmative action. Many of the programmes derived from the Civil Rights Act and the way it was to be interpreted. It was the Supreme Court which had to decide whether the Act was constitutional. Could equality of treatment be obtained by providing opportunities for some groups which were themselves inherently unequal?

> **busing**
> The transportation of children by bus from one area to another in order to create racially integrated schools.

The legality of affirmative action

Within the Supreme Court there has been uncertainty over affirmative action, just as there has been throughout the nation. The 14th Amendment to the Constitution laid down the notion of 'equal protection' before the law. The Court has, on occasion, argued that quota programmes in government or instigated by it, are a violation of that idea. The Burger Court (1969–86; see pp. 149–50) generally approved the principle of affirmative action (e.g. **University of California Regents v Baake**, 1978), but was unhappy with the details of particular programmes. The details can vary and the variations may be very important in their constitutional implications. In *Firefighters v Stotts*, 1984, it would not accept the principle as the only or even the most important consideration.

> **the Baake case, 1978**
> A landmark Judgement on affirmative action which stated that race could be taken into account in admissions decisions, as long as the institution did not set aside a specific number of seats for which only minorities were eligible.

In subsequent cases, there has been a division of opinion in the attempt to apply the 'equal protection' clause of the Constitution. Sandra Day O'Connor, herself the first woman to make it on to the Bench, has expressed grave doubts as to whether race-sensitive remedial measures can ever be justified, whereas others have taken the view that they can be necessary if the commitment to equality is to be honoured and past injustice righted.

Many votes have been very close, 5–4 or 6–3. In 1990, by 5–4, the Court upheld the right of Congress to adopt 'benign race-conscious measures' designed to increase the number of minority-held radio and television licences issued by the Federal Communications Commission. Similarly, with regards to women, the Supreme Court was usually willing to accept policies designed to help women overcome past disadvantages. In 1987, it upheld the California county agency's scheme which allowed consideration of gender in making appointments to positions where women had fared badly in earlier years. It recognised that there had in the past been an unfairness in representation and that it was therefore fair to use the issue of sex to correct the imbalance.

Bill Clinton was aware of the unpopularity of affirmative action, but generally resisted the temptation to trim his support. His appointments to the judiciary helped to ensure that the policy continued, and to overcome the hesitancy of the Rehnquist Court (see pp. 151–4). Rehnquist has long held doubts about the policy, once arguing in a dissenting submission that

> the Fourteenth Amendment was adopted to ensure that every person must be treated equally by each state regardless the colour of his skin ... Today, the Court derails this achievement and places its imprimatur on the creation once again by government of privilege based on birth.

The progress of American blacks in political life

By 2000, the total number of black elected officials had exceeded 7500, and although many of them served at the municipal level, more than 450 were in state legislatures, and more than 300 were mayors. Such figures indicate substantial progress, often the result of increased black voting in inner-city ghetto areas. But there were other areas in which a white majority was willing to elect a black representative.

Lyndon Johnson appointed the first black person to a Cabinet post and the first as an associate justice to the Supreme Court, Nixon appointed four black ambassadors, Bush the elder nominated Clarence Thomas to the Supreme Court and Bill Clinton proved himself to be more willing to put forward black appointees to the judiciary than any of his predecessors. George W. Bush has Colin Powell as his Secretary of State. In the 107th Congress, there are 39 blacks in the House, but none in the Senate.

Civil rights for women

For many years, American women experienced the same treatment as their counterparts in Europe. They were seen as goods and chattels, dependants of their fathers and husbands. They had few legal rights, and were unable to vote. Neither was there much opportunity to further their interests through educational advancement. This sense of powerlessness and dependency inspired some pioneering women to involve themselves in the women's movement. In the late nineteenth century, some states began to grant women the vote, and gradually it was extended across the country. In 1920, the 19th Amendment made it legally binding for all states to provide for the female franchise. Once women had a voice in political life, they were able to use it to campaign for other rights – on matters such as child welfare, anti-lynching and prohibition.

In World War II, the labour shortage created a demand for extra workers, and although many women were considered expendable once hostilities were over there were still six million in work, many of them wives rather than single women, and a number of them black. Since then, several factors have helped women advance their position in American society, similar to those which apply in Britain:
- the spread of education, especially higher education;
- the need for labour in the economy;
- the increased availability of labour-saving devices in the home;
- the increased ability of women to control their own fertility, via birth control.

The women's movement

The women's movement today is a broad umbrella, and within it there are several groups pursuing their own agendas. Even where there is agreement on the goals to be pursued, there may be differences of opinion about the means by which they should be attained. All agree, however, on the need to advance rights for women.

Among those who come within the women's movement are some who see women's inferior treatment as part of a more general problem of social disadvantage for minority groups, others who stress the right to work or the need for greater educational opportunity and yet more whose interest relates to a single controversial issue such as abortion or lesbianism. Even on abortion, there is a division of opinion, for whereas the majority would stress the mother's right to choose, a minority of activists emphasise the rights of the unborn child. Tensions over these differences surface in many campaigning organisations, but in the 1970s and 1980s there was a general recognition of the need to work for the passage of the Equal Rights Amendment, which was designed to guarantee 'equality of rights' under the law for both sexes. Passed by Congress, it was never ratified by enough states to become part of the Constitution. Ultimately, many Americans were too anxious about the extent of social change which the Amendment might unleash, to allow their support.

Despite the pressure of the women's movement for equal rights, only 7 per cent of public offices were held by women by the late 1990s, and women's wages remained on average considerably lower than those of men. They were more likely to work in white-collar employment, more than a quarter of them performing clerical or office-related work. Their jobs tended to be in sectors which paid less well (such as teaching), and management/industrial positions were and still are dominated by men. The fight to upgrade the level of female incomes is an important plank of the movement which points out that in 2002 twice as many women as men have incomes around the minimum wage.

The progress of women in politics

The number of women in elected office has traditionally been low, and several factors are involved. They are more reluctant to come forward as candidates, they have difficulty in getting nominated and the electoral system makes it harder for them to succeed if they are chosen.

In the federal legislatures, women are better represented in the Democratic Party which has been more willing to adopt them as candidates than the Republicans. In the 107th Congress, there are 13 women in the Senate, and 59 in the House. Within the 50 states, women fare better, so that a state such as New Hampshire, which has not had a female representative in either Washington chamber, has had a significant number within its legislatures.

Bill Clinton was more receptive to the claims for female representation in appointed offices than his predecessors. He included three women in his first Cabinet, appointed a second to the Supreme Court and made useful progress towards achieving a more balanced judiciary.

Civil liberties and civil rights in America: an assessment

The existence of civil liberties on paper is no guarantee that they will exist in practice. In times of peace and prosperity, they are more likely to be acted upon, although this was not true of the 1920s when – in a 'golden decade' – those suspected of adhering to a progressive creed were liable to be branded as 'reds' and treated illiberally. Such intolerance was again apparent in the early post-1945 era, when the **McCarthyite** witchhunt against alleged 'subversives' was at its peak. In the 1960s, some of the methods used by the FBI, including the phone-tapping of Dr Martin Luther King and the surveillance of other protesting individuals and groups, suggest that

McCarthyism

The practice of making unsubstantiated accusations of disloyalty or communist leanings, associated with the Republican Senator Joseph McCarthy. McCarthy led the notorious investigations into 'unAmerican activities' by members of the US government and other people prominent in public life such as artists and intellectuals, between 1949 and 1954. Many Americans of socialist or even liberal persuasion were hounded from public life as a result of the hysteria of his anti-communist crusade.

the civil liberties of those who dissent from American way of life are liable to be ignored. Few people will spring to their defence, especially when the cause is unpopular with majority opinion.

Such cases might seem to be a violation of the Bill of Rights, yet throughout American history they have occurred. The mere existence of freedoms on paper is no guarantee of their existence in reality. Much depends on the political climate of the day. The 1960s was a decade in which interpretation of individual rights often revealed a surprising latitude, but this has been less true of the 1980s and 1990s. The nation has been more conservative, as witnessed by the growing influence of the Christian Coalition and of the religious right, and by the advances made by the more cautious and conformist Republican Party in capturing the presidency for twelve years up to 1992 (and again in 2000) and gaining control in Congress in 1994. The Supreme Court has recognised this change of mood. On issues of individual rights, it has been less liberal.

This more conservative tide has not been widely reflected in rulings concerning First Amendment freedoms, which are still broadly defined. However, on freedom of religion, there has been a greater willingness to allow for an accommodation between church and state on key issues involving the establishment clause. On matters involving the protection of legal rights, judicial opinion has moved. The liberal decisions of the Warren and Burger Courts (see pp. 148–51) have not subsequently been overruled, but their application has been reduced in scope. New rules have placed more emphasis on the need of society for public order than on the rights of the accused.

If there is any sign of a trend, it would appear to be towards a more illiberal approach on matters of civil rights, because of the inroads made in areas of criminal procedure. Many Americans, alarmed by a wave of terrorism and of violent crime, are willing to accept new techniques such as greater electronic surveillance, helicopter searches, roadblocks and urine tests. A case can be made for many of these developments, but when viewed together they do suggest that respect for individual liberties and rights is less than it was a generation ago (see pp. 266–8).

Yet it would be wrong to see the United States as anything other than broadly liberal in matters of personal freedom. Few other countries have such an enviable record, whatever the occasional lapses. A human rights rating of 90 per cent was awarded in the 1986 Humana Guide, and it was accepted that there is a widespread respect for freedom, even if the position on matters such as capital punishment, homosexuality and abortion varies between the 50 states. The Supreme Court has recognised its duty to uphold the guarantees contained in the Constitution and Bill of Rights, and by its actions it has done much to strengthen liberal values.

The protection of freedoms in Britain and the United States: a comparison

Many Americans are aware of their liberties and rights, and can quote their constitution in defence of them. The Bill of Rights is part of the Constitution. As we have seen in the section on the Constitution, there is no guarantee that constitutional rights are always upheld. The Puerto Ricans of New York were long excluded from voting by a literacy test, though of course they may have been perfectly literate in Spanish. Rights clearly depend on other things, such as the tradition of liberty in a country.

In Britain, we have a negative approach to rights, few of which are guaranteed by law. We can do or say something, provided that there is no law against it. There is no Bill of Rights to set out our entitlements. We have traditionally relied upon what A. V. Dicey referred to as 'the three pillars of liberty' for the protection of our freedoms: Parliament, the culture of liberty and the courts. For much of our constitutional history, these arrangements seemed to serve us well, and politicians and commentators long believed that our liberties and rights rested on firmer foundations than any specific document. Ewing and Gearty[2] have pointed to the widespread British view that:

> If a country enacted a bill of rights, then it was likely to be acknowledged as a written but inadequate consolation for the absence of that commitment to liberty which appeared to seep unconsciously and effortlessly through the British system of government.

In the last few decades, some British politicians and several academic commentators have suggested that all is not well with the protection of basic freedoms in Britain. Breaches of rights are said to have occurred in many areas ranging from police powers to prisoners' rights, from immigration to official secrecy. As a result of Labour's change of heart on the adequacy of the available protection, the administration led by Tony Blair and elected in 1997 has carried out one of the demands of those who seek more effective means: it has incorporated the European Convention on Human Rights into British law via the 1998 Human Rights Act. Effectively, Britain now has a Bill of Rights, although not a home-grown one devised for the circumstances of the day.

One reason for British anxiety over the introduction of any form of Bill of Rights has been that such the existence of such a document would transfer power to appointed judges and away from elected, accountable politicians. Suspicion of judicial power is much greater in Britain than in the United States, for the British are not used to judges having a significant role in creating – as opposed to interpreting – the law. Americans are accustomed to the political role of the judiciary and from the 1950s to the 1970s an activist Supreme Court played a significant role in expanding liberties and rights.

In both countries, civil libertarians are alarmed by the scale of governmental action in the face of the terrorist threat following the attack on the World Trade Center in New York (see p. 11). Drastic counter-terrorism measures enable those in authority to act in a way which erodes personal freedom for the sake of national security.

CONCLUSION

The American Constitution is based upon key, underlying principles, notably:
- separation of powers, and checks and balances;
- limited government;
- judicial review;
- federalism (of which more in the next chapter).

These principles remain intact, but as a result of formal amendments, judicial interpretation and legislation the Constitution has been much modified. The changes made have enabled it to endure and retain acceptance, in a country whose circumstances are differ substantially from those of the late eighteenth century.

Documents depend upon their implementation and interpretation, and at different times the US Constitution has been differently applied. Sometimes its provisions have been ignored, much to the detriment of minority groups for whom the Bill of Rights has proved to be an inadequate form of protection.

Racial minorities have struggled for equality since the very beginning of the Republic. It was only when the Supreme Court decided in 1954 that segregation violated the equal protection of the laws (the 14th Amendment) that the tide began to turn in their favour. This landmark judicial decision marked the beginning of the era of civil rights for American blacks. By contrast, feminists have achieved more progress through legislation than litigation.

The civil rights umbrella is a large one. Increasing numbers of groups seek protection for their rights, be they older and younger Americans, those with disabilities, homosexuals, or victims of AIDS and other chronic and debilitating conditions. It is difficult to predict what controversies the new century will yield, but those categorised as belonging to disadvantaged minorities – blacks, Hispanics, gays, the disabled and the elderly among them – now constitute a very significant element in the population and are likely to be active in demanding greater recognition of their rights.

REFERENCES

1 A. Grant, *The American Political Process*, Dartmouth, 1994.
2 K. Ewing and C. Gearty, *Freedom under Thatcher*, Clarendon Press, 1990.

USEFUL WEB SITES

www.nara.gov/education/cc/main.html National Archives Classroom web site. Many key historical documents on American government can be found here, notably the Declaration of Independence, the Constitution, etc.

www.access.gpo.gov/congress/senate/constitution /toc.html Congressional Research Service, Library of Congress. Online copy of the Constitution, annotated with commentary and relevant Supreme Court cases, etc.

www.constitutioncenter.org/ National Constitution Center. A useful starting point for study of the Constitution.

www.americanstrategy.org/foundations.html An introduction to American constitutional history.

www.heritage.org The Heritage Foundation, a conservative group which campaigns to preserve liberties and rights. Has useful links to other conservative organisations with a similar agenda.

www.aclu.org The American Civil Liberties Union, a more liberal campaigning group on rights. Links to other more liberal organisations.

SAMPLE QUESTIONS

1 Has the American Constitution been an aid or an obstacle to good government?

2 Do the checks and balances written into the American Constitution still work today?

3 Should the American Constitution be rewritten?

4 Where would Americans look for protection of their liberties and rights? How well are freedoms protected in the United States?

5 Does the written constitution of the United States make the country harder to govern than Britain?

6 Are freedoms better protected in the United States or in Great Britain?

Federalism in theory and practice 3

Even the most authoritarian government would find it difficult to take all decisions at the centre. It would be impractical for any set of ministers to understand the needs of every area and to involve themselves in the minutiae concerning its public administration. Hence the need to allow some scope for regional or local initiative.

The Founding Fathers well understood that the structure and character of the governmental system which they were creating for the United States would shape the path of the country's development. It was important for them to strike the right balance between nationalism and states' rights. Since the Philadelphia Convention, that balance has changed and developed, and the emphasis on Washington DC has markedly increased. Yet in recent decades, there has been a movement to return power to the states, a tendency broadly encouraged by presidents from Reagan to Clinton.

POINTS TO CONSIDER

➤ Why did the US move away from its original system of 'dual federalism'?

➤ To what extent was there a conservative backlash against the growing power of Washington in public affairs in the 1970s and 1980s?

➤ By what label would you characterise American federalism today?

➤ Have the dangers and complexities of the modern world made it inevitable that national rather than regional or local government is the main focus of power in any political system?

➤ What are the differences between federalism and devolution? Is Britain experiencing 'creeping federalism'?

➤ Is local/state government better than national government because it is closer to the people?

The system of government devised by the Founding Fathers at the Philadelphia Convention (1787) resulted from the compromises necessary to reconcile conflicting political and economic interests. Federalism was seen as a 'halfway house' between the concept of a centralised unitary state, which was unacceptable to 13 states jealous of their independence, and the idea of a confederation which would have been a weak association of autonomous states.

As Alan Grant has written:[1] 'It arose out of a desire to bolster national unity whilst … accommodating regional diversity'. The Constitution does not mention the words federalism or federation, but the United States has always been recognised as a major example of this compromise form of unity. Other nations later adopted the federal principle, which Zimmerman[2] describes as 'a government system in which constitutional authority is divided between a central and state or provincial governments'. Wheare[3] wrote more elaborately of federalism as 'the method of dividing powers so that the general and regional governments are each, within a sphere, coordinate and independent'.

In other words, powers are divided between a general (that is, a national or federal) government, which in certain matters is independent of the governments of the associated states, and state governments, which are in certain matters independent of the general governments. Every American citizen is therefore subject to two governments which act directly upon the people; the system was not designed as a pyramid structure with the federal government

---

The division of power in American federalism: some examples

Delegated powers (powers delegated to federal government)
- Declare war
- Make treaties
- Coin money
- Regulate interstate and foreign commerce

Concurrent powers (powers shared by the federal and state governments)
- Taxes
- Public health
- Auto safety
- Drugs

Reserved powers (powers reserved for state governments)
- Draw electoral districts
- Intrastate commerce
- Creation of local units
- Police powers

at the apex, the states below it and then local government at the bottom. The Constitution lays down the binding division of power. In constitutional terms, the federal and state governments are seen as being of equal status within their own distinctive realms of authority. The Supreme Court settles any disputes about the division of powers between them. Its judgements are accepted as binding on the federal and state governments.

The relationship entails that no state may unilaterally secede from the Union, and a state cannot be expelled against its will. The interests of smaller states are protected in most federations by equal representation, or by additional members to those warranted by the size of their population. An important part of the Philadelphia compromise was to secure the support of the less populous states by giving them equal representation in the Senate – two seats per state.

Types of governmental systems: getting the terms right

In **unitary states**, legal power flows from one source, for instance the Queen-in-Parliament in the United Kingdom and the Knesset in Israel; most European governments are of the unitary type. Power is concentrated in national government, and the operation of lower tiers of government derives not from a written constitution but from the centre. In Britain, local authorities exist but they do so at the behest of Westminster, and they are entirely subordinate to it. Some devolution of power is possible (as in the case of Northern Ireland, Scotland and Wales), but this does nothing to breach the idea that control derives from Parliament; local and devolved power can be revoked.

Devolution involves the idea that there should be some redistribution of power away from the centre to subordinate assemblies which can, if necessary, still be overridden by the parent authority. It usually springs from dissatisfaction with centralised government when ministers appear to be unwilling to recognise local needs.

In **confederacies**, the regional authorities exercise much of the power, and central control is relatively weak. Historically, the best example of a confederacy was probably that found in the United States under the Articles of Confederation, but many years later the eleven Southern states seceded from the Union in the American Civil War and they too declared themselves to be a Confederacy. Switzerland today is often described as having confederal administration, its 26 cantons exercising much of the power in the country.

In **federal states**, power is shared between different tiers of government, a federal (central) government and regional governments – known as states in the US and Länder in Germany. Under federalism, the states have guaranteed spheres of responsibility, and the central government conducts those functions of major importance which require policy to be made for the whole country. Both tiers may act directly on the people, and each has some exclusive powers. Federalism thus diffuses political authority to prevent any undue concentration at one point. Under federalism, it is still likely that there will also be a system of local government, although it can vary significantly in form. In the US, the federal government has little role in regulating the functioning of this tier, which falls under the direction of the states.

The benefits of federalism today

With the growth of the federal government since the New Deal (see p. 21), it might have been expected that the states would become mere appendages of Washington. Yet despite the development of 'cooperative federalism' (see p. 47) and the fact that states were no longer 'coordinate and independent' as Wheare envisaged, in practice many writers could see them as a still important, indeed vital, part of the system. To Daniel Elazar,[4] writing in 1972, the states 'remain viable because they exist as civil societies with political systems of their own'.

Each state has its own distinctive history and traditions, and Americans identify with their state as well as with the nation as a whole; they are broadly popular as a form of government. In recent years, most of them have improved the quality of their services and the personnel who deliver them. Political institutions have been reformed and more efficient management of programmes has been introduced. They have, particularly in some cases, acted in an innovatory manner, and have been a testing-ground for experiments which others can follow.

They also provide an opportunity for involvement in the political process to many citizens, and have been a training ground for national leadership. It is through securing election in a particular state that national politicians build up their reputation, either by serving in the legislature, by becoming governor of the state or by representing the state in Congress.

The fifty states are important in their own right, and they are preferable to a more centralised system which would be unsuitable for a country of the size and regional diversity of the United States. Although there are ways in which the federal government can directly intervene to force the states into adopting certain adopting certain programmes and policies – as happened over the ending of racial segregation – nevertheless the central powers are limited. The relationship between Washington and the states is more one of negotiation and compromise, rather than one of coercion.

Americans think of their states as being important. Until well into the nineteenth century, they identified first with, say, Virginia and secondly with the United States. The motto of Illinois reflects the ambiguity of loyalty even today: 'State Sovereignty, National Union'. States are still a powerful reference point in their culture, and it is state laws which citizens encounter more frequently than any enactments of the federal government. Many federal laws are actually implemented through the states which modify them to suit their circumstances.

The development of federalism in the twentieth century

The influence of the federal government was much strengthened in the twentieth century, as the US became a world power. This led to huge increases in the budget and a massive expansion of personnel, both civilian and military. As a major contractor and provider of jobs, the federal government's decisions vitally affect the well-being of the states and of the people.

The Great Depression of the 1930s greatly increased the expectation that the federal government would intervene to deal with the major social and economic ills of the country. Washington's attempts to ease these problems by direct works programmes and various schemes of assistance for businessmen, farmers and whole areas in dire need, filled a vacuum. Given the scale of the task confronting the country, the states were unable to act themselves, as a result of the strain on their finances as well as out of an ideological unwillingness in some cases to do so.

Some rurally dominated state legislatures neglected the urgent difficulties afflicting the nation's urban areas, and not surprisingly the city administrations turned to the federal government for a lead. The lack of a positive response by many state governments to the crisis of the cities only served to increase the tendency towards centralisation. Indeed, the very nature of problems faced in a highly complex industrialised society provides a challenge to the federal system. The federal government has also often stepped in to coordinate governmental programmes when problems have cut across state boundaries

Such a combination of economic and social factors led to pressure over a century and a half for a change in the political and constitutional relationships within the federal system. Several methods have been adopted which have served to increase the influence of Washington over the states:

1 **Constitutional amendments**. Some amendments since 1787 affected the federal system – for example, the 14th Amendment provided 'equal protection' of the law to all citizens and the 16th gave the federal government the right to raise graduated income tax.

2 **Decisions of the Supreme Court**. At times, Court decisions have allowed a considerable expansion of national intervention by emphasising the broad and permissive character of some clauses in the Constitution – for example, the congressional power to 'tax for the common defence and general welfare of the United States'.

3 **The financial relationship**. After the passage of the 16th Amendment on income tax, the financial base of the federal government was expanded. This

led to a considerable increase in the size of its budget. Americans now pay the majority of their taxation to Washington, a smaller amount to the states and slightly less again to their local governments.

With the demands for more education, health and welfare, police protection and environmental services on hard-pressed local and state governments, the federal government increasingly stepped in with more financial aid. The dependence of the states on federal financial resources to support their services has inevitably coloured the relationship. Since the Great Depression, the main financial assistance has been in the form of **grants-in-aid**. Some existed before 1900, but most have developed since the 1930s, and this has led to federal supervision in areas not normally in its power. In other words, it is money 'with strings attached'. The federal government began to lay down minimum standards and to inspect the results of its funding, and matching funds had to be provided by the states to qualify for federal aid. The more a state was prepared to develop programmes, the more it was likely to receive national funds or contracts.

> **grant-in-aid programmes**
> Transfers of money from federal government to states and localities, in order to finance state policies and programmes.

Differing conceptions of federalism

In the US, there are, in addition to the national government in Washington DC, 50 states and more than 87,000 units of local government. How to balance the relationship between these elements has been at the heart of discussion about federalism every since the passage of the Constitution. Several descriptions have been used to describe that relationship which has fluctuated in different periods of American history.

Before the New Deal, America had a system of **dual federalism**. The Constitution had created two levels of government which were supposed to be independent, each with its own clearly defined sphere of influence and responsibility. The concept was interpreted in different ways, between those on the one hand who wanted a more nation-centred form of federalism and those who wanted a more state-based form. The version which emerged triumphant was the nation-centred one, the issue being finally resolved on the battlefields of the Civil War in the 1860s in which the Lincoln approach of keeping the country united was vindicated.

The label 'dual federalism' applies to the situation that existed in the nineteenth and early twentieth century. Such a model is a conservative one, for those who have supported it (right through until the present day) would prefer to see a strictly limited role for Washington. Supporters stress the importance of 'states rights', a large and secure place for the states within the federal system. Some writers would argue that such a situation never really existed in anything like its pure form. From as early as the nineteenth century, the federal government was 'stepping in' to provide grants for improvements on expensive and necessary items such as road-building.

Dual federalism proved to be inadequate to meet the needs of the Great Depression of the early 1930s. Roosevelt's energetic response to the deteriorating economic situation was to deploy the resources of the central government in a series of interventionist measures known as the New Deal, 'an extraordinary assumption of federal authority over the nation's economy and a major expansion of its commerce and taxing powers'.[5] More and more decision-making moved to Washington, with numerous grant-in-aid programmes bringing federal, state and local tiers into close, if not always harmonious, co-operation.

The New Deal programme inaugurated the era of **co-operative federalism**. This emphasised the partnership of different levels of government in providing effective public services for the nation. As Cummings and Wise put it:[6] the two levels were 'related parts of a single government system, characterised more by cooperation and shared functions than by conflict and competition'. Writing in 1966, Grodzins[7] did not view the American system as a 'layer cake' of three (national, state and local) distinct and separate planes, but rather as a 'marble cake', an inseparable mixture of differently coloured ingredients. In the nature of the relationship, the federal government supplements, stimulates and assist states, rather than pre-empting them. The distinguishing features of co-operative federalism were, then, a sharing of responsibilities over many governmental functions and the recognition that all the players were partners rather than adversaries.

The 1960s witnessed a marked expansion of the role of the federal government in initiating programmes and gaining state/local compliance. President Kennedy had promised to 'get the country moving again' with the use of federal money. The policy was vigorously taken up by his successor. In his Great Society programme (including such initiatives as the War on Poverty scheme), President Lyndon Johnson spoke of **creative federalism,** a more active form of co-operative federalism. This

> **categorical grants**
> Grants made from the central government to states and localities for specific, often narrow, purposes and to be used in specified ways; there is normally a clear procedure for applying, implementing and reporting back on the use of the money.

involved a massive expansion of federal aid, with grants to state governments increasing from nearly $7^1/_2$ billion in 1960 to $32 billion in 1978. Much of the funding came in the form of **categorical grants**, money being offered with the proviso that the recipient organisation carried out a specific task in such a way as to comply with detailed federal requirements.

The growing use of categorical grants	
Year	Number of grants
1900	5
1930	15
1960	132
1971	530

Creative federalism was not supposed to be a means of imposing programmes from the centre, although it did involve a great expansion in the role of the federal layer. The idea was that Washington, the top tier, would seek out and respond to local ideas and demands, and be able therefore to provide the type of service and the money which was wanted by those who lived in each locality. The role of state governments and legislatures was less important, and a wide-ranging series of civil rights and other measures imposed a greater degree of regulation upon state capitals. Johnson was able to work with his overwhelmingly Democratic Congress to carry out his programme. In the process, he was helped by a series of decisions taken by the federal judiciary which was in a mood to end racial discrimination and segregation, protect civil liberties, reform criminal justice procedures and grant new rights to both the accused and the convicted.

Some writers, particularly those opposed to the Great Society vision, wondered whether what had happened by the end of that decade was that creative federalism had become **coercive federalism**, a situation in which there was, in Kincaid's words:[8]

> unprecedented federal reliance on conditions of aid, pre-emptions of state and local authority, mandates, court orders, and other devices intended to ensure state and local compliance with federal policies.

Criticism of the growth in central power: the new federalism

States and localities had become ever more dependent on federal funding, and the conditions attached to the aid had become stringent. At the same time, the deteriorating state of the American economy led many people to believe that the country could not afford such vast and expensive social programmes. To Johnson's political opponents, the proliferation of policies and grants had brought about confusion and an excess of bureaucracy.

Conservatives never liked high-spending federal programmes which, in their view, involved an unnecessary amount of regulation and encouraged the states to initiate schemes which they did not want or need – simply to obtain the available federal funds. They claimed that problems were better tackled locally by people who understood the needs of the area, rather than through wasteful and inefficient programmes. They disliked the idea of federal interference in the affairs of states and local authorities, and argued the case for a preservation of 'states rights'.

As a conservative President, Richard Nixon had the opportunity both to preach and practise his ideas of a **new federalism**. To him, the relationship between all tiers of government was in need of redefinition. Yet his approach was not essentially about curtailing the amount of money which reached the localities, but more about how it got there. Money was provided by a **block grant**; the need was identified locally and the money then spent.

block grants
Discretionary grants handed over by the federal government to states or communities; recipients can choose how the money is spent within the broad area covered by the transfer.

Despite efforts of President Nixon to stem the flow of power from the states to Washington, it was still commonplace for academics and commentators to speak of the erosion of states rights until 1980. The growth of grants-in-aid, the expansion of federal regulations, and the decisions of the Supreme Court (especially on desegregation), had all signalled a decline of the states as a significant force. In the words of one exam question of the 1970s: 'States rights' are no more than an empty slogan for those who do not like the government in Washington'.

In January 1981, in his inaugural speech, Ronald Reagan observed that: 'Our government has no special power except that granted it by the people ... All of us need to be reminded that the federal government did not create the states; the states created the federal government'. He cast himself firmly in the dualist mode, emphasising his determination to 'demand recognition of the distinction between the powers granted to the federal government and those reserved to the states or to the people'. For him, it was not enough merely to adjust the delivery systems. He wanted to tackle the basic problem, namely that government was trying to do too much.

The Reagan version of 'new federalism' was more radical in its intention and in its impact. His intention was to bring about a restructuring of the federal system. In his vision of the future, the federal government would withdraw from several areas, the states would gain the right to take more initiatives and operate more programmes (if they so wished) and city governments would lose much of the power they had accumulated. He had little sympathy for 1960s schemes designed to help the cities. Of the War on Poverty, he observed: 'I guess you could say poverty won the war'. For him, this all added up to a 'new federalism', which would reverse a situation in which

> our citizens feel they have lost control of even the most basic decisions made about the essential services of government... A maze of interlocking jurisdictions and levels of government confronts average citizens in trying to solve even the simplest of problems.[9]

The changes on which he embarked included:
- a reduction of grants-in-aid;
- a merging of those grants directed to specific purposes into block grants, which allowed for far more state discretion;
- a removal of many federal regulations;
- An emphasis on urban and other problems being solved by a concentration on (a) achieving an increase in the overall prosperity and wealth of the country and (b) encouraging local private/public initiatives;
- a recasting of welfare arrangements, by which the federal government would take care of Medicaid health funding, whilst the states would look after the AFDC (Aid to Families with Dependent Children) and food stamp programmes.

What had been created by the end of the 1980s was not a replica of the pattern which existed before the days of Franklin Roosevelt and the New Deal. Federal funding may have been reduced, but the Supreme Court decisions which did so much to change the nature of American federalism survived intact. National standards were also largely preserved. The number of regulations was reduced and they were imposed with less zeal than was once the case, but in areas such as environmental regulation there remains a strong federal role. Americans are now used to turning to their President in Washington for a response to pressing national problems, and whether they are worried by rising crime, the system of welfare or any other aspect of policy, they expect a lead from the White House (and Congress) – even if they do not like the policy which emerges. The outcome therefore is a situation which, in Kincaid's words[10] is something of a paradox, combining

> federal dominance and state resurgence... If the states are so resurgent, why is the federal government [still] so dominant? The main reason is that the federal government has established a significant regulatory role in most domestic policy fields.

Bush, Clinton and federalism

At the beginning of the twenty-first century, states are more active than they were twenty years ago, and that is unlikely to be reversed. After Reagan had vanished from the scene, his successors had markedly less impact on the balance of the federal–state relationship. George Bush did not share the Reagan view of the appropriate role for government in the nation's life, and if anything there was a modest swing back to emphasising the role of Washington. But the scale of the budget deficit meant that there was unlikely to be a return to the heyday of co-operative federalism. In any case, in the words of David McKay:[11]

> Lower level governments had been taught to be more self-reliant and to cut spending and services rather than increase taxes or plead for aid from the federal government.

When Bill Clinton entered the White House, he was initially viewed by many commentators as a centraliser in intergovernmental relations. After all, he believed in more active national leadership than did Bush or Reagan. But as he was a Southerner, some hoped that the former Governor of Arkansas would be likely to be a defender of states rights. After all, he came from an area where there was a history of resistance to federal demands and had a reputation as an innovator who understood and appreciated the role of the states in the federal system. Moreover, he was not a traditional high-spending Democrat of the Kennedy–Johnson variety.

Once he was elected, one of Clinton's primary concerns was to cut the budget deficit which had grown dramatically in the 1960s and 1970s. By the time Nixon left office, more than a quarter of all spending at state and local level was provided from Washington. Jimmy Carter had begun to trim the amount of national support, but as we have seen it was Reagan who set about slashing it. Clinton continued in this vein, re-directing financial resources and responsibility for programmes back to the states, a process intensified after the Republican congressional successes of November 1994. He was more generous with federal money than Reagan had been and more than his Republican opponents desired, but the increased funding was modest by the standards of his party predecessors.

Clinton stressed the importance of improved co-operation between the federal and state/local governments, and spoke of increased opportunities for local experimentation. Within two weeks, he had invited the nation's governors to meet him so that he could listen to their complaints and ideas. Over the following years, he established a framework in which federal officials were able to loosen programme requirements to allow states and localities greater flexibility.

In the last few years, there have been numerous examples of states acting in an imaginative and more assertive fashion. They have advanced their own interests by effective lobbying in the national capital, have tried out different forms of revenue-raising and cost-cutting and developed alternative policy approaches. A spirit of innovation and vitality has spread through several state capitals, in many cases supported by both liberals and conservatives. As federal, state and local administrations vie with each other to provide the public services which the voters demand, the atmosphere is one of what Thomas Dye has called[12] '**competitive federalism**'. Washington is no longer seen as 'knowing best' and there has been a greater recognition of the role and importance of the states in producing effective government.

The Rehnquist Court has of late been instrumental in helping to shape the character of American intergovernmental relations. It has leaned to a more state-centred approach. In 1992, in *New York v United States*, the justices took the view that the national government could not 'simply compel' a state to take particular policy actions. In 1999, they decided that Maine was not subject to Federal Labour Standards legislation and a year later in *Kimel v Florida Board of Regents* they went significantly further in exempting states from the requirements of federal laws designed to prevent age discrimination.

These developments show that the debate about the appropriate level of federal intervention is unresolved, for the relationship cannot be fixed for all times. As Woodrow Wilson wrote back in the early twentieth century, the matter is not for 'one generation, because it is a question of growth, and every new successive stage of our political and economic development, gives it a new aspect, makes it a new question'. Arguably the devolving of power from Washington since the 1980s is the most significant change in the balance of the national–state relationship since the time of the New Deal. Federalism has proved to be a flexible system, suitable for the administration of a large and diverse country, and capable of adaptation to changing needs and interests as the situation requires.

The relationship between the centre and the states, today and in the future

The states have enjoyed a resurgence and renewal in recent decades. This has come about as part of a backlash against the activist government of the Great Society years. The Johnson presidency had some important achievements to its credit, not least for the poor and ethnic minorities who were its main recipients. These achievements came at a time when state and local governments often seemed inert and inefficient. But the changes generated opposition and political opinion turned against them. Americans have always been lukewarm about 'big government', and opponents found increasing evidence that too many programmes had been badly run, were wasteful and undermined individual and local initiative.

There were several reasons for the state resurgence in the late twentieth century, among them:
- The election to the presidency of former Governors – Carter, but especially Reagan and Clinton – who were well-versed in state perspectives on the appropriate national–state relationship.
- A feeling that the federal government has failed to respond to assorted economic and social problems, so that the states have had to act on their

own; the cutting of many grants-in-aids further enhanced the tendency towards state self-reliance, spurring state politicians to reform.

- The handing over of decision-making powers to the states on important subjects such as welfare, especially via the 1996 Welfare Reform Act. From then onwards, although there was a national framework, it was increasingly left to the states to decide whether to hand over money to individual claimants and the level at which help should be given.
- Rulings of the Supreme Court, a number of which have supported the states in their attempts to make important inroads on topics such as the availability of abortion.
- The increased willingness – indeed enthusiasm – of some states to experiment with new policies; state administrations have been notably more vigorous and creative than they were in the heyday of 'big government'.

The degree of government interventionism has tended to vary according to economic necessities and the tide of popular opinion. As the economy became national, there was an increasing need for national leadership to sort out problems such as urban decline, worker protection and the regulation of large corporations; state activity seemed inadequate to meet the challenge. When government became too big, then many voters came to see the federal government as part of the problem, rather than as part of the solution.

Sometimes people have had confusing aspirations, wanting smaller but yet decisive national leadership. Even those who deride big government and Washington 'meddling' sometimes find themselves calling for leadership on key issues. Robert Dole, a presidential contender in 1996, illustrated the ambiguity in a remark on law and order. He upheld states rights by saying that: 'Republicans... believe that our country's increasingly desperate fight against crime is an area where more freedom is needed at the state level'.[13] He went on to promise that the proposed 'crime bill will impose mandatory minimum sentences on those who use guns in the commission of a crime, and make sure the jails are there to lock them up'!

In the past, textbook writers have concentrated on the national scene at the expense of what happens in the states and localities. Examiners still tend to see American politics in this way. Yet not to be aware of the revival in subnational politics would be to underestimate seriously the importance of the trends of recent years and also to misinterpret the essence of American federalism. In the words of Hames and Rae,[14] 'states are the basic building-blocks of American life, and they remain highly individual and distinctive'. Some of the innovations for which they have recently been responsible are set out in the box on p. 56.

FEDERALISM AND DEVOLUTION IN BRITAIN AND THE UNITED STATES: A COMPARISON

When the British Labour party argued the case for devolution of power in the 1990s, its case was couched in democratic language. It accepted that the Scots wanted far greater control over their own lives and took up the devolution theme. It used decentralist rhetoric which showed that the truth of Gladstone's old maxim was appreciated: 'Making power local, makes it more congenial'.

In office, Labour ministers wished to satisfy nationalist demands, stave off the threat from the Scottish National Party (SNP) and ensure that the unity of the United Kingdom was preserved. Accordingly, the Scotland Act was placed on the statute book in 1998. First elections took place in 1999 and the Scottish Parliament began to function in 2000. A less-powerful version was made available to the people of Wales who were granted an assembly rather than a Parliament with tax-varying powers.

Devolution involves the ceding of power by Parliament to some new elected body. Bogdanor[15] defines it as 'the transfer to a subordinate elected body, on a geographical basis, of functions at present exercised by ministers and Parliament'. As such, it differs from federalism which

> would divide, not devolve, supreme power from Westminster and various regional or provincial parliaments. In a federal state, the authority of the central or federal government and the provincial governments is co-ordinate and shared, the respective scope of the federal and provincial governments being defined by an enacted constitution... Devolution, by contrast, does not require the introduction of an enacted constitution.

The merits and difficulties of devolution

Devolution is widely seen as democratic, in that it allows people to express their distinctive identity and have a say in the development of the life of their own particular regions. It has the merit of countering the dangers of an over-powerful, excessively centralised state. Indeed, in celebrating the referendum victory which preceded the passage of the Scotland Bill, Tony Blair observed that 'the era of big centralised government is over'.

Opponents see devolution as fraught with danger, often claiming that although in the United Kingdom the sources of unity are much greater than the sources of diversity, once parts of the whole are allowed to enjoy a measure of self-government then there is a danger of the whole edifice splintering apart. Moreover, the Conservatives, who resisted the Blairite proposals in the referendum in 1998, suggested that there was no real necessity for change, because unlike the situation in some other countries, the UK has not developed as a result of previously autonomous states coming together recently. They feared a 'Balkanisation' of the British Isles if parts were able to go their separate ways, because the Scottish Nationalists would not be satisfied with devolution which is a halfway house between unity and independence. The SNP is a separatist party, its long-term goal being national independence for Scotland. It would do its best to expose the flaws in devolution as introduced, and this would fuel pressure for separation.

One of the difficulties of devolution which is often mentioned by its critics is the West Lothian (now more usually referred to as the English) Question: 'Why should Scottish MPs at Westminster be allowed to have a say on purely English matters while English MPs will no longer have a say on Scottish matters?'. Such a dilemma would not arise if Britain had a federal system, for under federalism the division of functions is clear-cut. If ministers had opted for a system of elected regional councils for England, then each region (and Scotland and Wales) would have similar devolved powers, leaving the United Kingdom Parliament to deal with the residue of issues, those key ones affecting the four countries collectively. But as yet there is no public demand for legislative devolution across the UK. Even if this were ever introduced it is doubtful whether the powers granted to regional bodies would ever be equal to those of the Scottish Parliament, so that statutory responsibility for English devolution would probably remain at Westminster.

The question was never a source of contention when, prior to Direct Rule, Northern Ireland had its own Parliament at Stormont while the province sent members to the House of Commons. (The situation arises again under the Good Friday Agreement which provides for an Assembly and an Executive body.)

However, logic does not always apply in these matters, and there is a possibility that English people might feel disadvantaged. They may come to resent an issue primarily relevant to England being decided on the basis of Scottish votes in the House of Commons.

Bogdanor points out[16] that the difficulties inherent in the West Lothian Question have been resolved – or at least accommodated – elsewhere without much difficulty. Devolution has proved feasible in countries such as France, Italy, Portugal and Spain. For instance, in Italy 15 out of 20 regions have no exclusive legislative powers, but the other five have wide responsibilities in economic and social affairs; in Spain, 7 out of 17 have greater autonomy than the others. But 'there is no West Sardinian question nor any West Catalonian Question'. Be that as it may, the West Lothian Question does raise the issue of whether in a unitary state it is possible to devolve substantial powers which are denied to other regions.

Is Britain becoming a federal state?

As we have established, Britain is a unitary state. But there have been important changes in recent years to the pattern of government, and some of these seem to indicate a move in a more federal direction. Devolution has been the British route to decentralisation, so that power remains theoretically in Westminster's hands although it is politically hard to imagine any administration in London seeking to recover control over areas which have been delegated to Edinburgh or Cardiff.

Northern Ireland had a devolved assembly in the days before Direct Rule, so that the relationship between London and Belfast was essentially federal in character, with certain functions allocated to the national level of government and the rest to the provincial one. The new assembly formed as a result of the Good Friday Agreement (1998) has similar powers, so that Northern Ireland, Scotland and Wales all have devolved administrations, although Wales has strictly limited powers. Ministers have also allowed for the possibility that at some point in the future Regional Development Assemblies will be accountable to elected regional assemblies rather than as at present to an indirectly elected forum of local councillors (Regional Chambers). In some areas this is likely to happen, in others – where there is less of a sense of regional identity – it probably will not for many years. Hence the possible emergence of a Spanish-type structure, in which the peoples of some areas of the country have more control over their future than their fellow-Spaniards elsewhere.

Another area of likely development in Britain is the adoption of elected Mayors of the type to be found in American cities such as Washington and New York, and in European capitals such as Barcelona and Paris. London already has an elected Mayor in the form of Ken

---

Innovation across America

In general, matters that lie entirely within the borders of the 50 states are their exclusive concern. These include such things as:
- regulations relating to business, industry, property and utilities;
- the state criminal code;
- working conditions within the state.

Several states have been active in Washington DC in recent years, lobbying on their own behalf and employing professional lobbying companies to help them in their bid for federal help. However, they have also recognised the need to become more self-reliant. This has led to more creative thinking and some states have been fertile in devising initiatives:
- California has been restrictive on the rights of entry of illegal immigrants and the use of affirmative action programmes. These and many more policies have resulted from the widespread use of direct legislation, as described on pp. 190–4.
- Hawaii has introduced a British-style scheme of health care, and Oregon too has promoted a new system for the delivery health provision.
- Wisconsin has experimented with parental choice and a voucher system in state education.
- Several states have tried out different approaches to issues of law and order, the main common factor between them being that policies have generally veered towards 'toughness'. Texas is noted for its frequent use of the death penalty and its 'bootcamps' for young offenders; other states have employed policies ranging from 'zero tolerance' to registration of sex offenders.

Livingstone in this role. If London become the pattern of the future, then we will perhaps experience what Coxall and Robins[17] envisage:

> [the development from] a unitary state to a mosaic of federal, devolved and joint authority relationships between core and periphery, with the English core becoming more decentralised as regional and urban identities find political expression.

When commentators speculate on moves towards a federal structure in Britain, they do not usually imply a uniform division of power between Westminster and provincial units formally set out in a written document. Rather, they envisage a situation in which the policy of devolution is gradually applied to all parts of the United Kingdom, just as it is now applied to Scotland and Wales. Such a pattern is more akin to the model proposed by some Liberals in the late nineteenth century, a pattern then labelled as 'Home Rule All Round'. Bogdanor[18] seeks to distinguish this from a strictly federal system, and refers to it instead as 'federal devolution'.

Local government

Below the states, there is a mosaic composed of thousands of other units, many of which date back to the days of independence. They range from the counties which usually contain two or more townships and several villages (though so large is New York city that it contains five separate boroughs, each of which is a county in its own right), and they administer state and county welfare programmes to the towns and villages, which deal with strictly local needs such as paving and street lighting. In addition, there is a myriad of other governmental units, and school and other special boards handle specific problems as necessary.

CONCLUSION

Federalism is a form of government which divides political responsibility. Its underlying ideas are that:

- Too much political power is dangerous and it is therefore desirable that there should be diverse levels of government to prevent undue concentration.
- Particular powers are best assigned to particular tiers best suited to exercising them.

An understanding of federalism is crucial to unlocking the secrets of the American political system. It decentralises American politics, helps decide which president is elected, enhances judicial power and decentralises policies as well. The history of the federal system illustrates the tension between the national government and the states about policy – who controls it and what it should be. In the distant past, the debates were about whether the national government should regulate the railroads or adopt minimum wage legislation. Today, they are about whether it should regulate abortion, determine speed limits on highways or lay down that 18 year olds cannot legally drink alcohol. Policies relating to the economy, the environment and many other issues are subject to the centralising force of the national government and the dispersing force of the fifty states. Because of the overlapping powers of the two tiers of government, most discussion of policy is also a discussion about federalism.

The neat arrangements devised at Philadelphia have been adapted to changing circumstances at different periods in American history, because special situations have required a new approach. The broad drift has been towards a centralisation of power since the early days of dual federalism. But in recent years there has been a significant reversal in the flow of power and now it is meaningful to talk of states' revival and renewal.

REFERENCES

1   A. Grant, *The American Political Process*, Dartmouth, 1994.
2   J. Zimmerman, *Contemporary American Federalism: The Growth of National Power*, Praegar, 1992.
3   K. Wheare, *Federalism*, Oxford University Press, 1946 (reissued 1963).
4   D. Elazar, *American Federalism: A View from the States*, Harper and Row, 1984.
5   J. Burns *et al.*, *Government by the People*, Prentice Hall, 1994.
6   M. Cummings and D. Wise, *Democracy under Pressure*, Harcourt College Publishers, 2000.
7   M. Grodzins, *The American System*, Rand McNally, 1966.
8   J. Kincaid, 'American Federalism: The Third Century' in *Annals of the American Academy of Political and Social Science*, May 1990.
9   Quoted in G. Wesserman, *The Basics of American Government*, Longman, 1997.
10   J. Kincaid, 'American Federalism: The Third Century' in *Annals of the American Academy of Political and Social Science*, May 1990.
11   D. McKay, *American Politics and Society*, Blackwell, 2001.
12   T. Dye, *American Federalism: Competition Among Governments*, Lexington Books, 1990.
13   Quoted in G. Wesserman, *The Basics of American Government*, Longman, 1997.
14   T. Hames and N. Rae, *Governing America*, Manchester University Press, 1996.
15   V. Bogdanor, *Devolution in the United Kingdom*, Oxford University Press, 1999
16   V. Bogdanor, *Devolutionin the United Kingdom*, Oxford University Press, 1999.
17   B. Coxall and L. Robins, *Contemporary British Politics*, Macmillan, 1998.

USEFUL WEB SITES

http://newfederalism.urban.org/ The Urban Institute (a Washington think tank). Monitors changes in federal social policies that affect the states and local governments.

www.governing.com/govlinks.htm *Governing* magazine (published by Congressional Quarterly, Inc. The site has links concerning state and local government matters.

In addition, the web sites of particular state and local governments can be consulted.

SAMPLE QUESTIONS

1 Does the cry of 'states rights' have any meaning in the US today?

2 To what extent has there been a shift in power away from Washington and towards the states in the last two decades of the twentieth century?

3 'American federalism works well because although the constitutional structure has been largely unchanged, in practice the system operates with flexibility and in a spirit of partnership'. Discuss.

4 To what extent has there been a change in the relationship between the federal and state governments, and why has any change come about?

5 'In the twentieth century, federalism effectively disappeared from the American political system'. What did the author of the quotation mean and how accurate is his assessment?

6 'America has a federal and Britain a unitary form of government, but in reality the influence of the national government over the states and local and devolved authorities respectively is broadly similar'. Discuss.

The executive

4

The President is the head of but one of the three branches of government, but he is – in the words of one writer[1] – the 'superstar of the American political game'. As the only nationally elected official, other than the Vice-President, he is the symbol of both the federal government and the nation. Much is expected of American presidents, but in reality there are limitations to the power which any modern president can wield. He is an 'emperor with few clothes'.[2] Power is his for a fixed term only and is held on trust from the people who elect him. It is checked by the restraints of a separate legislature and an independent judiciary.

In this chapter, we will examine the executive branch of government, analysing the development of presidential power, the differing perceptions of the role presidents should play, the help available to the President and the difficulties he experiences in controlling the federal bureaucracy.

POINTS TO CONSIDER

➤ What do we mean by 'presidential power' and why has this power tended to increase over the last 100 years?

➤ 'There is a gulf between what Americans expect of their President and what it is possible for them to achieve'. How then can we measure the success of modern presidents?

➤ 'We hear a lot about the power of the modern presidency. We should think more about the limitations of the office'. Is this true and, if so, what are the limits of presidential power?

➤ 'An era of disappointment and ultimate failure'. Is this an unfair verdict on the Clinton presidency?

➤ How would you describe the present relationship between the President and Congress?

➤ Is the Prime Minister stronger within the British system of government than the US President within the American system?

➤ Has the position of Vice-President grown in political significance in recent years and if so why?

➤ In what respects are the British and American Cabinets (a) similar and (b) dissimilar?

➤ In what ways does the federal bureaucracy both support and limit the presidency?

THE MODERN PRESIDENCY

The role of the President as outlined in the Constitution

The American Constitution has relatively little to say about what the American President can and should do. What is said is rather vague, key terms such as the executive not being clearly defined. Furthermore, the functions set out are subject to restraints.

The actual powers outlined in the document are set out in Article 2:
- Article 1vii: to veto congressional legislation;
- Article 2ii: to act as Commander-in-chief of the US armed forces;
- Article 2ii: to grant pardons;
- Article 2ii: to make treaties;
- Article 2ii: to appoint ambassadors;
- Article 2ii: to make judges;
- Article 2ii: to appoint members of the executive;
- Article 2iii: to comment on the State of the Union;
- Article 2iii: to recommend legislation to Congress;
- Article 2iii: to summon special sessions of Congress.

The Founding Fathers had in mind a presidency of which the holder would stand above the political process and act as a symbol of national unity. He would not depend directly on the people or any political party for his support. This would enable him to act as a kind of gentleman-aristocrat, remote from the political arena. Congress was supreme, as far as the actual government of the country was concerned. In the words of Maidment and McGrew,[3] the presidency would be

> the brake, the restraining hand of the federal government; it would provide the balance for the congress, and the House of Representatives in particular.

It has not worked out in this way, for from an early stage presidents have stepped in to resolve national problems. In the twentieth century, wars and domestic crises provided the opportunity for assertive leadership from the man in the White House, so that there has been a broad, underlying trend towards greater presidential power. But as we shall see, the combination of weak presidents and variations in the national mood have meant that at different times the presidency has been a power-house and a motionless engine. There has been no continuous accumulation of power, more a waxing and waning of the degree of leadership and control.

The growth of presidential power

Presidential power has increased since the days of the Founding Fathers as people turned to the presidency for initiatives to get things done. Presidents filled the vacuum left by the inertia or inaction of Congress, the states or private enterprise. Presidential power is judged according to the ability of a president to achieve the identifiable goals he has set himself. Those presidents who set themselves clear priorities and manage to accomplish them are widely viewed as successful. Some do not set themselves clear objectives, or if they do so have difficulty in fulfilling them.

1933 to the 1970s: the imperial presidency

The modern presidency really began in 1933, for the Great Depression, created (or, at least, certainly accelerated) a fundamental change in political behaviour in the United States. The sheer scale of economic dislocation and hardship overwhelmed the states, and their inadequacy was revealed. The public and the special interests turned to the federal government to promote measures of recovery. The administration of Franklin D. Roosevelt was not reluctant to respond.

Since then, the American system has become a very presidential one and the political process now requires a continued sequence of presidential initiatives in foreign policy and in the domestic arena to function satisfactorily. Modern presidents impose themselves with far greater effect on the political environment than their counterparts of the nineteenth century.

The early 1960s saw the peak of enthusiasm for presidential power. A broad spectrum of commentators welcomed its expansion, for post-1945 there was a consensus about domestic and foreign policy which encouraged a delegation of power to the President. There was a greater degree of agreement about the fundamentals of policy-making, and the level and extent of debate over public policy was less intense and robust than at other times.

Of course, there was dispute and division, but many things were agreed. The legacy of the New Deal, the great postwar economic expansion, the growing confidence over the management of the economy, the belief in the solubility of problems and the increasing claims on the federal government combined to create a feeling of well-being. It was felt to be prudent to allow the president a relatively free hand to lead his country. There was broad agreement that the federal government should have a significant role in the nation's economy and in creating and maintaining a welfare system.

The Johnson era (1963–69) was the high point of the postwar domestic consensus which was about to crumble. Till then, there was a belief that social ailments were amenable to the application of money, and this confidence in the power of economic growth and social engineering enormously enhanced the presidency. It seemed to be the only institution which could solve problems. It had the expertise to devise new policies; Congress did not, and looked to the President for a lead.

In foreign policy, the postwar consensus aroused even less dissent than its domestic counterpart. Few raised a voice against the direction of American policy after Truman had laid down the 'Truman Doctrine' which outlined America's place in the world and was to become the foundation of foreign policy to the late 1960s. America was the world's policeman and had abandoned its prewar isolationism, stationed troops abroad and played an increasingly interventionist role.

Congress had willingly accepted presidential leadership, and gave Truman and his successors more or less *carte blanche* in matters of national security. The nation was united, and Congressmen had no desire to create an impression of disunity. A bipartisan coalition acquiesced in most presidential initiatives. Foreign policy was the President's policy, which received the almost automatic ratification of Congress. It was an unsatisfactory position, which opened up the possibility of the abuse of power.

Such abuses of presidential power did occur – Vietnam (see p. 83) and Watergate were but the most significant. In 1974, many Americans became aware for the first time of the tremendous accumulation of power in the hands of the president. The Separation of Powers principle had been incorporated into the Constitution to prevent a concentration of power in one part of the government. Watergate and the revelations of the misuse of power by the executive branch by several past presidents reminded people of the message spelt out by the Founding Fathers – a system that placed too much responsibility in the hands of one man must offer temptations for wrongdoing.

Watergate

The collective label for a series of abuses of power which began with a break-in at the national headquarters of the Democratic Party in the Watergate Building, Washington DC, in June 1972, as part of an attempt to find out the Democrat's election plans and thereby assist the chances of a Republican victory. As the story unfolded, many revelations were uncovered. Several members of the Nixon administration were indicted and convicted on charges ranging from burglary and wiretapping, to 'misleading testimony' and 'political espionage'. It became apparent that Nixon had been taping conversations in the Oval Office and that he had been tapping the phones of his political enemies. When parts of the tapes were released, many began to become more than ever suspicious that the President had himself been involved. With talk of him being impeached, he resigned in August 1974, the first president to do so. He left the White House in disgrace.

This growth of executive power did not happen suddenly under President Nixon. Arthur Schlesinger[4] argued that the concept of the constitutional presidency had given way by the 1970s to an **imperial presidency**, a revolutionary use of power very different from what had originally been intended. The presidency no longer seemed to be controllable via the constitutional checks and balances.

> **imperial presidency**
> A label for the increased authority and decreased accountability of the presidency, at its peak by the late 1960s.

The 1970s to the present day

In the aftermath of these concerns, power passed to two presidents, Ford and Carter, who were widely perceived as anything but 'imperial'. Neither projected the image of an assertive leader and each was rejected by the voters after one period in office. Observers began to refer to the limitations of the presidency rather than to the strength of the office, with Franck[5] writing of the 'tethered presidency', one too constrained to be effective of providing the leadership America required.

Ronald Reagan was the first postwar president since Eisenhower to complete two terms in office, and despite the lapses which occurred (in particular, Irangate – see opposite), he is widely perceived as having achieved much of what he wished to accomplish. Many Americans seemed to warm to his style, which is why he has been immortalised in numerous ways, with an airport, an aircraft carrier and highways being named in his honour.

The Reagan years (1981–89) were eventful in foreign and in domestic policy. In external relations, the President began with a reputation as a cold war warrior, deeply suspicious of the 'evil empire' of the Soviet Union. Yet in the second term, the unyielding attitude was softened, and his close working relationship with the Soviet leader Gorbachev helped to bring about an easing of international tension and an end to the Cold War. By 1988, the thaw in relations was well underway, and the most anti-communist president of recent years had reached an accommodation with the regime he had long detested.

At home, his agenda was to reduce the role of government in the lives of ordinary Americans, and he wished to return power to the states and downplay the influence of the federal government in Washington. His economic programme included a commitment to tax cuts, and the Reagan years witnessed an era of economic growth. There was also a huge expansion of the federal deficit, for lower taxes and increased military expenditure were not matched by cuts elsewhere of a proportionate nature. The US, the largest creditor nation in 1981, was the world's largest debtor eight years later.

The goal of substantially rolling back the sphere of influence of the federal government was not achieved. Federal expenditure actually increased marginally in the early years though non-defence spending – such as that on education – suffered sizeable cuts. But what Reagan was able to do was to make many Americans feel good about themselves and their country. After years in which its reputation had taken as severe blow over episodes such as Vietnam and Watergate, he was able to restore morale and there was a resurgence of patriotic feeling and confidence about the future.

Irangate

President Reagan's style of leadership was relaxed and detached, and he did not involve himself in anything but the broad generalities of policy. His aloofness from day-to-day activities had certain benefits, but carried the disadvantage that he was sometimes ill-informed and out of touch with events occurring in his administration.

The Iran–Contra affair, the major crisis of his presidency, occurred as a result of his method of managing the nation's affairs. Two officials within the National Security Council, John Poindexter and the more junior Lieutenant-Colonel Oliver North, were accused of pursuing a policy of selling arms to Iran in return for the release of American hostages detained in the Middle East. The proceeds of the arms sales were channelled to the Contras, rebel forces who were seeking to overthrow the left-wing Sandinista government of Nicaragua which the US Administration wished to destabilise and hopefully bring about its overthrow.

Both operations, the arms for hostages and the diversion of money to the guerrillas, were illegal. Congress had refused to agree to military aid for the rebel forces, though it was willing to grant humanitarian assistance and keen to see the regime toppled. Altogether, at least four main laws were breached, and the sale of weapons to states sponsoring terrorism was something which the President himself had publicly denounced.

George Bush was a Republican of a different kind to Reagan, and was uncommitted to the economic doctrines of the New Right. When he took over, he was confronted with the vast budget deficit, and contrary to his election promises he was forced to introduce increased taxation. He was not deeply interested in domestic problems, but found himself in office when many Americans began to worry about stagnation at home in domestic policy. His neglect of this area left him vulnerable to his political critics, and despite his successful conduct of the Gulf War abroad, he was unable to arouse popular enthusiasm when faced by the challenge of Bill Clinton and Ross Perot in 1992.

Unlike Bush, **Bill Clinton** was not initially faced by a Congress dominated by his political opponents, but the advantage was more apparent than real and his initiatives were rebuffed on several occasions. After the November 1994 elections, he was confronted by two Republican-dominated chambers, a situation which lasted throughout the rest of his presidency. Relations with Congress were often strained, the more so as the President became more deeply immersed in the problems which led to his impeachment. But in the eyes of many Americans he remained a likeable and attractive figure, whatever his personal lapses.

Bill Clinton: an assessment of his presidency

For many Americans, much of the Clinton presidency was a serious disappointment. His political opponents claimed to disapprove of both him and his lifestyle. But even many fellow-progressives felt disappointment, for the hopes he engendered of a fairer society seemed to evaporate early on as he embraced the Republican agenda in a modified way to win a second term. Even sympathisers saw the second administration as a time of missed opportunities, and felt that if months had not been wasted on the long investigations into tales of dissembling, lying and sexual/financial misconduct then more could have been achieved. The frustration was all the greater for Democrats to bear as they had not been in control of the White House for most of the previous thirty years.

There were many Americans who continued to like him, as an individual and a president. They believed that he lied and obstructed justice and that this was reprehensible, but they were also unattracted by the behaviour of the moral puritans who assailed him. Whatever the letter of the law, many preferred to act on their own beliefs and were unwilling to condemn him for personal weaknesses. They were willing to praise aspects of his presidency. They looked at the Clinton years and knew that as America entered the new millennium it was enjoying an era of general economic prosperity and social peace for which the President could – and did – take some credit. Economic growth was spectacular, inflation negligible and unemployment lower than for several years. The Dow Jones index continued to soar, standing at just over 3000 when he took over but nearer to 10,000 in late 2000. Even the crime figures were going down, with the murder rate the lowest in three decades. Clinton could say that Americans had rarely had it so good.

When he left office, the state of the Union was seemingly strong. A mountain of statistics could be assembled to point to the robust good health of the country, and he was able to highlight this contrast between the new golden age over which he believed he was presiding and what were – in his view – the unjustified proceedings against him.

As it reached its conclusion, supporters could claim that the Clinton presidency has re-asserted a role for government without relying on the lumbering machinery of bureaucracy past. Even in the midst of his troubles in January

1999, Clinton used his annual speech to the nation to spell out that the current revenue surplus should not be used for tax cuts but to assist the country's strained pensions system, cash for the elderly rather than assistance to the rich. He spoke of investing part of the social security pot in the stock market to generate a better return for pensioners and via his Universal Savings Accounts he promised to match the personal savings of Americans with money from the government, offering more money to those with smaller incomes.

After six years in which progressive politics often seemed to be on the back burner, he was beginning to flesh out the less-than-meaty bones of the Third Way which he and Tony Blair had often spoken about. Seemingly to the left of the British Prime Minister, he spoke of the 'vital centre' and began to advance an agenda for the future which was neither old left or new right. Future historians may yet look back on the Clinton years as a period of prosperity in which a form of practical progressivism was both preached and practised.

Undeniably Bill Clinton is a flawed human being, a point Americans realise. They knew they were not getting a saint in 1992 and he certainly lived down to their worst fears as far as personal lapses went. Yet in home and foreign affairs he was not a failure and if the scandals can be erased from the picture then in some respects he was quite an impressive president. He would be disappointed with the poll of American history professors (see p. 72) which ranked him only 21st out of 41 presidents. They classified him as strong on the pursuit of equal justice, economic management and persuasion skills, but weak on relations with Congress (36th) and bottom of the pile on moral authority, where he suffered the ignominy of finishing even below Richard Nixon.

In a recent survey of American presidential leadership styles, Fred Greenstein[6] has effectively summed up the mixed Clinton performance in this way:

> It is a tribute to Clinton's resiliency and political prowess that he has succeeded in serving two presidential terms. It is a commentary on his weaknesses that this talented political leader has not had more to show for his time in office.

The George W. Bush presidency: first indications

Critics have been quick to caricature the new president as a know-nothing, verbally challenged and not-very-industrious politician who has risen well beyond his abilities. They have also found plenty of evidence that he has shifted American politics sharply to the right. If this is so, it is a far cry from the 'compassionate conservatism' which George W. advanced in the election campaign. At the time, the allegation was frequently made that there would be little to choose between the two candidates; whoever won, little would change.

After polling day, many Americans indeed hoped that George W. would recognise his limited mandate and seek to govern from the centre, as a man of the consensus. This has not proved to be the case, for he and his supporters were serious in their intent to mark a distinct break from the Clinton years. They have won the support of the ultra-conservative Heritage Foundation, whose members are pleased to find that many items on the Republican wish-list are becoming reality. Its head[7] has detected that the new team are 'more Reaganite than the Reagan administration'.

The Bush technique seems to be to use the rhetoric of bipartisanship, humility and healing as a cover for the pursuit of a radically conservative agenda. The president's charm and seeming reasonableness have earned him some admiration, as have some of his early initiatives. For instance, he has:

- appointed Colin Powell, widely seen as a moderate, as his Secretary of State, and a black woman, Condoleeza Rice, as his national security adviser;
- selected an ethnically diverse cabinet which includes two black and two Asian Americans (one of the Asians is a Democrat, Norman Mineta), a Cuban American, an Arab-American, and four women;
- tried to break down social barriers in Washington by inviting liberal critics to the White House and also meeting black American political leaders and visiting black churches and schools;
- opted for an educational policy which Democrats broadly support, the emphasis being upon improving provision in the poorest areas of the country, with extra funding and greater teacher accountability; he has shown some willingness to negotiate over the principle and detail of his contentious educational voucher scheme.

The charm offensive has helped to blunt some Democrat criticism of the Bush agenda and performance, a task made easier because the last, scandal-ridden days of the Clinton administration demoralised the opposition. But behind the handshakes and smiles, the actions are tougher than the tone would suggest. Critics point out that the cabinet may be socially well balanced, but that its members are in several cases deeply conservative. They also note the importance of business in the administration, with millionaires at the cabinet table; for instance, Condoleeza Rice has a Chevron oil tanker named after her and chief of staff Andrew Card is a former leading lobbyist of General Motors. More partisan and controversial actions have included:

- appointing hard-liners such as John Ashcroft as his attorney general (his record includes strong backing for those who oppose abortion rights and affirmative action) and the hawkish Donald Rumsfeld as his defense secretary;
- widening the already-large gap between the position of the haves and have-nots, by a redistribution of wealth in favour of the rich; measures include:
  (i) the programme of $1,600 billion tax cuts which primarily benefit more

affluent Americans; and (ii) the proposal to drop inheritance tax, to the benefit of the top 2 per cent of Americans, who have estates worth more than $675,000;

- supporting faith-based social services, by offering aid to churches which perform welfare work; critics fear that this might lead to reductions in funding of secular social care;
- opposing a patients' bill of rights, which would remove legal immunity from private healthcare organisations;
- halting foreign aid spending on abortions, so that in future there will be no federal spending in support of international family planning organisations which back abortion;
- allowing prospectors to open up the Alaskan National Wildlife Refuge and relaxing environmental controls on old power plants;
- repudiating the Kyoto protocol signed by Bill Clinton on pegging greenhouse gas emissions;
- renouncing American support for the nuclear test-ban treaty, the anti-ballistic missile treaty and the ban on chemical weapons, and pursuing a costly and highly controversial national missile defence system known as Star Wars Two; opponents believe that narrowly defined national security interests and the commercial interests of the biotechnology sector are being allowed to take precedence over responsible multi-lateral agreements and global collaboration.

In May 2001, the new President received a setback, with the news that James Jeffords, a liberal senator from Vermont, had defected to the Democrats. Jeffords was born into a different Republican party and found that he could no longer find a home in the highly conservative party of today. There is a danger that some other moderates might follow his example, unless the Republicans become more accommodating and inclusive. Yet the President has shown little willingness to modify his programme and insists that his policies will not be derailed.

The defection of Jeffords means that the Democrats have taken control of the Senate. They will now take over major committee chairmanships, and have the opportunity to control what legislation proceeds and when. They will also be able to veto Bush nominees for top governmental and judicial posts.

A more assertive presidency

On 11 September 2001, there was a sudden terrorist attack on the World Trade Center in New York, a building which symbolised the business life of America. Hijacked aircraft crashed into the twin towers, causing thousands of deaths and massive destruction. Intelligence sources immediately pointed to Osama bin Laden (and his Al-Qaida organisation) as the guilty party.

Once the aggressor was confirmed, President Bush was under strong pressure from elements within the United States to act swiftly, but he did not take any drastic measures straightaway. Acting in concert with the British government, he attempted to create an international coalition to wage war on international terrorism. The war aims which he set the US and its allies were to apprehend Bin Laden and destroy his network, both of which are long-term goals. As the air campaign in Afghanistan (where Bin Laden was hiding) got underway, it became apparent that in destroying the Taliban regime there was another goal.

The collapse of the twin towers jolted the Bush presidency into uncharacter-istic vigour. It moved into a higher gear and Bush became more focused and purposeful. Washington reorganised itself around the executive branch and Bush reorganised his administration around the struggle against terrorism. Almost at once, he persuaded Congress to approve a substantial recovery package that also made additional provision to allow for strengthening of the intelligence and security services. It also quickly passed an anti-terrorism bill which greatly increased the potential of executive power.

Having long been suspicious of the power exercised by 'big government' in Washington, many Americans were in a mood to accept more assertive presi-dential leadership. They were unsure of what was happening to them and yearned for a sense of direction. This has given the President a chance to take a firmer grip upon events. He began to shape the political agenda, and his early actions were accepted with little dissent. Some commentators have begun to use phrases such as 'the revived presidency' or 'the imperialised presidency'. War – in this case on terrorism – has been the catalyst for change. It demands personalised control from the man who symbolises the unity of the country.

In seeking to wage war on terrorism, the President is engaged in a daunting task. In the short term, a crisis of the magnitude of 11 September tends to boost presidential prestige. It can serve to mature a new incumbent of the White House into an international statesman. This has happened and in its early days an American tragedy has proved to be the making of George Bush. In the words of a Washington correspondent, 'the sharpest learning curve in the history of the presidency has seen Bush mutate into a figurehead who has the people behind him'.[8]

The experience of Vietnam shows that if things were to go badly wrong, then presidential credibility could be seriously eroded. Bush walks a tightrope, having raised expectations which may be difficult to deliver without serious casualties. Whereas previous leaders could in theory have walked away from Vietnam, it would be difficult for him to withdraw from the task upon which he and his advisers have embarked. For the present, Americans are content to rally round the man who leads them. Should he fail in his objectives, then there could be another attempt to limit presidential power.

Presidential leadership today

As the size and influence of the United States in the world has developed so has the machinery of government and with it the informal power and influence of the President. He is a national leader and by many is seen also as the leader of the Western world, the person who will represent the country on the global stage.

The nature of the presidency at a particular moment depends considerably upon the incumbent. Great men make great presidents. Personality is important to the style and impact of the presidency, but the active presidential leadership of the 1960s and the habit of congressional compliance is out of fashion.

Popular expectations of presidents

Many Americans want more from their President than somebody who is merely efficient while in office. They also want someone 'presidential', and look for someone who can embody the American creed and reflect the 'spirit of the people'. Like the flag and the Constitution, the president is a symbol of national identity. Some have been successful in capturing the public's imagination and winning their support, as Kennedy and Reagan were able to do. If they can do this, then their influence and informal power will increase as well.

In the age of television, the personality and style of leadership of anyone who would be President have become all-important. The need to perform well is crucial, and Reagan, for all of his seeming lack of familiarity with some key issues and his occasional verbal stumbles, was a man who embodied the American Dream. His resolute optimism, his old-fashioned values and his promise to help America 'stand tall' after the malaise of the 1970s were very popular. His background as a film and TV actor enabled him to communicate well (his supporters called him 'the Great Communicator'), so that he represented a merger between the worlds of entertainment and politics.

In some respects, popular expectations are unreal. At different times, Americans have a different idea of what their president should be like. At times, they demand vigorous leadership, but they may then become troubled by the consequences of that assertiveness and yearn for a less active presidency. After a while, such inactivity can be portrayed as weakness and ineffectiveness. In Wasserman's words:[9] 'Americans have swung back and forth in how powerful they want their presidents ... [they] have walked a thin line between too much and too little power'. He illustrates this by pointing to the worries felt by many citizens about the abuse of power by Nixon, yet the perception only a few years later that Jimmy Carter was too weak to solve the nation's difficulties. In actual fact, it was the reaction against Vietnam and Watergate (as well as changes in the organisation of Congress) that made it difficult for Carter to stamp his authority on the legislature.

The reputation of past presidents

In early 2000, the findings of a survey of 58 American history professors were publicised for the public affairs TV channel C-Span. Ten qualities were tested, ranging from crisis leadership to moral authority, from vision to administrative skills, and from the pursuit of equal justice to performance in the context of the times. The top ten in the rankings were (in order) Lincoln, Franklin Roosevelt, Washington, Teddy Roosevelt, Truman, Wilson, Jefferson, Kennedy, Eisenhower and Lyndon Johnson, whose reputation has risen steadily in recent years.

What is clear from the tables to which we have alluded is that almost without exception the presidents considered 'great' by academic commentators have been 'leaders'. Most of the more passive ones have been long forgotten or remembered only because of the futility or scandals of their administrations.

The presidency is what its holder makes of it, being as large and important, or as weak and as insignificant, as the holders of the office. Academics have tended to divide past presidents into 'active' leaders of the nation or 'constitutional or passive' ones. The two views of presidential power can be seen in contrasting the approach of past incumbents and reactions to them.

Theodore Roosevelt remarked in his *Autobiography* that he 'did not usurp power but ... did greatly broaden the use of executive power'. He was of the Lincoln school and like him a Republican. He favoured a policy of active leadership, setting out national goals. Others of this type have wanted to make a mark on the national scene, not being content with mere stewardship of the presidency. Roosevelt, Truman, Kennedy and Johnson were of this type, as was Bill Clinton.

By contrast, the leaders of Lincoln's own party in the two chambers of Congress gave a warning in what has become known as the Wade–Davis manifesto: 'the authority of Congress is paramount ... if [the president] wishes our support he must confine himself to his executive duties – to obey, and to execute, not to make laws'. Those who take this view have a custodial view of the presidency, by which the incumbent confines himself to carrying out those powers expressly mentioned in the Constitution and leaves Congress to take the lead in deciding what is to be done. Examples included Harding and Coolidge in the 1920s – significantly, they were both Republicans many of whom tend to have a more sceptical view of the role of government.

Some writers[10] have detected a third genre, referred to as the 'Eisenhower type'. Exponents of this style combine elements of both the views described above. They tend to delegate responsibility (and thus shield themselves from blame when things go wrong), using the rhetoric of being 'above the political battle' to conceal a more active engagement with the political process. Sometimes called the 'hidden-hand' approach, its adherents have sometimes been willing to take a decisive stand and wield a surprising degree of power. Nixon tried to convey the impression of being a national figure and statesman beyond the heat of battle, whilst at the same time using the White House as a centre for powerful and partisan leadership.

Most modern presidents have by inclination been more activists than stewards. Bill Clinton began his period in office by taking several initiatives, helped as he was by his majority in both chambers of Congress. But his intentions were stalled in November 1994 and the political agenda was increasingly set on Capitol Hill rather than in the White House, with Clinton reacting to policies rather than shaping them. Some of his later 'triumphs' were more by way of fending off the impact of congressional inroads into social programmes, than as a result of his preferred lines of action. Yet in his case his qualities as an effective campaigner, with a knack for appealing over the heads of Congressmen to the nation at large, often enabled him to stage a comeback. He was able to use the presidential office as a pulpit from which to preach his values on issues which mattered to him, such as the family, race and even religion.

Presidential success?

It is unclear what constitutes presidential success. The views of academics (see p. 72) and the voters do not necessarily coincide, and the two groups do not necessarily share the same priorities. Success depends on what the president is supposed to do. If the criterion is dynamism and/or creativity, then Eisenhower was not a success. But in other respects, given his more limited conception as a steward of national affairs, he was arguably successful, being a popular national leader who was suitable for the mood of the times.

Certain eras require more vigorous leadership and legislative action than others. By the criterion of the proportion of his legislative programme achieved, President Johnson was an undoubted success. But he presided over a country which was becoming increasingly troubled and divided, and his memory has been tarnished by the events in Vietnam. Bill Clinton was able to speak to the hearts of many Americans at times of crisis and presided over eight years of economic success. Yet he stained the presidency as a result of his personal conduct and harmed his party's prospects in the 2000 election.

Factors in the growth of presidential power: a summary

1 **The growth of 'big government' in years after 1933**, as Roosevelt became identified with increased federal intervention in the Depression.

2 **The importance of foreign policy**, with the development of an American world role after World War II.

3 **The personality and conception of the office held by the incumbent:** sometimes, a passive president seems appropriate for the times, as in the twenties, whilst at other times an active presidency is required.

4 **The inertia of Congress and erosion of balance:** at times, Congress surrendered much influence, and allowed strong 'liberals' to achieve reform.

5 **The mass media:** the media can focus on one national office, for the president is news.

The limitations on presidential power

In *Presidential Power*, first published in 1960, Richard Neustadt[11] pointed to the limitations on the power of the president, as well as to the strength of his position. He was writing in the decade of the 'imperial presidency', before the post-Nixon era. In a subsequent edition, he was able to detect more evidence of presidential weakness and he reiterated his emphasis upon the importance of the personal qualities of the incumbent. It takes, in his view, a person of extraordinary temperament to make a really significant impact and achieve all the goals he sets for himself. Among the specific factors which he has highlighted are:

1 **Congress** (see also p. 83 below)

The President needs congressional support, and in the more assertive mood of Congress in recent years incumbents have found this difficult to achieve even with their own party in control. Faced by a hostile Congress, Bush and Clinton (in his last six years) had difficulties in carrying out their programme, resulting in 'gridlock', a situation in which the two branches of government were locked in conflict.

> **impeachment**
> The process by which Congress can remove officers of the national government, including the president. The House votes on a charge or series of charges and a trial on the charges is then conducted in the Senate.

The tendency of Congress to appoint special prosecutors to probe every aspect of a President's affairs, and the relentless media interest which this creates, has a paralysing impact on presidential policy. Investigations drag on, seemingly for partisan reasons, and – as Clinton found to his costs – there is always the ultimate horror of the threat of **impeachment** at the end of the road.

2 The Supreme Court

The Court can damage a president and negate a particular activity, as it did to FDR over his 'Court-packing' scheme (see p. 147) and to President Nixon over the Watergate Tapes. During the Clinton presidency too, it became clear that proceedings could be brought against an incumbent, with the President and his closest staff being compelled to give evidence under oath.

3 The Constitution and constitutional amendments

Any president seeking to bring about a measure of gun control faces the difficulty that the right to bear arms is written into the Constitution. In developing his New Deal programme, President Roosevelt found that the same document could be used as a barrier to social progress.

Some amendments to the Constitution in the last few decades of the twentieth century have weakened the presidency. The 22nd Amendment limited the president to two terms of office and the 25th provided for the removal of a person physically or mentally unfit.

4 The federal system

Whereas **1** and **2** above are limitations which derive from the operation of the Separation of Powers principle, so too are there hurdles for any President which reflect the operation of the idea of federalism. The fifty states have a large degree of fiscal and legislative autonomy, which acts as a check on the role of the federal government and therefore of the President who has to negotiate with state representatives in several areas of decision-making.

5 The mass media

Television can be a source of power to a telegenic president, but it can also act as a 'double-edged sword'. It can damage his reputation, for a poor performance or gaffe (e.g. the Ford in the presidential debates of 1976 – see p. 174) is seen by so many viewers that credibility is undermined. Press journalists can be vigilant in exposing presidential wrong-doings, as over Vietnam, Watergate, Irangate and Whitewatergate/Monicagate. The press was generally indulgent towards President Kennedy's personal indiscretions, but in the post-Watergate atmosphere it has been more disposed 'to seek out the dirt' in the private lives of politicians.

6 Pressure groups

Individual groups achieve prominence at particular times. Today, a Republican president has to contend with the Christian fundamentalists, pro-lifers and big corporations. A Democrat has to deal with the labour unions and environmentalists. In Bill Clinton's first few months in office, the clashes between groups concerned over 'gays in the military' inflicted serious damage to his reputation.

7 Public opinion

Levels of popular support can fluctuate, as they did for George Bush senior (high at the time of Gulf War, then down as the state of the domestic economy failed to impress Americans). Clinton was able to retain a high degree of public approval, in spite of his personal misdemeanours. He was able to bounce back after the disastrous 1994 elections and to win re-election. Many have been less fortunate, and this can be damaging not only because of the need to win re-election. A President who is losing popular backing or at least acquiescence may find that opposition in Congress, the media and the bureaucracy will increase, so that other checking mechanisms come into play.

8 Bureaucracy

The President has plenty of constitutional authority, but the problem is sometimes how to get the bureaucracy to work for him. He needs to be able to persuade as well as to direct, but even then he can find that his will is frustrated by bureaucrats who tend to see the world through a lens which is focused largely on their own departments. No modern president seems to have been able to stop the growth of bureaucracy, so that the majority of the agencies created since the 1930s have survived intact into the twenty-first century.

There are other factors ranging from the power of the federal reserve to determine interest rates to the current mood of detachment, some say neo-isolationism, which affects the conduct of foreign and defence policy: one area in which presidents – as commanders-in-chief – have always given a lead.

The American writers, Burns et al (11) make a series of fair observations when they write of

> one of the persisting paradoxes of the American presidency ... on the one hand, the institution is too powerful, and on the other, it is always too weak. It is too strong because in many ways it is contrary to our ideals of government by the people and decentralization of power. It is too weak because presidents seldom are able to keep the promises they make. Of course, the presidency is always too strong when we dislike the incumbent. And the president is always too constrained when we believe a President is striving to serve the public interest – as we define it.

Neustadt, as quoted above, makes the point that the power of the president always did depend upon personal leadership rather more than the formal position: 'powers are no guarantee of power'. This was true in the days of the imperial presidency. Indeed, it is easy to over-stress the power of presidents before Watergate and to over-emphasise the decline or difficulties of the presidency from the 1970s onwards. John Hart[13] reminds us that Franklin Roosevelt (FDR), the first of the so-called modern presidents, was untypical in the power which he exercised:

> None of his successors faced anything like the enormity of the Depression of the early 1930s, and none took over the White House during a national emergency so clearly and unambiguously defined. Neither has any post-FDR President had such a comparable level of public support for presidential initiative and leadership. As the beneficiary of a landslide election victory in a realigning election (one in which the voters opted for a complete change of direction and which resulted in a permanent shift in popular support), a strong coat-tails effect in the congressional races, and as head of a political party that behaved as a 'cohesive office-seeking team', FDR enjoyed a political environment that none of his successors have shared, and most could only fantasise about.

In other words, the Roosevelt presidency was the exception rather than the rule. Personality, ability and circumstance all play their part in determining presidential power, but whoever is in the White House operates in a system which specifically denies too much power to the Executive.

The differing roles of the President

Head of state

The President is the symbolic head of state and as such a focal point of loyalty. He has ceremonial functions, ranging from visiting foreign countries to attending important national occasions. These opportunities for favourable media coverage give him an advantage over his opponents, for he can be seen to speak and act in a 'presidential' manner.

Chief executive

The ability of the President to carry out or execute laws is laid down in Article 2 of the Constitution – 'The executive power shall be vested in a President of the United States'. He is the head of a vast federal bureaucracy, employing nearly three million civilians in the executive branch.

Chief legislator

Although the President is not part of the legislative branch of government, he has the constitutional rights to recommend measures to Congress. In the twentieth century, presidents increasingly found themselves in the position of producing a package to encourage the legislature. They have used the State of the Union address every January to present their annual programme and today most measures passed by Congress have their origins in the executive branch. As we have seen, much depends on the political situation. A president without a congressional majority – such as Bill Clinton in his last six years – is in the position of responding to and attempting to modify measures, rather than initiating them. In general, presidents are more successful in securing their legislation in the earlier than in the latter years of their term.

In this role, presidents make extensive use of arm-twisting techniques to impose their will or fend off policies which they dislike. This may involve invitations for Senators and Representatives to attend the White House or a round of golf ('killing opposition by kindness') or threats to obstruct public works projects in a congressman's district. Senator Byrd of West Virginia gave an indication of the sort of meeting that might occur, in the *New York Times* (26 July 1985):

> [President] 'I respect you for your opposition to that funding [for the Contras in central America], but I wish you would see your way to vote with us next time on that. Can you do it?'
> 'Well, I will certainly be glad to think about it, Mr President ...'
> 'Well, Bob, I hope you will. And by the way, that money for the heart research center in Morgantown that you have worked for, I will bet your people love you for that ... I have given a lot of thought to that. Be sure and take another look at that item we have, funds for the Contras.'

In addition to subtle and more blatant arm-twisting, presidents can also use the presidential veto (see box below), as a means of blocking unwanted policies.

The presidential veto

After passing through both houses of Congress, bills are sent to the White House for the President to sign. If the President fails to act within ten days (excepting Sundays), a bill automatically becomes law. But in the last ten days of a session, a failure to act amounts to a **pocket veto**; in other words, as Congress is not sitting and cannot fight back, the bill is effectively killed.

When a president vetoes a bill within the allotted time, Congress can override the decision, as long as two-thirds of those present in each chamber support the initiative. Presidents know that Congress only very rarely successfully overrides their vetoes, so that the mere threat of using the power is often enough to enable them to extract concessions from the legislature. As long as the power is sometimes used, the threat is a credible one. Presidents vary in their use of the veto, some using it extensively, as the figures suggest:

Number of vetoes and overrides for selected presidents 1933–96

President	Number of bills vetoed	Number and percentage of vetoes overridden
F. Roosevelt (1933–45)	635	9 (1.4%)
D. Eisenhower (1953–61)	181	2 (1.1%)
L. Johnson (1963–69)	30	0 (0.0%)
R. Nixon (1969–74)	43	7 (16.3%)
R. Reagan (1981–89)	78	9 (11.5%)
B Clinton (1991–95)	17	1 (5.8%)

Source: Figures adapted from those available from the Research Division, Congressional Quarterly, Washington DC.

Head of party

The president is the leader of his or her party, a role which itself involves several duties. The President:

- tries to fulfil its programme, the platform on which he or she was elected;
- is its chief fund-raiser and campaigner;
- appoints its national chairperson;
- distributes offices and favours to the party faithful.

As party leader, the President's control is limited, the more so given the decentralised nature of American political parties. He or she can use party identification to gain support in Congress, if they are of the same party, but in the case of Bill Clinton this did not guarantee support even in the first two years when he had a congressional majority. If members of either chamber oppose the President, there is little he or she can do about it, other than appeal directly to the people over their heads. The President has no formal disciplinary sanctions.

Presidents vary in their attempts to keep the party within their control. President Carter placed little emphasis on this party responsibility, which did

For many years, critics of the procedure argued that the presidential veto was a blunt weapon, for the President either had to sign or reject an entire bill. Knowing this, Congressmen sometimes attached extra (and unpalatable) provisions (**riders**) to a bill which they knew the president really wanted. By so doing, they were trapping him, for he either had to sign the whole bill with the unwanted features, or lose it altogether. After much discussion, Congress finally passed a **line-item veto** in 1996, giving the President the power to veto 'objectionable' parts of an appropriations (expenditure) bill, whilst agreeing to the rest of it. This innovation was soon tested in the Supreme Court. In *Clinton v New York* (June 1998), the judges were asked to decide whether Bill Clinton's rejection of some aspects of a tax bill was legitimate. They concluded that the line-item veto was unconstitutional, in that it violated the requirement that any bill must pass both houses and be signed by the President in the same form. If the President was allowed to strike out particular features, then in effect a new bill was being created.

The loss of the line-item veto means that presidents are left with one weaker power which they can employ if they are unhappy with a piece of legislation. Having signed the bill, they can withhold the funds (**impoundment**) appropriated by Congress for its implementation. Generally, impoundment has been used sparingly, but President Nixon used it regularly against a Democrat-dominated Congress, both as a means of controlling spending and as a means of controlling its behaviour. Congress responded by passing the Budget and Impoundment Control Act in 1974 (see p. 123). This laid down restrictions on the presidential use of impoundment. What remains is a much weakened alternative to the defunct line-item veto.

PRESIDENTS AND FOREIGN POLICY

Crisis management

The President's roles as Chief diplomat and Commander-in-chief are related to another presidential responsibility: crisis management. A crisis is a sudden, unpredictable and potentially dangerous event. Most occur in the realm of foreign policy. Crises often involve hot tempers and high risks. Quick judgements are needed, despite the availability of only sketchy information. Whether it is American hostages held in Iran or the discovery of Soviet missiles in Cuba, a crisis challenges the President to make difficult decisions. In origin, crises are rarely the president's doing, but handled incorrectly they can be the President's undoing.

With modern communications, the president can instantly monitor events almost anywhere. Moreover, because situations develop more rapidly today, there is a premium on rapid action, secrecy, constant management, consistent judgement and expert advice. Congress usually moves slowly (one might say deliberatively), is large (making it difficult to keep secrets) and composed of generalists. As a result, the President – who can come to quick and consistent decisions, confine information to a small group, carefully oversee developments and call upon experts in the executive branch – has become more prominent in handling crises.

Throughout the century, crises have allowed presidents to become more powerful, and crisis management is a natural role for most who assume the presidential position. Most have been only too willing to step in to the vacuum and seize their chance to lead, whether it be Kennedy over the Cuban missiles, Bush senior over the Iraqi invasion of Kuwait, Clinton over Bosnia or George W. Bush over the terrorist attacks on Washington and New York in September 2001.

The machinery of foreign policy

Presidents have their own style of management, and their own priorities. Some wish to be more involved with the detail of foreign policy than others, and wish to centralise decision-making on all aspects of foreign and national security matters into their own hands. The foreign policy-making machine in the United States is a vast one, with the President at the apex of the structure. He or she appoints key personnel such as the Secretary of State (SOS) and the Defense Secretary (SOD), and the heads of important agencies such as the Central Intelligence Agency (CIA).

In its original form, the Department of State was not concerned with overseas policy alone, but over the years most of its domestic workload was gradually transferred elsewhere. The Department retains the Great Seal of the United States, and if the President or Vice-President resigns it is to the Secretary of State that the resignation is officially submitted. The main work of the Department is concerned with:

- promoting of the security interests of the US and its allies;
- protecting foreign trade and commerce;
- helping negotiate and enforce treaties and other agreements with foreign countries;
- administering the Agency for International Development, and the Peace Corps, and most non-military aid to foreign nations;
- maintaining friendly contacts between the US and other countries, including such things as arranging the reception of new foreign ambassadors by the President and advising on the recognition of new foreign countries and governments;
- informing the American public about developments in the field of foreign policy, by publishing appropriate documents, official papers and other publications;
- protecting American citizens, their welfare and property abroad. (This last function involves the supervision of the Foreign Service of the United States, including the ambassadors, and administrative, consular, economic and political officers who manage the countries foreign relations. It is also concerned with the treatment of any Americans abroad, and it issues passports for their visits and processes visa applications for those entering America.)

In the Executive Office, see pp. 84–90, the President has his own advisers, and the Special Assistant for National Security Affairs (SA) has a highly significant position in the presidential team. Presidents like the advice and support of the SA, for not only is he conveniently located (in the White House) but he also owes prime loyalty to the person who chose him for the position. By contrast, the Secretary of State – once appointed – has a department to represent, the views of which can shape his or her own in a way which the President may not like.

The National Security Council (NSC), created by the National Security Act of 1947, meets irregularly to advise the president on foreign and defence policy. By the terms of the statute, it comprises the President, Vice-President and the Secretaries of State and Defense, along with advisers such as the heads of the CIA and the Joint Chiefs of Staff. Originally, the position of Special Assistant was little more than that of a secretary to the NSC, but it has grown vastly in scope. Today, some presidents prefer to rely on an informal group of advisers and the SA, rather than the statutory body.

Despite intentions to the contrary, Ronald Reagan allowed his SA unprecedented freedom of manoeuvre, and in the Iran–Contra affair his office operated what was in effect an independent foreign policy. The State Department and Congress were in the dark about the way in which the SA and some members of the NSC were engaged in trading arms with Iran in return for the release of American hostages, just as they were about using the proceeds of arms sales to supply the Contra guerillas in Nicaragua with weaponry – and thus evade a congressional ban on such a distribution of military supplies. 'Irangate', as it became known, illustrated the difficulties of establishing democratic control of the SA and his office. It also showed how powerful that office is, for the SA has special access to the President. Whatever they may say before assuming office, presidents like this source of extra and independent advice, for it frees them from the bureaucratic preoccupations of any department or agency.

little to ease his relations with Congress. At first, Clinton was more aware of party feelings and the need to 'manage' his legislative colleagues, but his policies came unstuck. By the time he was seeking re-election in 1996, there was an air of detachment between the presidential and congressional wings of the party.

Chief diplomat

The President has the power to develop relations with representatives of foreign powers, appoint ambassadors to those countries and sign treaties that become effective once the Senate has consented by a two-thirds majority. As we have seen, in the postwar years, presidents have become the initiator and executor of foreign policy. Although Congress officially declares war, there is presidential primacy in this area and this has provided incumbents with a formidable source of influence and power, doing much to enhance or diminish their political stature at home.

Commander-in-chief of the armed forces

Closely related to the role of chief diplomat is the position of Commander-in-chief, for it is the ability to use the might of the armed forces that makes a president's foreign policy credible. Presidents have very extensive powers in wartime, deciding when to intervene abroad. They have embarked on intervention in episodes ranging from wars in Korea to Vietman, deploying troops as necessary. In practice, much of the authority is delegated to the Secretary of State for Defense, who in turn normally delegate his command to leading figures in the military establishment.

In reaction to presidential war-making in Vietnam, Congress passed the **War Powers Act** in 1973 to curb presidential freedom. However, its effectiveness is questionable and presidents from Reagan to Clinton have basically ignored the limitations it was designed to impose upon them. It is often mentioned at times when troops are deployed, but in 1991 during the war with Iraq President Bush described it as being 'unconstitutional' and three years later, in sending troops to

War Powers Act

Imposed a 60-day limit on the time for which a President can keep American troops abroad without congressional approval. Without such authorisation, the troops have to be withdrawn; overall, 90 days can be allowed, to enable the withdrawal to be carried out successfully.

Haiti, his successor also did not seek congressional approval for his intervention. Originally the Act was passed over President Nixon's veto, and ever since Congress and a succession of presidents have failed to reach agreement over its status and relevance.

Others

The late Clinton Rossiter, an American political scientist, listed others – 'Voice of the People' in American affairs, 'Protector of Peace' (intervening in race riots etc.), 'Manager of Prosperity' and 'Leader of the Western World'.

The presidency and Congress

The Constitution places a joint responsibility on both the President and Congress to govern the nation, and real leadership is only easy to bring about when both bodies (and sometimes the Supreme Court as well) are facing in the same direction. Sometimes, as we have seen, Congress has the upper hand, but in the last sixty years of the twentieth century presidents were usually in control despite attempts to lay down specific restraints. The politics of shared power has often been stormy, and conflict can easily arise – whether over Watergate, the Iran–Contra affair, the confirmation to the Supreme Court of Clarence Thomas and of many other recent nominations, Whitewatergate and Clinton's health proposals.

In recent decades, one major area of contention has been over the conduct of foreign policy. Initiatives are usually launched by the president, but Congress still has an overseeing role. It has the power to raise taxes to fund a conflict, to create and maintain armed forces, to regulate arms sales and for the signing of treaties. It has the power also to make war. Johnson never formally declared **war against North Vietnam**, but the hostilities there led to Congress reassessing its position. The Nixon presidency saw a struggle between the White House and Capitol Hill over the control of foreign policy.

Vietnam War

The war began under Kennedy and escalated under Johnson to prevent communist North Vietnam from taking over the South and contain the spread of communism in South-East Asia. It ended with an American withdrawal in 1973, America's first defeat in war. In 1975, Vietnam was united under communist rule.

A hostile Congress can make life difficult for any president, by refusing his nominations, failing to fund his programmes and refusing approval to treaties he has carefully negotiated. If he has public support, he is much less likely to meet this degree of obstruction, and he can take to the media to rally public support on his side. Congressmen will watch the popular reaction with interest. Theodore Roosevelt was an exponent of the 'bully pulpit' approach, for he saw the opportunities for inspirational leadership if he could get his message across to the nation at large – as though it was a religious congregation. Wilson, Kennedy, Franklin Roosevelt and Reagan all knew how to 'preach' to the nation, and strengthen their position by winning acquiescence and support.

The President and the Prime Minister: a comparison of Britain and the United States

For years, it has been a regular part of discussion on the British and American systems of government to compare the two offices and to decide which is the more powerful, the Prime Minister or the President.

An obvious difference is that in Britain the ceremonial and political roles are separated, so that the Queen is the titular head of state while the Prime Minister is the chief executive or political head of the government. In America the roles are combined in one person, a consideration which imposes considerable demands on the incumbent, but means that he has many opportunities to appear on social occasions and attract favourable media coverage.

The prime minister is relieved of certain time-consuming duties, such as receiving ambassadors and dignitaries from abroad, and there may be an advantage in separating the ceremonial and efficient roles, pomp from power. Yet wearing both hats gives the President a dimension of prestige lacking in the office of Prime Minister, for he is only a politician whereas the President is both in and above the political battle, more obviously representing the national interest.

The holders of both offices have a similar responsibility for the the overall surveillance and direction of the work of executive departments of government, and there are advantages of the Prime Minister over the President and vice versa. The Prime Minister is part of a plural executive, and he and his Cabinet are collectively responsible to the House of Commons. He or she may, of course, have acquired a real ascendancy over his or her colleagues, and the impact of Margaret Thatcher's tenure in office showed the extent of prime ministerial dominance. Yet the British Cabinet is bound to be concerned in most major decisions during the lifetime of a government.

In the US, the Cabinet is much less significant, and several presidents – whilst not formally dispensing with the Cabinet – have been casual about holding meetings and and have treated its suggestions in a cavalier manner. Their Cabinet colleagues tend to be people drawn from the world of business, the ranks of academia or other professions, and return there once their term in office has expired; they have no personal following of their own in Congress or in the country. Cabinet members in Britain have a greater political standing in their own right, and are less easily ignored; they may be contenders for the party leadership.

A key factor in the comparison of Prime Minister and President is that the former is a more powerful party leader. He or she leads a disciplined party, whereas the President does not. This means that whereas the President can find difficulty in getting proposals enacted into

SUPPORT FOR THE PRESIDENCY

The Executive Office of the President

As presidential responsibilities widened in the years following the Great Depression, it became increasingly difficult for the President to cope with the law, perhaps because of states rights, the views of Congress or the Supreme Court, the prime minister, given a reasonable majority, is likely to get most of his or her programme through. In as much as the reputation of a government may depend on what it can achieve, the Prime Minister has far more chance of implementing the proposals he or she wants. Margaret Thatcher could reform the health service along the lines she favoured, whereas a few years later Bill Clinton could not. As Walles[14] observes:

> Whereas a Prime Minister ... with the support of party, is ideally placed for author-itative action, a President ... often lacking the full support of his party in the legis-lature ... is poorly placed to translate policies into working programmes.

In the area of foreign policy, both men are generally in charge of the direction of the Government's external relations. On their own or through the appropriate departments, they declare the tone of the nation's foreign policy. There are differences in their position, however, for the President must get any treaty approved by two-thirds of the Senate, and if the policy requires legislative back-up the President may have difficulty in getting this through the Congress.

On the other hand, whereas the President may decide administration policy alone in conjunction with the Secretary of State, a British Prime Minister is much more likely to put his or her policy before the Cabinet where views can be expressed. There may be individual opportunities for the prime minister to bypass the full Cabinet and take key decisions in a Cabinet Committee, but in most cases the Prime Minister appoints a Foreign Secretary with whom he or she is in agreement or on whom he or she feels can be imposed.

The Prime Minister is of course always liable to be defeated in the House, and therefore may not see out his or her term. Similarly, as with Margaret Thatcher, the incumbent of Number Ten can be removed when in office. In both cases this is rare. The occupant of the White House has a guaranteed fixed term in office, unless he or she does something very wrong, as over Watergate. The advantage in security of tenure is with the President, although when it comes to choosing the date of the next election (and manipulating the economy to create the 'feel good' factor), the advantage is with the Prime Minister.

Within the two political systems, the Prime Minister has the edge, because of his or her leadership of a disciplined, centralised party in a political culture which is orientated towards party government. This enables him or her to get things done. But the President has the greater power overall, for he or she is the leader of a more significant country in international terms, with enough nuclear capacity to wipe out civilisation.

demands of the job. He lacked the necessary support, a point noted by the President's Committee on Administrative Management, in 1937: 'The president needs help', it proclaimed.

A Commission on the Organisation of the Executive Branch of the Government, set up by President Truman and headed by Herbert Hoover, reported 12 years later. It was troubled by the lack of clear lines of authority from the president down to the civil service, and felt the modern president faced an impossible task unless there was an extensive regrouping of executive departments and agencies into a number of smaller, non-overlapping units, and an increased use of the Cabinet. These changes would give the President the chance to achieve an effective supervision of the governmental activities for which he or she was constitutionally responsible.

Both analyses drew attention to the burdens of the presidency, and argued the case that because executive power was centred on one person he or she needed help from better support services rather than from other people. The Cabinet might have seemed a possible choice to relieve the burden. But as the officers who serve in it are non-elected and therefore lack political or moral authority – and in any case, are not usually front-rank politicians – they have little incentive to relieve the President of any duties. In particular, they have little experience of managing relations with Congress. In other words, even if the President wished to make greater use of the Cabinet, several of its members have little interest in offering the necessary backing, for their reputation does not depend on the President's political success. Each Secretary looks after his or her patch; however, the President looks after his or her own duties, but also has to answer for any of their shortcomings.

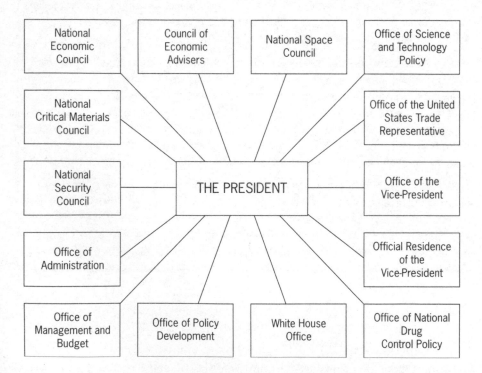

Figure 1 Executive Office of the President

Source: Based on an illustration from a US Government Manual, 1995–96.

The President is in a solitary position, with overall responsibility for the activities of an enormous governmental machine which he or she must direct and co-ordinate. To do this, the President requires information about operations, assessments of policy needs and means of ensuring that his or her decisions and those of Congress are efficiently carried out, in the ways and spirit in which they are intended.

The establishment and operation of the Executive Office

As a result of the recommendations of the 1937 Committee, Roosevelt agreed that new machinery should be established. Two years after it reported, an enlarged presidential office was created, far larger in scale than had existed previously. Instead of a few clerks and secretaries, there was to be a new Executive Office of the President. In the words of Clinton Rossiter,[15] the presidency was converted 'into an instrument of twentieth century government … it gives the incumbent a sporting chance to stand the strain and fulfil the constitutional mandate as a one-man branch of our three-part government'. In his view, the innovation saved the presidency from paralysis, and the Constitution from radical amendment.

From the earliest days, it was obvious that the new Office would be highly significant, but even so the extent of its eventual impact on American government could not have been judged. At the time, it comprised barely 1000 staff, whereas at the beginning of the twenty-first century the total exceeds 5000. But the extent of its operations and of its importance is not to be judged by numbers alone, but more by the centrality of its position in the workings of the executive branch. It has become what Maidment and McGrew[16] call 'the principal instrument of presidential government'.

The modern president relies on the Executive Office to come up with the background information, detailed analysis and informed policy recommendations that are needed to enable him or her to master the complexities of a task. It has taken its place at the heart of the administration, giving the President the advice he or she depends upon, conducting many dealings with Congress, and helping to publicise and supervise the implementation of presidential decisions. The President is freed to deal with top-level matters of the moment and to engage in future planning.

The component parts of the Executive Office change from president to president, for it is the President's personal bureaucracy. Individuals have varied in the use made of it and amended its internal organisation to reflect their own priorities, interests and needs. New parts of the Office have been established, some have been developed or transformed from their original character, and others have become redundant.

The Executive Office is an umbrella under which exist a number of key agencies which cover the whole range of policy areas and which serve him directly. The Office of Management and the Budget already existed in 1939, but otherwise only the White House Office has been there since the original

ELEMENTS OF THE EXECUTIVE OFFICE

The White House Office

The President's closest aides, his personal staff, work in the White House Office, the nerve centre of the Executive Office. Of those located in the White House, only a few dozen of the most senior advisors will see the President regularly. There are special assistants to advise on foreign and domestic affairs, speech writers, liaison officers who maintain contact with Congress, and, of course, the Press Secretary. There is nowadays a Special Counsellor to the President, and also many whose services are more concerned with basic personal needs, such as a personal secretary, a social secretary and a physician.

The Office ensures that urgent priority issues reach the President's desk quickly, and members seek to ensure compliance by the departments with presidential policies, and so obtain for the President control over the federal administration. These assistants obtain their real authority from their closeness to the President, and the trust which he or she places in them. By deciding who should see the President and the issues to prioritise, they have much discretionary power. The danger is that the office can so 'protect' the President that he or she becomes remote from the political world. He or she becomes surrounded with 'yes-men' who say what they think the President wants to hear, and thus prevent him or her from making a balanced assessment.

Under Kennedy, several members were used more to help the President carry out the tasks he set himself, rather than to act as key advisers. In contrast, other presidents have given this inner circle enormous influence, so that some administrations are remembered in terms of the President himself and the immediate associates with whom he surrounded himself – Nixon had Haldeman and Ehrlichman, Carter had Jordan and Powell, and Reagan had Baker (later his Secretary of State), Deaver and Meese. During the Nixon presidency the size of the White House Office grew substantially, with well over 500 personnel. Nixon downgraded his Cabinet, and so to get the co-ordination of policy which he required he established the post of Counsellor to the President. The appointee was given the prime responsibility for co-ordinating the handling of home and overseas affairs, and was included within the Cabinet – a status denied to previous White House aides.

The Office of Management and Budget (OMB)

Nixon reconstituted the Bureau of the Budget into the Office of Management and Budget in 1970, as a major managerial instrument for the President. Its main task is to prepare a federal budget to submit to Congress, and all appropriations requests from the departments come through the Office for approval. The departments use their influence to retain

machinery was set up. Elements have changed in different administrations, but central to the work of the Office are the White House staff, personal appointees who are likely to be the closest advisers for general and particular policies (see below).

maximum financial autonomy, and the President needs support if he or she is to keep overall control of their plans. The Office can be a powerful instrument, for it also provides a mechanism by which the President can co-ordinate governmental activities, and ensure, in his or her role as manager of the executive branch, that programmes are carried out as efficiently as possible.

The National Security Council (NSC)

Established in 1947, the Council was given the role of advising the President on domestic, foreign and military matters relating to national security. Its duty was to consider 'policies on matters of common interest to the departments and agencies of the government concerned with national security, and to make recommendations'. As with the Cabinet, the National Security Council does not make decisions for the President, but it provides evidence and advice from which the President can come to his or her own conclusions. At times of crisis, the Council does not usually seem to be the place where key assessments are made.

The Council of Economic Advisers

Economic policy is increasingly important to the performance and reputation of any administration, and for presidents, few of whom are economic experts, assistance is needed. Since 1946, a three-person panel of professional economists has been appointed with the consent of the Senate to advise on key issues. Often they are university academics, but new presidents select people of their own persuasion and outlook. It is a purely advisory body, but it is an important counter to the Treasury and the OMB, which have a narrower and more immediate focus. Such advice helps presidents to bear in mind longer-term considerations in their economic thinking. One specific responsibility is to assist in the preparation of an annual economic report to be given by the President to Congress; this outlines the Administration's view of economic trends.

The Office of Policy Development (OPD)

Since 1981, the Office has had an important advisory role in the conduct of domestic policy. President Nixon had his Domestic Council for this purpose, but like some of his other innovations its reputation was damaged as part of the general discrediting of Nixonian methods – following the Watergate revelations. President Reagan's establishment of the new OPD is a further reflection of the presidential need for systematic and coherent advice on matters of internal policy.

There are other bodies in the Executive Office, such as the *Council on Environmental Quality*, the *Office of Science and Technology Policy* and the *Intelligence Oversight Board*.

Assessment of the Executive Office

It was because of the growing demands on the President that some help was necessary if he or she was to be adequately equipped for the necessary tasks. As the President's responsibilities grew, so did his or her need for expert assistance. At the time of the creation of the Executive Office few commentators realised just how important it would become. It is now far larger than in the year after its establishment, and its influence has grown even more dramatically than its number of personnel. What makes it so important for the president is that it is beholden only to him or her. Its members are appointed by the President, and they know that they owe their position to him or her and therefore seek to serve him or her loyally.

The Executive Office is the main instrument of presidential government, and all modern presidents rely upon it to a greater or lesser degree, for information, analysis and policy recommendations. In some cases, their dependence is greater than others, and certain key aides emerge as the linchpin of the administration. For them, their focus of attention is inevitably the presidency, as it must be. It is easy for them to become so obsessed by the protection of the President that they ignore the limitations of the office designed by the framers of the Constitution. In other words, the Executive Office – and especially those assistants who serve in the White House Office – can become out of touch with the viewpoints and requirements of those who inhabit other areas of the system of government.

The danger can be that, having appointed an advisory team of people who share his or her personal and political preferences, the President receives advice only from those who share the same outlook. Other people in different branches of the governmental process also have insights worthy of an audience, and some Congressmen and bureaucrats may find that their route to the President is barred. Presidents can come to rely too much on those around them, and in that way allow themselves to become out of touch with the views of a wider section of the American public.

The vice-presidency

For many years the office of Vice-President ('Veep') was viewed as little more than a joke. Its first incumbent, John Adams, spoke of it derisively: 'My country has in its wisdom contrived for me the most insignificant office that ever the invention of man contrived or his imagination conceived'. The majority of his successors would probably have shared his view, and a disillusioned John Nance Garner, Franklin Roosevelt's deputy, suggested that the office was 'not worth a pitcher of warm spit'.

The office was only created as an afterthought by those who devised the Constitution. It simply says that he will be chosen by an electoral college, outlines the circumstances when he will be acting president and lays down that he will preside over the Senate. Given that there are so few formal responsibilities, some vice-presidents make little of it. One such occupant was Charles Dawes, who served under President Coolidge. He declared that his position was 'the easiest job in the world'.

Choice of the Vice-President

Presidential candidates want a running-mate who will be an asset to the ticket and boost their electoral prospects. Ideally the person chosen will balance their own background and characteristics, so that geographical, demographic and ideological factors come into play. It may be that the choice will be pleasing to an area, to a group of voters or to some faction within the party. Kennedy, a Northern liberal and a Catholic, chose Johnson, a Texan Protestant likely to appeal to southern conservatives. Nixon chose Spiro Agnew (a Maryland Governor) to please the same group. Clinton chose Al Gore, for although he came from a similar geographical background and shared many similar beliefs, he offered definite advantages which might extend the appeal of the ticket. In particular, he was seen as a 'Mr Clean', reassuring on the topic of 'family values', a subject on which Bill Clinton was thought to be vulnerable. George Bush Jnr opted for Dick Cheney, who had served in this father's Cabinet and was expected to provide some experience and weight to the presidential challenge in 2000.

Responsibilities and role

The Vice-President assumes some of the ceremonial tasks of the President, and represents him or her on formal occasions, whether it be the funeral of a foreign leader or the commemoration of some past event. The Vice-President is formally the presiding officer of the Senate, refereeing its proceedings and interpreting the rules. Usually, vice-presidents put in few appearances, for there is little kudos to be won and little chance to exert political influence – given that he or she is not a member of the chamber. Otherwise, vice-presidents take on *ad hoc* assignments, their number and character depending on the use which the President wishes to make of them. Bill Clinton gave his deputy the task of conducting a national review of the workings of the federal democracy. Other presidents were much less willing to use their running-mate than he was.

The significance of the position

The importance of the role varies according to who is in the White House. For some presidents, their deputies can be useful in an advisory capacity on matters of politics and policy. Jimmy Carter made more use of Walter Mondale than had been usual in the past, because he needed the support of a Washington 'insider' who could give good advice based upon his knowledge and experience. Reagan allowed Bush to attend many meetings and to represent him in many engagements. However, activity and influence are very different, and whereas Mondale was allowed more say in the decision-making process this was much less true of his successor.

Al Gore was probably the most influential Vice-President in American history. Not only did he preside over important projects such as the 'Reinventing Government' initiative, he also took an active interest in issues ranging from the environment to science and technology, and gave Bill Clinton his advice upon them. Often, he would remain in the Oval Office when all other advisers had departed, so that his voice was the last the President heard. He is said to have been allowed considerable influence over the composition of the revamped Cabinet at the beginning of the second term, the idea being that this would give him influential supporters in key positions to help him prepare his bid for the November 2000 contest.

Two Constitutional Amendments have helped to raise the status of the office. The 22nd limited the president to two full terms in office, and thereby increased the chances of the Vice-President taking over. The 25th, in 1967, confirmed the previous practice of making the Vice-President not an acting one but the real thing, in the event of a national emergency such as the incapacity of the president to fulfil his or her tasks. A procedure is laid down to determine if and when the deputy should take over, as it is to determine for how long and under what conditions he or she should exercise presidential duties. (In 1985, George Bush was the first Vice-President to assume such responsibilities, when President Reagan had an operation for skin cancer.)

There has been discussion in recent years of 'a new vice-presidency'. Yet in spite of the growing trend towards providing vice-presidents with a more worthwhile role, for much of the time they are effectively 'waiting in the wings' in case their services are called upon to assume the burden of the presidency. They stand in readiness to assume command, in the event of death (either through natural causes or assassination), or through resignation or removal from office. Nine presidents have failed to complete their allotted terms, eight through death, and one (Nixon) because of his forced resignation. The possibility of assassination is a real one, four presidents having been killed, two in the twentieth century (McKinley and Kennedy) – several others have been the victim of life-threatening attacks. Because of this, Vice-President Adams was right in his summary of the strengths and weaknesses of his position: 'I am Vice-President of the United States. In this, I am nothing, but I may be everything'.

A frustrating role

For those with presidential ambitions, the post takes them that much nearer the White House, and there is always the chance that their services might be needed should a death or assassination occur, or electors choose them as the next president. About one-third of vice-presidents eventually become president; five have done so since World War Two: Truman, Johnson, Nixon, Ford and Bush Snr.

Yet it is still difficult for vice-presidents to carve out a useful and distinctive role. The job is a frustrating one, particularly when the administration is nearing its end – even more so, if it is unpopular. On the one hand, the 'Veep' is expected to remain loyal and act as a mouthpiece of the presidential team. On the other, he may wish to carve out a distinct persona and, if things are going badly for the President, to show a degree of detachment. Hubert Humphrey was in such a dilemma over Vietnam, in the latter days of the Johnson presidency. Whatever his personal reservations, he was unable to oppose official policy whilst he remained a member of the White House team. Al Gore faced a similar problem. In his case, there was no dispute over political direction, but he was embarrassed by the scandals which so damaged the Clinton reputation. Especially in the latter days, he kept himself as detached as possible when it was apparent that the administration was in political difficulty.

The office provides the incumbent with an opportunity to see the workings of government at the highest level, and gain a useful insight into the problems which arise and the way in which they are handled. But it is easy for the occupant to seem faceless and lacking independence of outlook. Few presidents would appreciate an outspoken understudy, or one who diverted too much attention from them. Many have preferred to keep their number two in the dark on key issues. Roosevelt took this isolation of his Vice-President so far that he did not even tell him that America was developing the atomic bomb.

Nixon did not find work under Eisenhower fulfilling, and neither did Johnson under Kennedy. In both cases, the relationship was a poor one before they were ever chosen as running mates. Presidents rarely feel that they can totally trust the person they have chosen to run with, for such associates have their own ambitions. It is usually a 'marriage of convenience' on the part of the President, rather than an expression of deep regard for the person selected. Political rather than personal considerations dictate the original choice.

The Cabinet

The Constitution allows the President to invite the opinions of the main officers of the executive departments of government, but there is no mention of summoning them together as a cabinet. Yet this has always happened, from George Washington onwards. The influence of **the Cabinet** has varied according to the tastes and inclinations of the President. As a broad generali-sation, it was a more powerful body before the 1930s than it has been subsequently. Yet the 'decline' has not been a continuous one, and from time to time individual presidents have promised to use such gatherings more. A very few have fulfilled their initial promise.

> **The Cabinet**
> Cabinet meetings comprise the President, Vice-President, the officers who head the 14 departments, plus a few other officials whom the President considers to be of appropriate rank.

Abraham Lincoln is usually credited with the comment 'seven noes, one aye – the ayes have it', following a cabinet discussion in which his proposal was unanimously rejected by those around the table. True or otherwise, the remark indicates the view which most presidents have of the people they appoint to serve under them. Presidents tend to view them as spokespersons for their departments who have nothing to contribute on other matters.

This means that presidents lack the political support which the British Cabinet gives to the Prime Minister. The American Cabinet does not contain party notables, high-ranking members with a power-base and standing in their own right. Neither do cabinet members have a place in the legislature, and so they are of little assistance to the President in pushing his or her programme through Congress. An American cabinet bears little relation to one operating in a parliamentary system. It does not work as a team as the British one does, and American and British cabinets share little in common other than the name.

Some presidents have begun their presidency with the intention of using the Cabinet more, but as with Richard Nixon the number of meetings called tends to decline as the years go by: by 1972, he was down to eleven meetings in the course of the year. As Watergate enveloped his administration, he came to regard the Cabinet with intense suspicion and conceived a strong dislike for its individual members, whom he had originally appointed. Jimmy Carter's similar intentions were never fulfilled, and the number of his cabinet meetings declined significantly.

Especially in the early years of his administration, Reagan was keen on the idea of Cabinet government, and at meetings was likely to go round the table and invite individual views. He also made use of cabinet councils of five or six cabinet members on topics such as Economic Affairs and Human Resources, and these worked with White House staff to provide a source of new ideas for the President – a system which was analogous to the British system of cabinet committees. Bill Clinton formed committees of cabinet and sub-cabinet members, as in the case of the National Economic Council. Again, the purpose was to better integrate departmental heads and White House officials around particular policy areas. The original precedent for such committees was the National Security Council formed shortly after World War II with the intention of providing the President with quality advice on matters concerning the security of the nation against external threat.

Choosing the Cabinet

One of the first tasks of a new president before the inauguration is the choice of the Cabinet, and the selection is watched by commentators eager to get an indication of the likely tone and style of the administration. The President can choose whom he or she wishes, although it is wise to nominate people who are likely to be acceptable to the Senate. The Cabinet is the President's personal creation, and he or she will seek out people felt to be useful, and effective within their departments. Few people can assume that they will be included, for it does not follow that prominent people in the presidential election campaign will be rewarded with a position in the Cabinet; other rewards may be awarded and preferred.

The President will want to include people who are loyal to him or her and to presidential programmes. Other considerations include the need to reward prominent politicians who helped the campaign nationally and within the President's state. There are often political debts to repay. Kennedy, as a northern liberal, was even prepared to include a southern segregationist within the cabinet – though this seemed to be in direct contradiction of his expressed support for civil rights. The choice did enable him to achieve a geographical balance, with representation of regions different from his own. A broad social balance is desirable, and recent presidents are aware of the desirability of acknowledging the existence within the US of women and of different racial groups such as the black and Jewish communities.

The President will also want people of administrative competence who may bring expertise and specialist knowledge to their work. It does not matter if they have not previously served in a government position, and many have no political background. There will sometimes be an attempt to persuade Congressmen from either house to serve the administration, but in most cases figures who have won re-election are unlikely to be interested in forsaking the legislature for administrative responsibilities which are lacking in influence over the overall direction of policy. Moreover, from their own experience they will know what it is like to grill members of the administration, and may be unwilling to submit themselves to the procedure. Republican Cabinet appointees often come from a business background. Eisenhower, Nixon, Bush and Reagan all plucked people from the worlds of commerce and manufacturing. Those chosen may be elevated from obscurity, and when the administration comes to an end they often return to such a status – having made little impact on the public mind.

The role and practice of American cabinets

As we have seen, the Cabinet is not even mentioned in the Constitution, although the 25th Amendment lays down a procedure to be followed in the light of the President's incapacity. Congress determines the lines of succession after the Vice-President, and beyond the Speaker and Senate president *pro tempore*, the Cabinet personnel are listed in order of status, starting with the Secretary of State.

The Cabinet is an advisory body only, and in the final analysis the President consults whom he or she wishes and may choose to ignore what the cabinet members say – assuming they are consulted in the first place. As the President does not have to refer to the Cabinet in times of crisis, the sole responsibility for decision-making rests with him or her. The role can be a lonely one. The President may choose to seek out the advice of individuals whose counsel is trusted, but for many members there is little incentive to offer backing and support. There is no question of the President seeking and feeling the need to act upon the advice of all of the cabinet members. He or she may prefer to seek the advice of the White House Office, and the Office of Management and Budget when advice is needed. Presidents use the Cabinet as they feel appropriate or necessary. They may choose to hold meetings regularly as Eisenhower did, or perhaps allow the Cabinet to meet only irregularly, and consult individuals where they are likely to be in a position to contribute usefully. Kennedy felt that full meetings were usually unproductive. He posed the question which sums up the way in which many presidents regard Cabinet discussion: 'Why should the postmaster sit there and listen to a discussion of the problems of Laos?'. In other words, members can more usefully employ their time on the work of their own departments rather than engage in general discussions.

Cabinet unanimity does not exist in the sense to which we are accustomed. It may be desirable where it can be achieved, but it is not a constitutional principle such as Collective Responsibility in Britain. Members do differ in their views, and may do so publicly, as happened at the time of the Vietnam War and at the time of the Argentinean dispute with Britain in the early 1980s. In both cases, spokespersons reacted in different ways when questioned about their reaction to policy decisions.

No cabinet member feels he or she has to rush to defend a colleague (or president) under attack, and when there are disagreements no one feels obliged to resign – though members may choose to do so, if they are at odds with the President. Disagreement is not in itself an automatic reason for resigning, and Congress would not call for resignation as cabinet members are not responsible to the legislature, only to the President.

Cabinets in Britain and the United States: a comparison

- In both countries, cabinet membership is usually around 20.
- In Britain, members are elected politicians, answerable to the House of Commons. US cabinet appointees have not been elected, are not figures of prominence within the party and are not members of Congress.
- In Britain, the Cabinet is the main decision-making body. It takes decisions, co-ordinates policy and acts as a court of appeal when agreement cannot be reached in the Cabinet Committee. Even if the Prime Minister is very powerful, the role of the Cabinet is still a major one, although commentators debate the balance of power between the premier and his or her colleagues. Ultimately, prime ministers need cabinet backing. The President looks elsewhere for policy advice, co-ordination and support. He or she may choose to consult the Cabinet, but does not feel bound to do so.
- In Britain, the doctrine of Collective Responsibility applies to cabinet members. In the US, there is no such doctrine and disagreement in public is more apparent. For instance, in the George W. Bush administration, the Secretary of State and the Defense Secretary have taken a different line on European Union defence policy.

The bureaucracy

Bureaucracy refers to what Burns *et al.*[17] describe as a 'professional corps of officials organised in a pyramidal structure, and functioning under impersonal, uniform rules and procedures'. By the term bureaucrats, we refer to people who operate in the executive branch, whose career is based in government service and normally work there as a result of appointment rather than election; they work for presidents and their political appointees. They serve in government departments, and in the more than 50 independent agencies embracing some 2000 bureaus, which are sub-units of the agencies.

Who is part of the federal bureaucracy?

- Some 5 million people work in the Executive Branch.
- 60 per cent of them are civilians; the rest are military personnel.
- About 12 per cent of them operate in Washington.
- The rest are based around the country.
- In California, there are more than a quarter of a million federal employees.
- Of the 3 million civilians, about 1 million work in the area of national security – for the air force, army, navy and various defence organisations – and nearly half a million work for the welfare agencies.
- There are some 15,000 different categories of federal employee. The majority are white-collar workers, ranging from inspectors and engineers to secretaries and clerks.

It is sometimes assumed that the administration is primarily concerned with putting into effect decisions taken elsewhere, so that politics and adminis-tration are separate compartments. According to this view, bureaucrats are the neutral instrument of elected politicians and their concern is only to pursue their tasks with the utmost efficiency, free from considerations of personal gain or political advantage. Such a view is naive, and the executive branch is deeply involved in politics at many levels.

Much of the legislation which goes before Congress begins its life in the departments and many agencies of government, and pressure group activists and Congressmen realise this and may seek to influence proposals from the Administration at an early stage. Equally, much discretion is granted to those who implement the law when enacted, and they seek to influence Congressmen on matters such as appropriations. In the same way, they seek to influence other agencies and departments whose interests conflict with their own, and so administration and politics cannot be isolated from each other.

Key positions in the American bureaucracy are held by persons appointed by the President (see below), and because these are normally people who share his or her outlook this might be expected to result in presidential control of the bureaucratic process. Yet this often does not happen, for once in position, those appointed may 'go native' and become part of the administrative machine – rather than agents of the President's will. As with relations with Congress, presidents soon find out that it is important to persuade, for they lack the power to command. In the frustrated words of President Truman: 'I

The presidential power of appointment

At one time, political appointees made up the vast majority of the federal bureaucracy. Appointments were made on the basis of patronage, 'who you knew, rather than what you knew', and membership of the successful party was important in gaining government jobs. Andrew Jackson (1829–37) developed the patronage system to its maximum extent, for he believed that 'to the victor go the spoils'. By the 'spoils system', employment was given to members of the party that won political office, not just as a reward for political support but also as a way of ensuring that many offices were opened up to ordinary citizens.

The Jacksonian approach survived for several decades and it helped to make the federal bureaucracy responsive to the needs of the White House. However, it later came to be associated with corruption. Congress tackled this problem by passing the Pendleton Act (1883), which limited the number of political appointments that a president could make and established a merit system for about 10 per cent of federal jobs. This stressed ability, education and job performance as the key criteria for appointment, rather than political background. The merit system now applies to some 95 per cent of federal civilian jobs.

thought I was the President, but when it comes to these bureaucracies I can't make 'em do a damn thing'.

The importance of political appointments can be exaggerated. They may seem to provide the President with an opportunity to change the direction and character of government policy, but in reality the number of appointments which he or she can make amounts to only a small percentage of those who work for the federal bureaucracy. For his first administration, President Clinton was able to nominate 222 personnel in the Department of Commerce, less than 1 per cent of those working in the department; overall, he chose less than 0.2 per cent of the total civilian, non-postal federal work force. Moreover, the appointments have to be made in the brief period between the day of the presidential election and Inauguration Day. Inevitably, the presidents must concentrate their attention on appointments at cabinet level and leave many of the rest to other members of their team.

The American bureaucracy has a large degree of autonomy, each agency having its own clientele, power base and authority. Much of that authority derives from Congress, which creates or destroys agencies, authorises and approves reorganisation plans, defines powers and appropriates agency funds. Yet even Congress is unable to control the operation of bodies once they are established, and many of them have a life of their own. Walles[19] sees the bureaucracy as 'an active and largely independent participant in the political process, negotiating and bargaining with Congress, groups and the presidency alike'.

Today, the President has an opportunity to influence the nature of the bureaucracy via his power of appointment over the most strategically important positions in government. He or she can nominate more than 3000 senior civil servants to serve in the Administration and these include the heads of the 14 major departments (the secretaries), as well as assistant and deputy department secretaries, deputy assistant secretaries and a variety of other appointive positions. Nearly 700 of the top presidential appointments have to be confirmed by the Senate. Once in office, their tenure of office depends on how the White House judges their performance.

The President is likely to choose personnel whom he or she regards as loyal and competent, and who share his or her political outlook. Abernach[18] notes that whereas in the past many appointees had been people who had established good connections with interest groups or congressional committees, in the Reagan era 'ideology was the key'. Before coming to office, he established an appointment system which ensured that appointees would be faithful to him and pursue his objectives of reduced governmental activity.

There are some 2000 federal agencies, which are not directly amenable to presidential command or congressional directive! There is no collectivity of purpose, and the decisions and actions of one body may easily conflict with those of another. The Federal Reserve Board, which supervises the private banking system of the US and regulates the volume of credit and money in circulation, may pursue policies which are at variance with those of the Administration, just as the Secretary of the Treasury may publicly cross swords with the Director of the Office of Management and Budget.

The types of organisation involved

The federal administration is organised around most of the same vital functions which exist in any other national bureaucracy. The administrative apparatus responsible for fulfilling them is divided into three broad categories:

1 Government or executive departments

The heads of departments (or ministries) are picked by the President and hold office at his pleasure. As we have seen, they constitute the American Cabinet, although they do not share collective responsibility for government policy as they do in Britain. There are 14 cabinet-level departments, which vary greatly in size. They are sub-divided into bureaux and smaller units, often on the basis of function. Within the Commerce Department, there is the Bureau of the Census, and others such as the Patent and Trademark Office.

By far the most important department is the State Department (see pp. 80–1), but others include the Treasury, the Defence Department, and the Justice and Interior departments. Others include Agriculture, Commerce, Labour, Health and Human Services, Education, Housing and Urban Development, Transportation and Energy.

2 The independent agencies

In addition to the executive departments, which are the major operating units of the federal government, there are many other agencies which help to keep the government and economy functioning smoothly. As they are not part of the executive departments they are often known as 'independent agencies'. They are powerful and important bodies in the executive branch: *in* it but not *of* it. They include several types of organisation, and have differing degrees of independence. They carry out functions laid down in statute, but have a complex set of formal and informal relationships with President and Congress, unlike those of a normal executive department.

These agencies vary considerably in character and purpose. Some provide special services either to the government or to the people (the 40 or so

executive agencies, such as the Veterans Administration), whilst others are supervisory, monitoring sections of the economy (**regulatory commissions**, such as the Federal Reserve Board and the Environmental Protection Agency). Some have substantial independence, others rather less so. In many cases, the agencies have been created by Congress to tackle areas or issues that are too complex to come within the scope of ordinary legislation.

The independence of regulatory commissions is considerably greater than that of the executive agencies, this substantial autonomy having been deliberately arranged by Congress. Regulatory commissions have a different function: they remove supervision of particular areas from presidential hands, and are run by independent boards of commissioners. Often there are only five to seven commissioners, who serve for a fixed term of anything varying from three to fourteen years.

Such Commissions are part of the executive branch, but they are not under direct presidential control. When vacancies arise, the President appoints appropriate personnel. However, once their appointment has been confirmed by the Senate, incumbents have security of tenure, and remain in office until their term of office has expired. Commissioners are not responsible to the President for the work of the Commission, and because of their autonomy they can pose considerable problems for any President. Such Commissions are sometimes described as the 'headless fourth branch of government'.

Commissions have quasi-judicial and quasi-legislative functions, as well as executive ones. Their number grew considerably during the twentieth century, for as new problems arose so new machinery was needed to watch over developments and resolve problems as they arose. Congress established these commissions in a way designed to keep them free of White House influence. It has given them much power, but their relationship to the President is unclear. Any President will be concerned with their activities because of the way in which they regulate economic activity, but presidential power over them is limited, given their conditions of appointment.

A new President will be confronted with a complex number of commissions whose leading figures have been selected by a predecessor, and it may be two or three years before he or she can tip the balance of agency thinking by making new appointments on the retirement of existing officials. President Kennedy felt particularly limited by the fact that eight years of Republican patronage under Eisenhower meant that he was unable to get his own people in important offices, and direct policy along the lines he favoured. Crucially, the President lacks the power of dismissal over such appointees. Moreover, the legislation regulating the commissions requires that members should be drawn from both political parties, a further limitation on presidential control of their operations.

3 *Government corporations*

The United States avoided nationalisation of the type that was introduced in Britain by the postwar Labour Government. However, the federal government has become involved in conducting numerous activities which are commercial or industrial in nature. For this purpose, the Corporation has been seen as the most appropriate form to enable activities to be carried out according to commercial or industrial needs. The intention was to give those directing such corporations the same sort of freedom to take decisions as that enjoyed by a director of any private enterprise organisation. As such, they are a cross between business corporations and regular governmental agencies. Examples of corporations include the Panama Canal Company, the St Lawrence Seaway Development Corporation and the Tennessee Valley Authority (TVA).

These and other bodies have a huge annual turnover and are responsible for projects of massive importance. The attempt to allow them freedom of manoeuvre has not always worked, for as with British nationalised industries there is a temptation for the Administration and Congress to seek to exert control over the decisions taken. The 1945 Government Corporation Control Act was passed to integrate them more closely into the normal machinery of the executive branch.

Making the bureaucracy function better

Reform of the bureaucracy is difficult to achieve, for as soon as a proposal is made specific, its implications for particular groups are understood and they may then lobby against change. Efforts to make the bureaucracy more efficient and more responsive are regularly mentioned at election time, but they continue to run into difficulties. Ronald Reagan was deeply sceptical of bureaucrats and their work, and he committed to a series of changes. These included privatisation of some operations, contracting-out, and handing over federal programmes to the states as part of the New Federalism project. The outcome was less dramatic than he had anticipated, but there were some successes such as bringing in private-sector enterprise to root out inefficiency and waste. In as much as cuts in personnel were made in areas such as welfare, they tended to be balanced by increases in staffing in the Justice, Defence and State departments.

The *Reinventing Government Report*, September 1993

In 1993, President Clinton gave Al Gore the task of reviewing the bureaucracy and making recommendations for promoting efficiency and flexibility, and improving morale.

Al Gore's National Performance Review (NPR) made several criticisms of the federal bureaucracy, including:

- the wastefulness of many governmental organisations;
- their traditional preoccupation with familiar working practices;
- the lack of incentive for them to experiment and innovate;
- the relative absence of penalties for inadequate performance.

The Gore Report (known as the *Reinventing Government Report*) made wide-ranging recommendations which among other things stressed the need to cut red tape, place more emphasis on customer service, give more authority to those operating at lower levels of employment and prune unnecessary expenditure. The broad thrust of the review was accepted, but it was less easy to command agreement when individual measures were to be implemented. Critics made the point that many changes were impossible to achieve, for it was not in the interest of Congress or the White House to insist on measures which were upsetting to groups of voters across the country.

The NPR has had some modest successes, not least in pruning the number of federal employees by more than 300,000, transforming the Federal Emergency Management Agency into a highly efficient disaster-relief unit and removing thousands of pages of governmental rules and regulations written in largely incomprehensible language. Progress was made and meaningful reform of the bureaucracy has occurred in recent years. But other factors have been at work besides the Gore review, notably:

- The ending of the Cold War. The reduction in personnel was at least in part related to the defence cuts which followed from the thaw in international relations.
- The fact that both parties supported the Government Performance and Results Act of 1993 which required every government agency to publicise its performance criteria, to enable Americans to have a more effective assessment of how well public bodies were performing.
- The political climate created by Republican stress on 'smaller government' following the 1994 mid-term elections. Promises were made to axe departments such as Housing and Urban Development (HUD) and Energy, but they were not abolished. More modest ambitions were to lessen the impact of the Food and Drug Administration and to privatise some NASA programmes; these were fulfilled. Overall, however, the changes made in the 1990s were fewer than many Republicans had wanted to see.

The term 'bureaucracy' conjures up an image of 'red tape' and inefficiency, and in the 1990s it was fashionable for many Americans to deride 'faceless bureaucrats' whose actions were wide-ranging and difficult to control. Anti-government politicians (many of whom were to be found in the Republican Party) were able to capitalise on this mood and urge the need for smaller government. There are problems in large and complex bureaucracies, for those working in them tend to acquire expertise in their own area and in the immediate problems confronting them, and also to extend their sphere of activity. Presidents have always found difficulty in ensuring that federal

---

THE BUREAUCRACY IN BRITAIN AND THE UNITED STATES: A COMPARISON

Government departments

Government departments are organised differently in the two countries. Their heads (Secretaries of State, often known as ministers) have a more directly political role in Britain. They:
- are in most cases elected members of Parliament;
- not only run their departments, but take part in cabinet and cabinet committee meetings, have parliamentary duties such as answering questions and taking part in debates, and perform a constituency role as members of Parliament;
- are able to introduce legislation in the likelihood that it will become law, because of the strength of party support;
- are used to the rough and tumble of party politics, in some cases becoming figures of party standing in their own right;
- may have already served in several other departments as a junior minister and perhaps taken charge of one or two;
- are liable to be reshuffled from time to time, collecting as they go a wealth of experience in office.

American secretaries:
- are not usually prominent party figures;
- often return to relative obscurity after they have served the president who appointed them;
- have no regular constituency or congressional duties, although from time to time they will talk to Congressmen about legislation which they wish to see enacted and testify before congressional committees;
- are less sure of seeing their legislation on the statute book.

Below head of department level, there are key differences in the two systems. In Britain:
- Ministers are advised by permanent secretaries: career civil servants whose role is prestigious and powerful. They may serve for several years and acquire a wealth of knowledge and experience, derived from functioning under different party administrations. There is no comparable job in US government departments, for senior departmental figures such as heads, under secretaries and assistant secretaries are political appointees of the incoming administration.
- Almost all senior civil servants are permanent employees who are expected to be loyal to the government of the day.
- Less use is made of political advisers, although governments of recent years have employed more than ever before. As we have seen, secretaries of American departments are surrounded by a coterie of appointees, political figures who help the departmental heads to impose their will on the career civil service below them.

employees at all levels relate their expertise to the wider public interest. In the twentieth century, they initiated eleven reviews to try and make bureaucracy more responsive and efficient, and less costly and intrusive.

British constitutional theory makes a clear distinction between the political role of ministers and the administrative role of civil servants. Under the convention of individual ministerial responsibility, each minister is responsible to Parliament for the conduct of his or her department. Ministers, the elected politicians, are in charge, civil servants, the appointed officials, advise on policy and the implementation of ministerial decisions. Traditionally, the British civil service has been known for having three characteristics:

1 Permanence

Unlike ministers, civil servants do not change at election time; this allows for continuity of administration between governments and the development of expertise.

2 Neutrality

Civil servants do not allow their political opinions to influence what they do and they carry out the policies of whatever party is in power; this enables an incoming government to have confidence in what they do.

3 Anonymity

No one is supposed to be able to identify civil servants; this enables them to give impartial and frank advice without fear of public reaction. It is the minister who is responsible for taking the praise or blame for actions and policies.

In the last few years, the organisation of the British civil service has been overhauled and its character has undergone changes.

1 Much of the administration has been handed over from government departments to agencies established under the 'Next Steps' programme, and the vast majority of civil servants now work for appointed chief executives rather than elected government ministers. The agencies and their chief executives are not accountable to Parliament or to the electorate, as government ministers and their departments used to be.

2 A unified, career civil service no longer exists, many chief executives and top civil servants being brought in from outside Whitehall to introduce new thinking. The traditional permanence of the civil service, which underpinned its public service ethos and methods and its commitment to serving the needs of the government of the day, has been eroded, with the hiving off of officials into agencies, a new emphasis on market testing and contracting out and the increased importance of political advisers. The Blair government has doubled their number, in a bid to ensure that the political will of ministers is reinforced as they seek to impose a sense of direction on their departments.

3 Civil servants have also become less neutral and anonymous. A frequently encountered observation among critics such as Hennessy[20] is that there has been a 'politicisation' of the civil service, with many senior civil servants owing their positions to the preference

of prime ministers from Thatcher to Blair to have people in top positions who share their outlook. They are:

- alleged to tell ministers what they wish to hear, rather than offer unpalatable advice based on careful and impartial analysis.
- said to be increasingly drawn into the political arena, being used by politicians to draft party political speeches, prepare briefings for party events and help ministers in their policy presentation.
- more likely to be named if mistakes occur, as ministers have become ever-more-reluctant to assume responsibility for the mistakes of their officials.

Other bodies

The Next Step agencies are only one example of the way in which British governments are making more use of unelected persons of dubious accountability. A further development in Britain has been the growth in the number of quangos (quasi autonomous non-governmental organisations) in the last few decades. According to Hall and Weir,[21] the total quango count in 1996 amounted to 6424 public bodies. These are involved in government, but operate at arm's length from it. They comprise many state-related organisations which are influential in making or applying government policy, and are executive or advisory in

CONCLUSION

Many Americans have an ambivalent attitude towards the presidency. Like the framers of the Constitution, they both fear and admire leadership. At times, they seem to expect their president to rise above the party battle and represent the broad consensus of the nation at large. At others, they expect to see him provide a lead, both to Congress and the people.

The presidency has been described by Malcolm Walles[22] as 'the focal point of the United States system of government'. The Constitution may have shared power between the Executive and the Legislature, but it is the President who symbolises the nation. When people think of the achievements or failures of any particular epoch, they see these in terms of presidential rather than congressional eras. The curtailment of the imperial presidency accelerated during the 1990s. It is a trend which is widening the gulf between the electorate's expectations and a president's capacity to deliver. Presidential aspirants scatter promises on the campaign trail, but find them increasingly hard to fulfil.

The President needs and gets support from a multitude of advisers – the Vice-President, the Cabinet and the Executive Office of the President, which

character and may have important regulatory functions. Examples include the Arts Council, the Countryside Commission and the Commission for Racial Equality, as well as NHS trusts and police authorities. The appointment of members to quangos has become another form of political patronage for whichever party is in power.

American civil servants also work in hundreds of agencies, ranging from those which are part of cabinet departments, to others which operate independently. Others are to be found in the regulatory commissions and government corporations. The profile of the federal bureaucracy is not a single, monolithic institution, but rather a network of hundreds of distinct organisations employing millions of individuals.

In some respects, therefore, the workings of the British bureaucracy in the last few decades have taken on characteristics more familiar in the United States. Some of the traditional differences have been removed, in that:
- there has allegedly been a 'politicisation' of the senior civil service, with appointments increasingly made on a 'one of us' basis;
- more use is made of political appointees or 'aides' to advise and bolster ministers;
- more use is made of agencies and other unelected bodies;
- appointment of key personnel in these agencies such as chief executives is in the gift of the government of the day.

includes the smaller White House Office. The policies deriving from the decision-makers in the executive branch are implemented by the federal bureaucracy, which has grown in size as its responsibilities have expanded. All who work in the area of making and carrying out governmental policy spend their time trying to match the expectations of a demanding electorate.

REFERENCES

1 G. Wasserman, *The Basics of American Politics*, Longman, 1996.
2 T. Hames and N. Rae, *Governing America*, Manchester University Press, 1996.
3 A. Schlesinger Jnr, *The Imperial Presidency*, Houghton Mifflin, 1973.
4 R. Maidment and D. McGrew, *The American Political Process*, Sage/Open University, 1992.
5 T. Franck, *The Tethered Presidency*, New York University Press, 1981.
6 F. Greenstein, *The Presidential Difference: Leadership Styles from FDR to Clinton*, Martiin Kessler Books (The Free Press), 2000.
7 Quoted in *The Guardian*, 20 August 2001.
8 E. Vullami, *The Observer*, 23.11.2001.
9 G. Wasserman, *The Basics of American Politics*, Longman, 1996.

10   G. Wasserman, *The Basics of American Politics*, Longman, 1996.

11   R. Neustadt, *Presidential Power: The Politics of Leadership/Presidential Power and the Modern President*, Wiley & Sons/Free Press, 1960/1990.

12   J. Burns et al., *Government by the People*, Prentice-Hall, 1994.

13   J. Hart, *The Presidential Branch: Executive Office of the President from Washington to Clinton*, Chatham House, 1995.

14   M. Walles, *British and American Systems of Government*, P. Allan, 1988.

15   C. Rossiter, *The American Presidency*, Harcourt Brace, 1960.

16   R. Maidment and D. McGrew, *The American Politics Process*, Sage/Open University, 1992.

17   J. Burns et al., *Government by the People*, Prentice Hall, 1994.

18   J. Abernach, 'The President and the Executive Branch' in C. Campbell et al. (eds), *The Bush Presidency: First Appraisals*, Chatham House, 1991.

19   M. Walles, *British and American Systems of Government*, P. Allan, 1988.

20   P. Hennessy, *The Hidden Wiring Unearthing the British Constitution*, Gollancz, 1995.

21   W. Hall and S. Weir, *The Untouchables: Power and Accountability in the Quango State*, The Democratic Audit/Scarman Trust, 1996.

22   M. Walles, *British and American Systems of Government*, P. Allan, 1988.

USEFUL WEB SITES

www.whitehouse.gov/ Official presidential site for the White House. Useful for following the day-to-day activities of the president, including daily briefings and press releases.

www.whitehousehistory.org White House Historical Association. General overview of the presidency and the White House; offers a virtual tour of the White House, showing its *objets d'art*.

SAMPLE QUESTIONS

1 President Truman argued that his only significant power was 'the power to persuade'. Is this a valid description of presidential power today?

2 What factors determine the ability of a president to exercise control over Congress?

3 Assess the effectiveness of presidential power in relation to either (a) domestic or (b) foreign policy?

4 The presidency was described as 'imperial' in the 1960s and 'tethered' in the 1970s. How might we categorise presidential power today?

5 What factors determine the power of the President? In what ways are his powers limited?

6 How successfully do Presidents direct and co-ordinate the work of their administrations?

7 Examine the evolution and present importance of the Executive Office of the President.

8 How important is the Cabinet in American government?

9 Which is the more useful to the President, the Cabinet or the Executive Office?

10 'In this, I am nothing, but I may be everything' (John Adams). Evaluate the role and importance of the vice-presidency, in the light of this remark.

11 Examine the part played by the federal bureaucracy in government and policy-making in the United States.

The legislature: Congress

5

Congress is a bicameral legislature, comprising two bodies: the Senate and the House of Representatives. They are law-making chambers, and both have broadly equal powers, making the Senate the most powerful upper house in the world. Both chambers are directly elected by the people. Although representation and law-making are the primary roles, Congress has other duties. For example, the Senate approves or rejects the US President's choices for the heads of government departments, Supreme Court justices and certain other high-ranking jobs. The Senate also approves or rejects treaties that the President makes.

In this chapter, we are going to investigate the role and status of Congress and its members in the American system of government, the way it is organised, and the attempts at reform in the past and proposals for further reform in the future.

POINTS TO CONSIDER

➤ What factors have led to the resurgence of Congress in recent decades?

➤ Why might an ambitious American politician prefer to serve in the Senate rather than the House of Representatives?

➤ What are the major stages through which legislative proposals must pass before they become law?

➤ What factors influence members of Congress as they make legislative decisions?

➤ How might Congress be usefully reformed?

➤ In what ways do the duties and responsibilities of US Congressmen coincide and conflict with those of Members of Parliament?

How Congress is organised

Congress is bicameral. In other words, it has two chambers:

- **The Senate** consists of two senators from each of the 50 states.
- **The House of Representatives** has 435 members. Members of the House Representatives are elected from congressional districts of about equal population into which the states are divided. Every state must have at least one House seat. For example, Alabama has two senators and seven House seats, Delaware two senators and one House seat, and New York State two senators and 34 House seats. Representatives are often called Congressmen or Congresswomen, though technically the term applies to senators as well.

The Democrats and the Republicans have long been the only major parties in Congress. In each chamber, the party with more members is the **majority** party, the other the **minority** one. Before each new session of Congress, Republicans and Democrats in each house meet in what is called a caucus or conference to choose party leaders and to consider legislative issues and plans.

Committees form an important feature of each chamber's organisation. They prepare the bills to be voted on. The committee system divides the work of processing legislation and enables members to specialise in particular types of issues. The majority party in each chamber elects the head of each committee and holds a majority of the seats on most committees.

The Vice-President serves as head of the Senate and presides over its proceedings. In fact, he or she usually only appears on special occasions or to break a tie, and for everyday work the Senate elects a president *pro tempore* to serve in the Vice-President's absence. The Speaker of the House serves as presiding officer and party leader. He or she is chosen by the majority party, the choice then being ratified by the whole chamber. The Speaker is the most important member of Congress, because of the broad powers the post provides within the assembly.

A new Congress is organised every two years. Voters elect all the Representatives at that time, and about a third of the Senators come up for election every two years. The Senate is therefore a continuing body because it is never completely new. The two chambers elected in November 2000 form the 107th Congress.

The 107th Congress: party representation in January 2001 (and % of the vote won by party candidates across the country)

	Democrats	Republicans	Independents
House (one vacancy)	211 (47.9%)	221 (47.9%)	2
Senate	50 (49.5%)	50 (48.5%)*	0

* The subsequent defection of Senator James Jeffords in May 2001 left the Democrats in control.

The powers of the House and of the Senate

The two primary functions of Congress are to represent the will of the people and to make laws for the country. The two tasks overlap, for if the laws do not represent the people's wishes then the lawmakers may suffer defeat at the next election.

Which chamber has the higher status?

Whereas, in Britain, one chamber is dominant, this is not so in the United States. In powers, they are virtually co-equal, although some writers would argue that the Senate's responsibilities with regard to treaties and ratification of appointments, gives it a greater degree of authority. Even the restriction that all bills on revenue-raising must originate in the House is hardly a limitation as the Senate has the same full power of amendment as it has with other types of bill.

Indicative perhaps of the Senate's higher status is the fact that candidates for the presidency tend to come from the upper house (or after serving a period in office as a state governor). Few come from the House of Representatives. Senators tend to get higher levels of media coverage and so find it easier to build personal reputations. Richard Pear[1] has elaborated in this way:

> Great senators have made the Senate great, and have influenced the course of American history in ways which can be recorded in the history books... [Some] sitting for safe seats have spent their lives in the Senate, becoming the embodiment of national or regional thinking on certain topics. Great senators are competitors for the limelight with presidents. They know their power and can use it for long term objectives.

An important difference is the length of service of a senator and a representative. Senators have the opportunity to acquire a working knowledge of their subjects of concern, without the problem of constantly having to campaign for their return to Washington. They can take part in a genuine debate rather than speaking and listening with the likely reactions of the voters in mind. Also, they have been elected by the whole state rather than a district of it. By comparison, members of the House are at a disadvantage. Maidment and McGrew[2] quote the example of one newly elected representative, who described his four years in the House in this way: 'The first two years, I spent all of my time getting re-elected'. Two years is perhaps too short a time in which to achieve anything substantial. For this reason, membership of the lower chamber is not a particularly satisfying form of activity, nor a particularly honoured position. Every two years, there are some representatives who do not seek re-election, but return from whence they came. Some are put off by the nature of their work, which they may find unrewarding. Little can be achieved by a 'freshman' unless the committee on which he or she serves suddenly bursts into prominence, because of a sensational investigation or contentious bill. For many of them, the job leads no further.

Americans are healthily sceptical about all those who represent them in Washington, and all politicians are held in low esteem. They tend to have a higher regard for those who have improved themselves by their own industry and perseverance in the fields of business, law and the other professions, rather than for those who operate in government.

Each house of Congress has the power to introduce legislation on any subject, except revenue bills, which must originate in the House of Representatives. The large states may thus appear to have more influence over the public purse than the small states. In practice, however, each chamber can vote against legislation passed by the other house. The Senate may disapprove a House revenue bill – or any bill, for that matter – or add amendments which change its nature. In that event, a Conference Committee made up of members from both houses must work out a compromise acceptable to both sides before the bill becomes law.

The Senate also has certain powers especially reserved to that body, including the authority to confirm presidential appointments of high officials of the federal government as well as to ratify all treaties by a two-thirds vote. Unfavourable action in either instance nullifies the wishes of the Executive.

In the case of impeachment of federal officials, the House has the sole right to bring charges of misconduct which can lead to an impeachment trial. The Senate has the sole power to try impeachment cases, and to find officials guilty or not guilty. A finding of guilt results in the removal of the federal official from public office.

The 18 broad powers of the whole Congress are spelled out in the eighth section of the first article of the Constitution. The first 17 are specific duties, but the 18th sets out the task of making

> all Laws which shall be necessary and proper for carrying into execution the foregoing Powers, and all other Powers vested by this Constitution in the Government of the United states, or in any Department or Officer thereof.

The functions of Congress

The overall role of Congress is extensive. As with any other Western democracy, it performs a key representative task. People choose representatives to make decisions for them, and if they do not like the decisions made they can reject those previously chosen at the next election. In this way, a link between the people and the national government is formed, and the consent of the governed is achieved. Representation is a difficult concept, and is open to a number of interpretations, but it involves the basic idea that legislators are responsive to those who put them in their position (see also p. 119).

The work in which Congress is engaged can be conveniently classified according to three main headings: legislation, investigation and finance. It is the legislative role which is the prime function, for it is this aspect which affects the lives of the American people most directly. An efficient and

---

Committees in Congress: main types

Committees are the principal means via which the House and Senate carry out their legislative work. There are several types of committee, notably:

1 Standing committees

Permanent committees with fixed jurisdictions which operate from one session of Congress to another. These are the most important committees and the focus of much of the work performed by the legislature. In the House, the Rules Committee has a crucial role, with the power to delay or even stop legislation. The Ways and Means Committee raises money; the Appropriations Committee deals with how government spends that money. Many members of the House Budget Committee are drawn from these two bodies, with one member from each of the other Standing committees. In the Senate, the Appropriations, Budget, Finance and Foreign Affairs Committees are prestigious

2 Select committees

Temporary committees which cease to exist unless specifically renewed at the beginning of each new Congress. They may be asked to study or report on a particular topic, but they do not receive or report bills.

3 Joint committees

Include members drawn from both houses and have continuing oversight over a particular area of policy. They may initiate legislation and often carry over from one Congress to another.

4 Conference committees

Again drawn from both houses, are charged with resolving the differences between legislative proposals dealing with the same topic.

---

responsive legislature has the power to further national goals at home and abroad, by the way in which it handles its law-making task.

Legislation

Bills are introduced by a variety of methods. Some are drawn up in standing committees, some by special committees created to examine specific legislative issues, and some may be urged by the President or other executive officers. Individuals and outside organisations may suggest legislation to congressmen, and individual members may themselves have ideas they wish to see pass into law.

Such is the volume of legislation proposed by senators and representatives that much of it has no chance of getting any further. It is introduced in the first place more as a way of securing the goodwill of lobbyists or constituents than with any expectation of further progress. After the initial introduction, bills are sent by the leadership to designated committees, where many of them die.

Ninety per cent of those before a sub-committee get no further, for lack of time or lack of support. This is the justification for the existence of committees. They act as a screening mechanism for the flood of measures presented, and thereby prevent the Senate and House being overwhelmed.

For those bills with significant backing, the committee schedules a series of public hearings which may last for weeks or months, and allow for an outside input from interested bodies. The sub-committee then discusses and amends the bill, and – assuming there is a vote in its favour – it is sent ('reported') to the full chamber where it is debated, and again a vote occurs. (In the House, the bill will first go to the rules committee, which determines the time limits to be allowed and decides whether or not amendments from the floor will be allowed.)

The Rules Committee

The House Rules Committee is the most influential committee in the lower chamber. Comprising some of the most senior members of the House and having a 2:1 membership in favour of the majority party, it organises the timetable of the House and thereby effectively determines the fate of proposed legislation.

The committee decides on a rule, which sets the time limit for debate and states whether amendments can be allowed on the floor of the House. It may decide that there can be debate and amendments subject to the overall time available ('open rule') or it may limit debate and insist that only members of the reporting committee may offer amendments ('closed rule', usually used only for tax and spending bills). Normally, without such a rule, the bill will not reach the floor.

Before Congress was reformed in the 1970s, the committee was even more powerful than is the modern committee. The 'old guard' (a coalition of Southern Democrats and Republicans) used their influence to block proceedings. The committee was then much disliked by liberals and those who wanted to see reform; they saw it as dictatorial and unrepresentative.

Today, the committee is less controversial and more representative of the membership of the majority party. If it wants a bill to be passed, the committee can expedite its passage, by sending it quickly to the floor of the House for immediate debate.

Usually, both chambers consider their own bills, at approximately the same time. To succeed, the approval of both the Senate and the House is necessary. If there are differences in the versions passed, then a conference committee will seek a compromise.

The bill must have successfully endured the procedure of both houses, and have been approved in identical form, for it to become law. If this does not happen in the lifetime of one Congress, the attempt has failed: the whole process needs to be started again.

ST. DOMINIC'S SIXTH FORM COLLEGE

At this point, the bill goes to the White House for the approval of the President. He may sign it, veto it or do nothing. If Congress is sitting and he does nothing, then after ten working days the bill becomes law without his signature. If the Congress has adjourned and the President waits ten days before signing, then this is a pocket veto. Other than in this case, a vetoed bill is returned to the Congress, with the reasons for rejection. The presidential veto can be overturned, if both chambers can muster a two-thirds majority against it.

Figures produced by Professor Davidson[3] show that only about 3 per cent of bills received by the President are vetoed, and only about 4 per cent of all vetoes are overridden by Congress. Presidents may veto a bill for several reasons – perhaps because it differs from their own legislative preferences, or because they feel it is unconstitutional, costs too much, or is hard to enforce.

The role of the Administration in legislation

The amount and character of legislation has changed significantly over the years. In the 1960s and 1970s, there was a burst of legislative action, but in the following decade the pace of change – especially on substantive issues – slowed down.

Federal governments cannot in theory make laws, and their proposals have no priority in congressional procedure. Presidents can propose legislation, but if congressional leaders prefer their own then the White House has no means of redress. Departments, in consultation with committee chairpersons and party leaders, draw up the measures seen as desirable, and they are then introduced by sympathetic members.

Although most successful legislation now originates in the executive branch, the Administration cannot be sure of its passage in the form which it favours. Whereas, in Britain, the system of party discipline ensures that a government with a parliamentary majority may get its way, this is not the case in the US. Presidents cannot depend on congressional support, and Congress remains a major force in determining the shape and timing of legislation.

The legislative procedure of Congress has often been described as an 'obstacle course', for bills have to get past the appropriate standing committee, be given time by the rules committee and then survive the debate on the floor of the House or Senate. To have got this far, there must have been a substantial degree of support, but in the Senate this is no mere formality and the bill can always be subject to a filibuster, by which senators hold the floor of the chamber, speak at length and seek to delay proceedings to avoid a vote being taken. The aged Strom Thurmond holds the record: in seeking to delay the 1957 Civil Rights Act, he spoke for 24 hours 18 minutes!

It is not surprising that few bills successfully navigate the procedure. In 1993–94, fewer than 6 per cent of those introduced went on to become law.

The procedure is not without advantages. The Separation of Powers is there to stop the domination of one section of the governmental machinery by another, and the law-making process reflects this aim of preventing tyranny. It is impossible for the whips to force through changes at the wish of the executive branch, and there is no elective dictatorship of the type often said to exist in Britain. Instead, those who seek to get a bill passed onto the statute book need to build a consensus in its support, and if it does pass it is likely to have substantial backing.

However, in a crisis the machinery is less responsive than the situation demands. Franklin Roosevelt and Lyndon Johnson, each aided by a Congress controlled by his own party, were able to introduce a package of measures speedily, but their experience is untypical. The system offers a built-in advantage to those who would thwart legislation, and at key points enables a dissenting minority to prevent the passage of bills by their obstruction at several access points – and thereby kill the proposal off.

Investigation

One of the most important non-legislative functions of Congress is the power to investigate. This power is usually delegated to committees, either the standing committees, select (special) committees set up for the specific purpose, or joint committees composed of members of the two houses. As the legislative initiative in Congress has diminished in recent years, so the investigatory role has assumed a greater importance.

It is in the scrutiny of the executive that the extent of congressional power becomes most apparent. Two factors give Congress greater power than the British Parliament. The first is the Separation of Powers, which was designed to prevent undue concentration of power in one location, and which denies the executive the chance to sit in Congress. Secondly, the absence of strong party discipline means that Congressmen can act as free agents, and act and vote as they please; they do not feel beholden to their party leaders for their advancement.

Investigations may be conducted to gather information on the need for future legislative action, to test the efficacy of laws already enacted, to enquire into the qualifications and performance of members and officials of the other branches of government, and to lay the groundwork for impeachment proceedings. Often, these hearings will involve the use of outside experts to assist in conducting the investigation, and to enable a detailed study of the issues involved.

Most of these hearings are open to the public, and they are widely reported in the media. Witnesses can be compelled to testify, and those who refuse may be cited for contempt; those who give false testimony can be charged with perjury. Investigations of a special type (such as that by the 1987 Joint Committee on the Iran–Contra affair) attract much publicity and through their findings can provoke much public and political controversy. Congress can examine anything it considers appropriate within the legislative sphere, and added to the overseeing aspect of investigation (i.e. acting as a watchdog on the executive), this indicates the power of the two houses in the political process. Investigations over the years have covered topics such as drug addiction, the Ku Klux Klan, foreign aid programmes, the American role in NATO, foreign commitments in China and Vietnam, and the possible abuses of power involved in the Watergate/Irangate operations. Whitewatergate (and allied/other scandals) was the subject of investigation during the Clinton years.

Finance

The presidential budget proposals may begin their existence in the White House, but they have to survive the detailed scrutiny of Congress. Most policies cost money, and thus require congressional authority to raise and spend it. Once the President and Congress are agreed upon a programme (authorisation), it is Congress which has to appropriate the funds to pay for its implementation. Such appropriations are processed by a committee in either house, and until the President signs the annual appropriations bill the original authorisation of expenditure amounts to nothing.

In recent years, the federal budget has been a continuing source of controversy between the President and Congress. The conflict originally dates back to the growth in the costs of federal programmes in the Great Society programmes of the 1960s, and in the years since then there has been an insufficient amount of revenue to match the expenditure. This has resulted in budget deficits, which by the 1990s were increasingly viewed with much alarm by many commentators and politicians.

Congress could accept the increase in military spending in the Reagan years, for it shared the goal of keeping America strong. It also liked the idea of low taxation. But the growing deficit could only be tackled by reduced spending in other areas, and this posed political difficulties for Congressmen. A large part of the expenditure could not be cut without tackling the controversial social security and medical programmes which used up so much federal money, but were popular with recipients. These programmes and other entitlements such as pensions (adjusted for annual cost-of-living increases) were difficult to control.

Without cuts in defence spending, welfare and other areas, there was little scope for tax cuts unless the deficit was allowed to increase – which is what happened. The reason, as given by President Reagan's Director of the Office of Management and the Budget, was that:

Deficits create many winners and few losers ... Every legislator is in a position to confer benefits on his or her favourite constituencies, and the incentive for any individual legislator to refrain from such behaviour is virtually non-existent.

Representation

The House of Representatives was originally viewed by the framers of the Constitution as the body which would **represent** the wishes of the mass of the people. The Senate, not directly elected, was seen as a more detached, dispassionate body that could operate as a check upon the House, which was liable to be influenced by considerations of short-term popularity. When direct election of the Senate was introduced, the House lost its unique position as the body which reflected the mood of the mass electorate. Since 1913, both chambers can claim to be representatives of the people.

representation
Has several meanings in political science. Usually, it means the authority to act on behalf of another, as gained through the process of election; in this sense, the representative acts to safeguard and promote the interests of the area represented. It can also mean the extent to which a representative mirrors or is typical of the characteristics of the person he or she formally represents – e.g. is the House representative: does it have an appropriate balance of women and ethnic minority members? (see pp. 128–30).

The importance attached to this function of representation is one of the distinguishing features of Congress, compared with other legislatures. The Senate and the House have always attached the highest priority to the attitudes and concerns of those who elected them, and other considerations such as party figure much less in their thinking. This leads us conveniently into a consideration of the roles and responsibilities of Congressmen.

The work and responsibilities of Congress members

Any Senator or Representative is concerned with five broad spheres of responsibility, the national interest, the constituency interest, the party interest, the lobbyists and the Political Action Committees who supported his campaign, and his own personal convictions. In Congress, he or she must seek to balance their importance to him or her.

Several Congressmen represent areas where their re-election is likely. They know that party discipline is much looser than in Britain, and the party label counts for less. Some of them may not feel particularly beholden to special interests. In other words, they can make up their own minds on issues, in the light of what they think is best for the country, best for their constituency and most in accordance with their own wishes. Independence of judgement in the light of their own conscience and beliefs is still a determinant of their vote.

The party has never claimed the allegiance of Congressmen as it does the Member of Parliament (MP) in Britain. The MP sees support for the party, except on rare occasions, as a primary duty. In the United States the situation is different. As Walles[4] puts it: 'While party membership provides a natural starting point for action, ultimately it may well take second place to activity related to committee and constituency pressures'.

Parties are of course the route via which the senator or representative reaches Congress, but as Mayhew argues,[5] once the journey is successfully accomplished 'it is the pressure for re-election which colours congressional activity'. In pursuing this goal, Mayhew distinguishes three forms of likely activity which to a greater or lesser degree might influence a congress member's behaviour:

1 Self-promotion, via postal communication and diligent attention to social and other occasions in the constituency.
2 Credit-claiming, as members point to what they have done for their district (jobs, contracts, support for local industry, etc.), and for individuals. This is especially relevant to the representatives, facing as they do the prospect of a re-election battle within two years, although no Senator wants to antagonise important interests within the state.
3 Position-taking, undertaken to help promote a favourable image of what the representative really believes in – what Mayhew calls 'the public enunciation of a judgmental statement on anything likely to be of interest'.

The constituency 'welfare' role

In the last two decades of the twentieth century, it has been constituency responsibilities which consume much of the time of the legislators. They hire more staff to work in their state and local offices, make more trips to the constituency, receive and send more mail to the voters and generally treat such work as a priority demand upon their time. For many of them, it has come to be a more important responsibility than drafting legislation.

In American government, there has always been talk of 'pork-barrel' politics, by which Congressmen are judged according to the success with which 'they bring home the bacon'. It used to mean 'delivering the goods' in terms of bringing rewards to the constituency. Today, constituency service has a wider connotation than merely gaining 'pork' or advantages. It is also about assuming the role of welfare worker or ombudsman, as citizens feel that they need assistance in their dealings with those who work in government offices and who are part of what is seen as an unresponsive bureaucracy.

Helping constituents in difficulty is more likely to ease the path of re-election than speaking and voting on controversial issues. Christopher Bailey[6] has highlighted this change of emphasis, and quotes the example of a Democratic senator from Alabama, who observed:

> Many freshmen view their role differently than 25 years ago, when a Senator was only a legislator. Now a Senator is also a grantsman, an ombudsman, and a caseworker, and cannot ignore [these activities] ... When we are asked by our constituents to help, we can't say we don't have time because we are focusing on national and international issues.

Bailey concludes that 'the increased emphasis on constituency service has transformed members from national legislators to narrowly focused ombudsmen'. He shows how many of them see themselves as lobbyists furthering the interests of their constituents in dealings with federal bureaucrats, by interceding on their behalf.

The danger of such an approach, in which Congress members see themselves as acting as advocates for the people, is that they may be tempted to act more forcefully on behalf of those who are the most influential persons in the community, particularly those who have contributed to campaign funds. The Ethics Committee of the House advises that the member must treat all constituents equally, 'irrespective or political or other considerations', and warns against favouritism or arm-twisting tactics. This has become the more important in recent years given the number of cases involving questions of ethics.

Bailey also makes the point that, in spending more time on matters of welfare and other matters of constituency service, Congress members may boost their reputations but do so at the expense of their effectiveness:

> By ensuring that grandma gets her social security cheque, the member may enhance his chances of gaining re-election, but the consequences are profound. Mismanagement and corruption within the federal agencies go unnoticed, and federal benefits are distributed on the basis of political clout rather than need. The cost to the taxpayer of the expanded notion of constituency service runs into billions of dollars, and the cost to the American people is a Congress filled with ombudsmen rather than legislators.

Congressmen are acutely aware of their prospects for political survival. They know that these depend to a large extent on their ability and effort, and accordingly they spend a large part of their time in discovering, assessing and acting upon the wishes of those who sent them to Washington. Maidment and McGrew[7] quote a Republican who described his task in the House as: 'Taking care of home problems, Case work, not necessarily having anything to do with legislation at all. Taking care of constituents'. He continues:

> if Senators and Representatives are to be believed, they are constantly looking over their shoulders for guidance. Few, if any, are willing to ignore the interests of their constituents. In that sense, the Congress is an extraordinarily representative legislative body. It is sensitive to the slightest shift in electoral opinion.

The roles of Congressmen: conflicts involved

There is no easy answer to the question of which is the most important responsibility of Congressmen. Many voters expect that they will represent the wishes of the people of the district, for that is why they are sent to Washington in the first place. They are there to voice feelings 'back home', and not to take an independent line based on some perception of the national interest or personal feelings. If the needs of the US as a whole happen to be in line with those of the folks 'back home' so much the better, but if they are not then constituents will draw this to the attention of their elected representative.

In the eyes of the voters, this is not just a matter of constitutional theory, but one of tangible benefits which the Congressman can and should be able to win. The title representative is therefore not lacking in significance – they do or should represent the people of their district.

Congressmen inevitably perceive their roles differently. This was highlighted by the findings of the final report of *The Commission on Administrative Review* (in the House, 1977), which analysed the responses of 140 Representatives about what they saw as their most important responsibility. The priorities were:
- per cent the nation only;
- 28 per cent the nation and district;
- 24 per cent the district only;
- 3 per cent unsure.

When a conflict arose between these differing pressures upon them,
- 65 per cent professed to following the dictates of conscience;
- 25 per cent thought it depended on the issue;
- 5 per cent wished to follow the wishes of the district;
- 3 per cent were uncertain.

In practice, any Congressman, senior or junior, must react according to the pressures of the moment. It is unrealistic to expect that he or she will ignore the chances of re-election in making a decision, and for that reason he is likely to pay heed to the prevailing mood of fellow citizen's – especially those in his or her locality. Yet on many issues where there is no clearly expressed constituency view or obvious local involvement, the congress member can argue a more exalted case as a trustee of the national interest.

Congressional reform: the 1970s onwards

Congress can be, and often is, very parochial, run as it is by senators and representatives who have their own individual ambitions and constituency problems to preoccupy them. Because of this, it can seem as though it is more concerned with safeguarding its own interests and those of the members' localities, than of acting for the general good. Several presidents have criticised the preoccupation with immediate local pressures which has prevented Congressmen from seeing what needs to be done over the longer term. Since the 1970s, Congress has become much more assertive, but some writers (and some presidents) wonder if it has become any more constructive.

Legislative curbs

The struggle in the Nixon years over the bombing of Cambodia made Congress act. It overrode the President's veto and passed the 1973 **War Powers Act** (see p. 82), which reasserted congressional oversight of foreign policy by curbing the scope for the Commander-in-Chief to wage war abroad. Another limitation which Congress imposed was the **Budget and Impoundment Control Act**, which was an attempt made in 1974 to allow a more effective check on the President's budgetary and economic planning. Congressmen objected to the way in which the President impounded (refused to spend) huge sums of money set aside for social programmes. Both chambers set up their own budget committees, and a Congressional Budget Office, with its own specialist staff, was created, to boost their expertise, and enable them to seek out and acquire the sort of information which presidents tended to deny them.

The internal workings of Congress

Apart from the legislative control over the presidency, the other changes made were more to do with the internal organisation of Congress itself. The time was appropriate for an expansion of internal democracy.

Problems with the committee structure

Many younger Congressmen felt that the workings of their chambers were beyond their control. Power lay with the committee chairpersons, and in the hierarchical structure new entrants saw little chance of being able to play a significant part and wield real influence for many years. Yet they were elected to look after the position of their constituents, and could not do so as effectively as they wished if they did not have the backing of powerful committee chairpersons.

Congressional committees are very important, and the House in particular has always devolved much power to them. Even though there is more debate on the floor of the Senate, its committees are also what one writer[8] has called 'the nerve centre of its legislative process'. To serve on one of the more prestigious committees is an ambition of many Congressmen, and the position of Chair is regarded as especially influential.

Until the 1970s, Congress operated via a **seniority rule**, so that length of service was the main determinant of committee allocation. It favoured the Congressmen who came from areas where their party always won, so that they would gain the opportunity for years of unbroken membership (as long as they could survive their party's primary election). For the Democrats, it paid to represent the South or the northern cities, for the Republicans advancement came for those who hailed from the agricultural Midwest. Representatives and senators who were elected for these areas were accordingly over-represented on committees.

The seniority rule applied especially to advancement within the committees, and those who became Chairmen were those who were the most senior members of their party on the committee. This provided enormous influence, for it was the chairperson who determined the agenda for discussion and the number and composition of sub-committees. The Democrats were the victorious party in almost all of the congressional elections from 1930 to 1970, so that many chairpersons were unrepresentative, and often conservative, Southern Democrats. This had a significant bearing on legislation, for too much influence lay in the hands of those who represented rural – and white – America.

The old system had few defenders, but it had one main advantage. The existence of an 'inner club' of senior members whose attitudes and behaviour could be predicted meant that presidents knew who to do business with. These people counted, for they had so much influence over congressional proceedings. If their approval was sought and won, then Congress could be managed. When reform finally came, this was not the case – as President Carter found to his cost. No longer were the reactions of Congress as coherent as they once were. Anything could happen, without the strong will of senior chairmen to steer legislation and impose control.

Reform of the structure

In 1973 the Democrats in the House decided, at a caucus meeting, to abandon the automatic use of the seniority system. In future, chairpersons would be nominated by the steering and policy committee of the party, and the nominees would then be subject to an election by secret ballot of all Democrats in the chamber. Most of the senior members were actually elected in the first elections, but there was now an opportunity for change. Two years later, with an influx of younger and more liberal Representatives, three elderly chairmen were removed.

Another change prevented chairpeople of key committees from serving as the chair of other significant ones. They also lost some of their control over the sub-committees, which became less beholden to the parent body. The Republicans saw the need to exhibit a similar 'democratic' interest, and implemented similar changes within their party.

Nowadays, less-senior members of Congress have more authority, sub-committee Chairs are more independent and, especially in the Senate, sub-committee chairs may be offered to Congressmen who have only served for one or two terms.

Often, chairpersons are still chosen on the basis of seniority, with the longest-serving majority-party member on the committee being selected.

Since the 1980s, Democrats from the South have lost their disproportionate strength, and those from safe northern industrial areas have frequently been chosen. Whereas once the system discriminated against organised labour, civil rights and urban-based interests, that is no longer the case. Over time, women and members of racial minorities ought to benefit from the seniority rule as it now operates, whereas if there was a free choice without recognition for long service they might get selected only rarely.

Power in Congress has become more dispersed than ever before, and the seniority rule for choosing chairpersons is much less of a bone of contention than it used to be. In the Senate, most members who belong to the majority party chair a sub-committee, several a full committee. In the House, many Republican Representatives now have such a responsibility.

Improved staffing

The formation of the Congressional Budget Office (via the Budget and Impound-ment Control Act, p. 123) was an indication of the wish of many congressmen to improve their professionalism and acquire a new expertise. An Office of Technology Assessment had already been formed two years earlier, and the General Accounting Office and other research services were reformed to allow for the use of more analysts and experts.

The number of aides to Congressmen in both houses has been increased, as has the staffing of committees. Maidment and McGrew[9] estimated that by the end of the 1980s there were some 40,000 staff serving members, committees and various support agencies. Congress ought to be able to perform its task with greater efficiency, having equipped itself with an increased capacity to handle and investigate presidential initiatives.

Letting the cameras in

Reforms of the legislative procedure in 1970 allowed each house to decide whether to televise its proceedings. A new generation of legislators was more comfortable than its predecessors with television, and eager for coverage of floor debate. Members quickly agreed to experiment with a closed-circuit debate. The House first opened its chamber to television in 1979; the Senate held out for a further seven years. But long before there were broadcasts of floor debate, television had been allowed to record more impressive and/or dramatic events on Capitol Hill, among them the State of the Union messages and Senate committee hearings such as those concerned with the possible impeachment of Richard Nixon.

Representatives and senators have learnt to exploit television by consenting to interviews, appearing on news programmes and crafting photo-opportunities with constituents. Some of them now devise a video version of their press releases, so that they can be sent – or beamed via satellite – back to local stations.

What more can and should be done?

By the turn of the twenty-first century, the balance of power had significantly altered from the situation a generation earlier. Congress became assertive, and the change in overall party control in both houses (from Democrat to Republican) meant that there was a much greater willingness – indeed enthusiasm – to challenge presidential policy. As the continuing saga of Whitewatergate and alleged sexual lapses unfolded, great damage was done to Bill Clinton's authority, but also – some would say – to the presidency itself.

Congress now has the expertise and will that it has lacked for many years, and if it wishes to challenge the President it has the capacity to do so. Yet the reforms carried out, especially the weakening of the importance of seniority, have actually made it less easy to organise Congressmen to act in concert and produce a united response. If anything, they are even more free to concentrate on acting in a way pleasing to their constituents, and are an easy prey to the special-interest groups who lobby for their support.

Much of what is done is designed to enhance the chances of re-election, and this does not make for effective long-term thinking. It does, however, ensure

---

Legislatures in Britain and the United States: a comparison

Both countries are bicameral. Whereas the US has two elected chambers, in Britain only the lower house is elected. The House of Lords, as at present constituted, contains appointed life peers, bishops and archbishops, law lords and an elected element chosen from the ranks of the hereditary peerage. The Blair government has put forward proposals to eliminate the hereditary element altogether and to establish a predominately appointed body, with a small elected element. In America, the upper house is based upon regional representation, but as yet this is not a prescribed feature of the British second chamber.

All four chambers have legislative responsibilities and in both countries criticism is often voiced about the effectiveness of law-making procedures. Congress is widely portrayed as an inefficient, 'do-nothing' legislature, whereas sometimes the allegation against the British House of Commons is that it has too vast a programme which – because of intense party whipping – it is able to force through Parliament.

Fundamental to the comparison, of course, is the system of government. Under the Separation of Powers, Congress is designed to be an effective check upon the executive.

that Congressmen think about the wishes and needs of those who elected them, and this helps to ensure that there is continuous accountability.

Criticism still surfaces from time to time of a 'do-nothing' or 'obstructive' Congress, which is sometimes portrayed as being timid, obsessed with internal bickering, narrow-minded and self-interested. Several questions are asked by those who seek further congressional reform:

1 **Is Congress efficient?** Congress has to deal with a vast number of complex bills, and criticism often relates to the pace of legislation. David Brinkley, the TV anchorman, expressed public frustration[10] when he said that 'it is widely believed in Washington that it would take Congress thirty days to make instant coffee work'. There is much talk of a 'paralysis in Congress', brought about by the number of sub-committees and their overlapping jurisdiction. Again, with more independently minded members less committed to the party line, it makes it more difficult for leaders to create coalitions to get business conducted and the agenda kept on time. For instance, much-needed reforms on health care have been particularly difficult to achieve.

2 **Does Congress defend the national interest?** Are legislators so anxious to ensure their re-election that they neglect to think of the national interest? Are they willing to tackle controversial issues which may be unpopular with their constituents? One House Republican leader[11] suggested that congressional behaviour was too concerned with 'perpetuating the longevity and comfort of the men who run it'. Are those representatives too concerned with the views

In the traditional absence of strong party loyalty among its members, it has sought to curb presidential ambitions – particularly if a different party controls the two arms of government. Since the 1970s, Congress has been described as 'resurgent' and its ability to hold the executive to account has been strengthened, as a result of internal reforms and the passage of legislation.

The British Parliament is often said to be 'in decline'. Commentators write of 'the passing of parliamentary control' and sometimes seek to boost the power of the House of Commons, in particular, to act as an informed and effective critic of government. It is often alleged that instead of Parliament controlling the executive, it is now the executive which controls Parliament. Not all academics would accept that Parliament is as ineffective as its critics suggest. Philip Norton[13] regards it as 'not just significant', but also 'indispensable'.

'Legislative decline' is a theme much discussed in relation to many liberal democracies. Power has passed from the legislative to the executive, as governments have needed to be able to pass laws to please the mass electorates. However, whereas the broad trend in Britain has been inimical to Parliament, in the US it is the presidency which has been subject to numerous limitations in recent years.

of special interests? Think of the way in which expensive congressional elections are financed. Are Congressmen beholden?

3 **Is Congress representative?** In both parties, there is a notable over-representation of middle- and upper-middle-income groups. Women and racial minorities remain seriously under-represented. Such questions are often asked and the responses are invariably critical. If it is true that Congress does not often perform its legislative and investigative tasks as effectively as it should, this perhaps reflects the fact that it is, in Walles' words,[12] 'better organsied for obstruction than for promotion'. The overlapping jurisdictions between committees and sub-committees provide opportunities for affected interests to delay or halt action. He suggests that the machinery seems 'ill-equipped to establish priorities which can be readily translated into action'.

Dominated by 535 sets of individual considerations, Congress can be an ineffective body, unable to devise policy initiatives coherently and pass them into law. It can sometimes seem that those 535 interests take precedence over the overall needs of the nation, and this is why major national problems – from tax reform to energy policy, from welfare to gun control – have been so difficult to resolve.

Issues for consideration

Is Congress socially representative of the nation?

By this use of 'representative', we mean 'typical of a class'. Sociologists use the term this way when they speak about a 'representative sample' of the people. In the case of America, the suggestion is that Congressmen should possess characteristics which are broadly similar to those possessed by the people as a whole. If this is the case, then Congress as a whole will be a microcosm or mirror-image of the nation.

Congress is not such a microcosm, for Congressmen – judged by attributes such as socio-economic status, education, race, gender and age – are not representative of Americans as a whole. Like the House of Commons, Congress is overwhelmingly white, male, middle class and middle aged.

Most senators and representatives are professionals: lawyers, business people, accountants, journalists, doctors, teachers, university professors or farmers. Lawyers are a sizeable contingent: their numbers are lower than in the 1970s, but still some 40 per cent of the 107th Congress. Next come business and banking. There are few blue-collar workers, and the poor, the underclass of the big cities and others near the bottom of the social pile are unrepresented in this sense, although this does not mean that present Congressmen are incapable of representing their interests. Some rich senators – Edward

Kennedy among them – are active in seeking to protect the under-privileged, and can be vociferous advocates of their cause.

Black Americans and Hispanics are present in smaller numbers than is justified by their presence in the community. At present, there are 39 blacks and 21 Hispanics in the House, none in the Senate. They and other ethnic minorities as a whole still have a long way to go to achieve anything like equality, as do women. In the 107th Congress, there are more women than ever before. Prior to the 2000 elections, there were 58 women in the House and 9 in the Senate. After the contests, there are 59 and 13 respectively. Groups such as Jews and Catholics are now represented in greater numbers than in the past, but still under-represented.

Representatives and senators particularly are older than the average of all Americans. Senators are usually older than representatives, partly perhaps because of the minimum entrance qualification (30, as opposed to 25), but also because many senators build up a reputation over six years and then, as incumbents, are difficult for opponents to remove. They may survive for many years, as the example of Strom Thurmond illustrates. He was originally elected in 1954 and celebrates his 100th birthday in December 2002.

It is very doubtful whether any freely chosen assembly ever could constitute a cross-section of electorate, for the choice is largely at the mercy of the voters. But having said this, the discrepancies between different groups and categories and their representation in Congress is clearly a considerable one.

This under-representation obviously matters to the groups who feel largely unrecognised. It becomes all the more important that if such groups are not well represented among the membership, then at least there need to be members who in their approach can show an empathy with those unlike themselves. In the nineteenth and twentieth centuries, there have always been legislators who – whilst socially untypical of and unlike those whom they seek to serve – can nevertheless imagine what it is like to be disadvantaged and are prepared to articulate their concerns for such people.

For the practice of their profession, Congressmen need the education and skills normally associated with middle-class professionals. In a system reliant upon volunteers to come forward, it is unlikely that the least educated, those from the poorest backgrounds and the majority of people who do manual work are likely to put their names forward. Few would wish to forsake their existing lifestyle and live the life of a Congressman who spends much of the time in Washington, away from the family. That being the case, it is all the more important that those who are chosen as candidates, and who are victorious, should reflect in their own experience and understand the conditions and outlook of all 'walks of life'.

The social backgrounds of legislators in Britain and the United States: a comparison

- In general, legislatures in European democracies and the United States tend to be male, middle aged, middle class and white.
- The number of women has increased in most assemblies, although the situation is patchy. It is poor in the US and in some European countries such as France, Greece, Ireland and Italy. In Britain, the representation of women moved forward in 1992 and significantly so in 1997 (120/635). It fell back slightly in 2001, to 118.
- Most representatives attain their position only after doing some other job and making a mark in their chosen careers. This may give them experience of life, but it also means that the voice of the young is largely excluded. Since 2001, the average age of Conservative members in the House of Commons is 48, of Labour members 50. (Labour had 10 members who were under 30 at the time of the election in 1997, 4 after 2001.) In the US, it tends to be slightly higher, so that the average age of representatives at the start of the 104th Congress was 50.9 and of senators 58.4.
- The middle-class nature of elected representatives is more marked now than it used to be in Britain. Labour evolved as a party to represent the working classes in Parliament. In 1918, the Parliamentary Labour Party (PLP) had 87 per cent working-class membership. Since the 1960s, the parliamentary party has been dominated by members with a university education and middle-class professions, many of them in higher education. Following the 2001 election, the manual worker element diminished to 12 per cent, the lowest ever. The Conservatives have always found it difficult to get working-class candidates to stand, and if this happens it is usually in unwinnable constituencies. Business people, managers, lawyers and other professional employees (particularly from the communicating professions) are well represented in Britain. So too are the law, business and academia strongly represented in the US.
- Twelve British MPs elected in 2001 belonged to ethnic minorities, including two Muslims and three Sikhs; 21 Jews were successful. Hispanic and black Americans fare badly in Congress, but among religious groups again Jews are well represented.
- Of course, both countries use the 'first past the post' electoral system. This does not encourage the representation of minority groups, for everything is staked on one candidate in a single member constituency. Parties encourage the choice of candidates who are likely winners and fear a possible loss of votes by deviating from the norm.

Should there be term limits for Congressmen?

In the 1990s, there was renewed interest in 'term limits', although the debate on how long any incumbent should serve has a much longer history. The Founding Fathers considered limiting the period for which any member of the executive or legislature should sit, but decided to avoid setting a limit on the number of terms anyone could serve.

In the nineteenth century, however, it was customary for elected politicians to limit themselves. It was only in the twentieth century that Congressmen began to exceed two terms in the House and one in the Senate. The development of the seniority rule for committee chairmanships inspired representatives to seek a longer term. The introduction of direct election for Senators in 1912 encouraged them to seek an extra six years.

Recent developments

Term limits were approved in the 1990 elections in Colorado, and thereafter in several – mainly western – states. In the 1994 elections, the tenth item in the Contract with America (see p. 221), the Citizen Legislature Act, dealt with the issue. It urged the need for a first-ever congressional vote to place limits on career politicians and replace them with citizen legislators.

In 1993 an Arkansas judge found the term limit approved in that state in 1992 'unconstitutional' in that it established a new qualification for congressional membership – besides age, citizenship and residency which are laid down in Article 1 of the Constitution. The same happened in Washington where the limit would have allowed senators a maximum of 12 years' service and representatives only six. The court would not accept this, even though on the expiry of their official maximum term there was provision for the voters to 'write-in' their names on the ballot paper so that they could serve again. The question was taken to the Supreme Court. In 1995, it ruled in the case of *US Term Limits, Inc. v Thorton* that states could not impose term limits on their congressional delegations, but the ruling did not apply to state legislators. Twenty states now have limits on legislative service, but there is little uniformity in their application.

Why the interest today?

Several factors have inspired a desire to curb career politicians from staying in power on Capitol Hill. Among them are:
1 All politicians – and Congressmen foremost amongst them – are increasingly viewed with disdain by many voters who have a deep scepticism about the motives of those who serve them. They wish to 'throw the rascals out', and believe that they can 'clean up' a sleazy Congress by ensuring that fresh faces appear to replace older, seasoned Washington politicians who can 'play the system'. Yet despite this distaste for Congress and many Congressmen, voters seem more than happy to re-elect their own representatives in either chamber, a point which leads to the second explanation.
2 In recent years, incumbents have been re-elected with great regularity. In 1994, no Republican incumbent was defeated in any gubernatorial, Senate or House race, and even the Democrats lost only two incumbent scalps in

the Senate – though they lost 34 in the lower house. For a variety of reasons, incumbency presents an advantage over opponents, so that once elected some Congressmen have stayed on Capitol Hill for a long (too long?) time.

3 Allied to the point about long-time career politicians is the feeling that there are too many incentives for Congressmen to stay 'on the Hill'. Perquisites and salaries are generous: too lavish for the many Americans who have a much less comfortable life.

A beneficial change?

Against:

1 Term limits are unnecessary in that the American system provides a check on those in power through regular (in the case of the House, frequent) elections. The incumbent can be challenged from within his/her party in a primary election, and by the voters as a whole in the general election.

2 It seems undemocratic to impose limits on the electorate's right of choice, for limits on Congressmen are actually limits on voters. They cannot reward able men and women who have given good service.

3 If there are problems of low ethics and scandalous or self-interested behaviour, the answer is to legislate against the evil or to vote against the offending Congressman.

For:

1 Term limits would weaken the stranglehold of long-servers in Congress, people who command excessive influence by virtue of their seniority. Fresh faces may be talented, as well as less 'corrupted' by long-service in the system.

2 A 'citizen legislature' would replace a chamber of career politicians. Congressmen would be more in touch with those who elect them, and contain 'ordinary people'.

3 Applying term limits to Congressmen is a logical extension of the curbs on presidential service. In 31 states, governors also have a limited period of office.

3 Are Congressmen paid enough and do they have good facilities?

Members of Congress are paid $145,100 per year, as at January 2001. The figure is high by most American standards, but well below that of several corporate presidents who earn several times as much.

In addition, members have awarded themselves a variety of expense allowances, which are generally considered a necessary accessory to members' regular salaries. They range from generous staff assistance and accommodation, to free use of video recording facilities and sophisticated computer services. Congressional leaders receive additional remuneration. Once they leave office, they receive handsome retirement benefits.

Pay and facilities of elected representatives in Britain and the US: a comparison

- In terms of accommodation, equipment, staffing, library assistance and other amenities, Congressmen are notably better placed than their British counterparts.
- Each senator and representative has a suite of offices in a building connected to Capitol Hill by an underground railway, and the member has access to office equipment, gymnasia and many other facilities, as well as generous expenses.
- For many years, it was customary for MPs to lament their inadequate facilities, the vast size and splendour of the Palace of Westminster being little consolation for the conditions in which they had to operate. Today (January 2002) an MP has a salary of £49,822, as well as a range of allowances for office help and accommodation. Some members still voice criticism of the lack of constituency help they receive, whilst others feel that they could do with more research assistance at Westminster. The lack of office equipment and particularly of information technology services are frequently condemned, for the House makes no central provision for such facilities.

CONCLUSION

Congressional reform has been a topic of periodic analysis in recent decades and the changes of the 1970s seemed to enhance Congress's powers and make it more assertive in relation to the presidency. Yet there are still doubts about the performance of Congress and its membership, reflected in the 1990s preoccupation with 'term limits'.

The public expects that Congress will be both responsive to popular needs and efficient. Many Americans lack confidence in the performance of those who represent them and feel that Congressmen are too swayed by lobbyists and party leaders and insufficiently committed to serving their interests. They also decry a 'do-nothing' Congress, complaining that it is often slow to identify, define and effectively tackle the problems facing the nation. But if Congress is sometimes slow to act, this may be because the American people themselves do not agree on what the problems are and how they should be resolved.

REFERENCES

1 R. Pear, *American Government*, MacGibbon & Kee, 1963.
2 D. Maidment and D. McGrew, *The American Political Process*, Sage/Open University, 1992.
3 R. Davidson and W. Oleszek, 'Congress and its Members', *Congressional Quarterly* (Washington DC), 1998.
4 M. Walles, *British and American Systems of Government*, P. Allan, 1988.
5 D. Mayhew, *Congress: The Electoral Connection*, Yale University Press, 1974.
6 C. Bailey, 'Ethics as Politics: Congress in the 1990s' in P. Davies and F. Waldstein (eds), *Political Issues in America*, Manchester University Press, 1991.
7 D. Maidment and D. McGrew, *The American Political Process*, Sage/Open University, 1992.
8 G. Wasserman, *The Basics of American Government*, Longman, 1996.
9 C. Bailey, 'Ethics as Poitics: Congress in the 1990s' in P. Davies and F. Waldstein (eds), *Political Issues in America*, Manchester University Press, 1991.
10 D. Brinkley (TV anchorman), as quoted in T. Conlan *et al.*, Taxing Choices: The Politics of Tax Reform, *Congressional Quarterly*, 1990.
11 J. Rhodes (one-time House Republican leader), *The Futile System*, EPM Publications, 1976.
12 M. Walles, *British and American Systems of Government*, P. Allan, 1998.
13 P. Norton, *Does Parliament Matter?*, Harvester Wheatsheaf, 1993.

USEFUL WEB SITES

www.thomas.gov/ Thomas (named after Thomas Jefferson, the Library of Congress). The congressional site which offers a comprehensive look at at Congress in the past and today; useful information about current activities.

www.house.gov/ (House of Representatives) and **www.senate.gov/** (Senate). Both give valuable details about the work of both chambers, reports about current legislation, the activities of Congressmen, their conditions etc.

www.vote-smart.org/ Vote Smart. An easy-to-understand guide to current legislation going through either chamber.

SAMPLE QUESTIONS

1 Why is the US Senate more powerful and prestigious than the House
   of Representatives?

2 Examine the role of Congress in making the law. Is Congress an
   efficient law-making body?

3 What reforms might lead to an improvement in the public perception of Congress?

4 Is it true that the real work of Congress is done in the committee rooms? How does the
   American committee system compare with that in the British Parliament?

5 Why is Congress a more powerful legislature than the British Parliament?

6 Compare the background and roles of MPs and Congressmen. What might an MP like
   and dislike about the American legislature?

The judiciary: the Supreme Court 6

The judiciary wields considerable political power in the US and for this reason must be considered in any discussion of the political process. Its members may not act overtly in the manner of a politician seeking election or re-election, but in a more passive way their influence is highly significant. They do not take the initiative, but rather wait for cases to be brought before them. At that stage, in the light of the facts presented, they can make their judgements which may have important political implications.

In particular, the Supreme Court has a key role in making the Constitution relevant to modern needs and circumstances. It is not bound by past precedent, and it can specifically or implicitly over-rule, ignore or modify judgements made in previous cases. Its decisions have important political significance. In this chapter, we examine the judiciary in general, but our attention will be particularly directed to the Supreme Court, its history, judgements and personnel.

POINTS TO CONSIDER

➤ Why is the presidential choice of justices on the Supreme Court considered so important?

➤ Is the Supreme Court still a strong defender of the rights of the individual?

➤ Has judicial activism gone out of fashion?

➤ How and why did the idea of judicial review develop in the United States? Why and in what sort of cases has it become important in Britain?

The range of state and federal courts

There are today two parallel systems of courts in the United States which between them cover the range of **civil and criminal** cases. There are the state court systems established under the individual state constitutions: these decide actions and settle disputes concerning state laws. Secondly, there is also the federal judicial system, which has become relatively more important as the country has expanded and the amount of legislation passed by Congress has increased. In effect, there are therefore 51 different judicial structures.

civil and criminal law
Civil law relates to private and civilian laws, and deals with relationships affecting individuals and organisations (e.g. family or property matters).
Criminal law relates to crimes against the state. It is concerned such things as theft, violence and murder.

The practice of state courts may vary significantly, for it is the essence of federalism that the states may run their own affairs in the way best suited to their own wishes and requirements. Differences of operation and terminology are inevitable, and this makes general comment on their structure more difficult. For instance, judges are elected in approximately three-quarters of the states, whilst in others they are appointed.

States are responsible for passing and enforcing most of the civil and criminal law of the United States. For every person in a federal prison, there are at least eight times more in a state one. The vast majority of cases are resolved in state municipal or justice courts in town and cities, with a right of appeal to the state appeals courts or, in a small minority of cases involving the interpretation of the state constitution or basic constitutional rights, to the state supreme court.

Federal courts enforce federal law and state courts enforce state law, but the relationship between the two systems is more complex than this. The federal Constitution is the supreme law of the land, and if state law conflicts with it or with federal laws made under that Constitution, then state law gives way. This is made clear in the 'supremacy clause' of the Constitution (Article vi). Because of it, decisions made in the federal courts can have a broad impact on those made in the state courts.

We are primarily concerned with the federal judicial system, the structure of which is relatively simple. There are three layers of courts. At the bottom of the pyramid are the district courts, above them are the circuit courts of appeal and at the apex of the system is the Supreme Court, the highest court in the land.

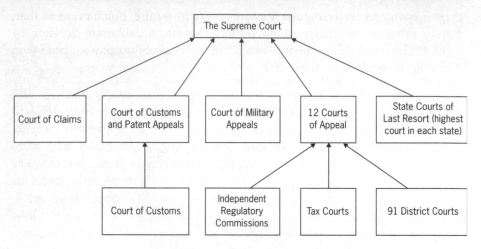

Figure 2 The structure of the federal judiciary

The appointment of judges in federal courts

Federal judges are appointed by the President, who is advised by the Department of Justice and the office of the Deputy Attorney-General. This power of appointment is highly significant. As Vile[1] puts it: 'No president can afford to ignore either the partisan advantages of such appointments or the fact that the men he appoints will be able, to say the least, to give a particular emphasis to the way in which policy is carried out'.

The power of appointment gives the President the opportunity to influence the balance of opinion in the courts. By 1940, Roosevelt had achieved a Democratic majority among federal judges, but the high point was reached during the presidency of Johnson when more than 70 per cent were of his party. In his 1980 election campaign, Reagan undertook to choose conservative judges who would abandon the social activism of many earlier appointees. His more overt concern with the ideological stance of judges was in line with the Nixon approach, but a departure from the usual practice whereby party label was a more important consideration. For Reagan, Republican leanings alone were not a sufficient guarantee of suitability.

In his two terms as President, Ronald Reagan made 344 federal judicial appointments, 4 to the Supreme Court, 6 to special courts, 76 to circuit courts and 258 to district ones. As with presidents before him, he made partisan appointments, but two factors were particularly significant about his choices:

1 He had the opportunity to appoint more lower-court judges than any of his predecessors since Franklin Roosevelt – he filled about half of all the judgeships at that level.

2 His appointees were singularly conservative by nature, much more so than most previous Republican nominations. This was a deliberate decision by the President to choose people of a different legal philosophy to those who had in the past sat on the bench.

George Bush followed a similar approach in his selection of another 187 judges. The effect of the appointments made in the 12 years from 1981 to 1993 was to transform the type of personnel who sat in judgement on legal issues. Overwhelmingly, the nominees were young, white males who were deeply conservative. Few women, African Americans or members of other minority groups were selected, but in one respect the choices were unusual for Republican administrations. More Roman Catholics were chosen than usual, probably because the Justice Department was in sympathy with the Catholic stance on the controversial matter of abortion, and saw a chance to win some popularity with the Christian Right on the topic.

In the first term of the Clinton era, appointments were quite distinctive. As a result of a rush of retirements, he was able to nominate almost a quarter of all federal judges, and he used the opportunity to diversify the composition of the judiciary. Almost all of his nominees were Democrats, but many of them were more moderate and less ideological than some party members would have liked. The figures below illustrate the different approach of the three presidents since 1981 (those for Clinton based on the 200 of his first term):

Presidential appointments to the judiciary

	Reagan	Bush Snr	Clinton
% of female appointees	7.6	19.0	31.0
% of black appointees	6.0	11.0	19.0

The Supreme Court

Courts tend to have a reputation for conservatism. Often, they resist the tide of innovative enthusiasm, interpreting the law as it is, guarding precedents and securing rights which have been traditionally recognised. The American Supreme Court has at times acted in a remarkably radical way, and rather than reacting to the wishes of politicians it has sometimes forced them to deal with great issues of the day. In particular, it was the Court which was instrumental in the drive to establish the rights of American blacks on a firmer footing in the postwar era. By so doing, it was effecting a major change – one resisted by a large section of the population.

The Court has not regarded the American Constitution as fixed and unalterable, but rather as an evolving body of ideals. It has preserved the fundamental principles which underpin the whole political system and create its basic character, but it has sought to reformulate them at various times in a way which makes them relevant to the problems of the day. It was not expected to exhibit such extraordinary influence when the Constitution was devised.

The Constitution said little about the judiciary, and the status of the Court is only briefly sketched. Judicial power was vested in one Supreme Court 'and in such inferior courts as the Congress may from time to time ordain and establish', but it was unclear as to how important the main Court was to be. Few specific powers were set out, but neither did the document seek to limit its role. The expectation in the very early days of the Republic was that it would play a lesser role in the newly established governing arrangements than the other two branches of government.

Much of the Court's present-day influence stems from a series of remarkably vigorous interpretations of the law and Constitution by the fourth Chief Justice, John Marshall, who was the leading figure on the bench from 1801 until his death in 1835. He established the Court's pre-eminence in judicial matters, and helped to make it a major influence in American politics. His contribution was threefold. He:
- helped to establish the independence of the judiciary from other branches of government;
- developed the role of judicial review (see p. 145);
- ensured that the Court's decisions were supreme over all courts in the land. He firmly believed in the importance of upholding national power over that of the states, and from this it followed that it was the duty of the Court to see that states did not infringe the sovereignty of the federal government.

Size and composition

The Constitution is silent on the qualifications for judges. There is no requirement that judges be lawyers, although, in fact, all federal judges and Supreme Court justices have been members of the bar. Since the creation of the Court more than two hundred years ago, there have been just over 100 justices. The original Court comprised a Chief Justice and five associates. Thereafter, the number varied until, in 1869, the total was fixed at one Chief Justice and eight associates, and nine has been the figure ever since. Each justice has one vote, and rulings do not have to be decided unanimously. The Chief Justice is *primus inter pares* (first among equals), in relation to his colleagues.

Prior judicial service is not essential for service on the Court, and some 40 per cent of all appointees since 1789 have had no kind of previous judicial experience in federal or state courts. Some leading figures on the bench have had a mainly political background. Earl Warren was a Californian politician, state Attorney-General and Governor before his elevation, and several others have been actively (some controversially) involved in political struggles before they gained recognition. It can be argued that such a background is more of an asset than a liability, for many of the decisions to be taken by the justices are essentially political ones.

In making appointments to the Court, it follows that presidents have not been primarily concerned with the judicial expertise of their nominees. They want to choose people who share a broadly similar political outlook and judicial philosophy to their own, so that the passage of contentious legislation has an easier ride both now and in the future. John Adams did not appoint John Marshall solely because of the brilliance of Marshall's mind, but because he shared a number of beliefs in common. Ever since then, presidents have been interested in finding people who broadly share their own opinions.

Appointments are an opportunity to change the direction of the Court's approach, and thereby to influence the evolution of public policy. For any president, therefore, the primary concern is to find someone who represents his or her own thinking (almost certainly someone of the same party) and who will be acceptable to the Congressmen who have to confirm the appointment. Beyond these considerations, other factors may come into play, all of which have the merit of maximising the President's political advantage. Presidents may wish:

1 to make a gesture of recognition to some disadvantaged group, by appointing someone who is a member of, or sympathetic to, that community. In the past, it was sometimes considered prudent to ensure that there was a Catholic or Jew on the Court, and in 1967 Lyndon Johnson saw the advantage of appointing a black Justice (Thurgood Marshall). In 1981, President Reagan appointed the first woman, Sandra Day O'Connor. In such a way, the President might hope to boost his or her standing with the under-represented group.

2 directly to influence the Court's direction, as did Roosevelt with his Court-packing scheme, and Reagan with his attempt to curtail **judicial activism**.

3 to give favours in recognition of some past service. Warren backed Eisenhower at the 1952 Republican Convention, and in return was given a seat on the bench.

> **judicial activism**
> The view that the courts should be active partners in shaping government policy – especially in sensitive cases, such as those dealing with abortion and desegregation. Supporters are more interested in justice, 'doing the right thing', than in the exact letter of the text. They see the courts as having a role to look after the groups with little political influence, such as the poor and minorities.

Richard Nixon consciously set out to change the balance of the Court, for like many conservatives he had become increasingly irritated by the persistent judicial activism of many who sat on the bench. He wanted to tip the balance by appointing people who would exercise **judicial restraint:** whose interest was in interpreting the Constitution and the law, rather than in breaking new ground via their adventurous decisions. 'Strict constructionists' were his preferred type of judges: in his words, those who would be 'caretakers of the Constitution … not super-legislators'. He was fortunate in having the opportunity to nominate four out of the nine justices on the Court at the time of his departure, and indeed if he had continued his presidency in the normal manner he would have been able to make another choice, and thereby gain a theoretical majority in his favour.

> **judicial restraint**
> The idea that the courts should not seek to impose their views on other branches of government, except in extreme cases. Supporters of this view are constructionists: those who want the courts to limit themselves to implementing legislative and executive intentions. They want a passive role for the courts.

The plans of presidents do not always work out in the ways intended. In the Nixon years, two of his nominees – Harold Carswell and Clement Haynsworth – fell foul of Senate approval, the first time this had happened since the 1920s. Carswell had been involved in a conflict of interest, and Haynsworth was seen as a mediocre figure with a marked tendency towards racial bias. In 1987, Robert Bork, a distinguished former Professor of Law and later a well-known judge of conservative persuasion, was rejected following heated battles over his confirmation. The Senate Judiciary Committee questioned him for five days, before it came to its verdict. The choice proved to be too controversial, for he had been associated with the dismissal of the Special Prosecutor during the Watergate scandal, and was seen as having contentious views and a too partisan a past. Bork aroused deep suspicion among American liberals who pledged millions of dollars in an attempt to fight the nomination; conservatives were willing to spend freely to defend his cause.

Other Republican nominees also had difficulties. The preferred replacement for Bork, Douglas Ginsberg, was rejected. He was withdrawn by President Reagan, when it became apparent that many senators were worried about his earlier use of marijuana. Clarence Thomas – accused by Anita Hill, a Professor of Law at Oklahoma Law School, of sexual harassment – was only confirmed after 12 days of embarrassing revelations at the Senate hearings in 1991, as graphic descriptions of his sexual habits were laid before the national television audience.

Altogether, 28 presidential nominees have failed to receive the necessary majority vote in the Senate, nearly 20 per cent of the total. Timing is often a consideration, for whereas most nominations in the first three years of a presidency are confirmed, the chances are less favourable in the fourth. The general trend is for hearings to be longer than was once the case, and in the more intensive scrutiny which takes place a candidate needs to have a very clean record to get an easy passage. Controversial nominations inevitably are more likely to fail.

President Clinton was aware of the importance of his decision when his first opportunity arose to make an appointment. The existing Court had been chosen entirely by Republican presidents, and he faced a body which had become markedly conservative in character. He wanted to arrest the rightward drift of the Court's membership, and find someone who would take a pro-choice line on abortion as he had pledged to do in his campaign. Yet he was aware that an overtly liberal person could easily be 'Borked' by conservative opponents in either party.

When Byron White retired in 1993, this was the first opportunity for a Democrat to make an appointment for 26 years, and Clinton set out to find 'a person that has a fine mind, good judgement, wide experience of the law, and in the problems of real people, and someone with a big heart'. His selection of Ruth Bader Ginsburg was readily confirmed by the Senate, for she had a reputation for fairness and moderation, was obviously well-qualified and was seen as someone who would interpret the law rather than become an advocate of special causes. A Carter nominee to the Court of Appeals in the District of Columbia, she had been a Professor of Law and an active supporter of women's advancement. Clinton's second nominee, Stephen Breyer, similarly survived the hearings without damage to his reputation or credibility.

Sometimes presidents find that the choice they have made turns out to be a wrong one from their own point of view. Harry Truman claimed that his biggest mistake was putting 'that damn fool from Texas' (Tom Clark) on the bench. Earl Warren proved to be a talented and innovative Chief Justice, but Eisenhower had not selected him as such, and never imagined that the Court would move in such a liberal direction under his leadership when he appointed him. 'Ike' was equally disenchanted with another of his appointments, Justice Brennan. Nixon was similarly disappointed with the performance of his appointees Blackmun and Powell. Appointed primarily for short-term political reasons, justices have a habit of becoming more independent and sometimes more creative when they are safely installed in office.

Procedure

The Court term begins in early October and runs through until June or July, depending on the workload. Throughout the term, it alternates between two weeks of open court, known as sessions, and two weeks of recess, during which the justices read petitions and write opinions. In the period when the

Court is in session, the justices attend from Monday to Wednesday to hear oral arguments presented by the attorneys whose presentations are strictly time-limited. *Briefs* (written documents) will have been presented before the hearing, so that in the oral sessions attorneys are supposed to discuss the case rather than read from a prepared text.

The more crucial stage is the *conference work,* during which the justices meet on two occasions a week to discuss and decide cases. The Chief Justice will initiate the discussion of each case, by outlining and commenting on the main issues as he or she sees them. Then, in order of seniority, the other eight members of the court are invited to comment. If the position of some justices is not clear at this stage, a formal but still preliminary vote will be taken. After the vote, the Chief Justice assigns the writing of the opinion to one of his or her colleagues. Others may decide to write *concurring opinions* (in agreement with the conclusion but not the reasoning of the majority) or *dissenting opinions* (that disagree with the majority conclusion). As the drafts are completed, the others comment upon them and may suggest changes in wording and reasoning. Sometimes this is a time-consuming procedure, for opinions may sharply diverge. The opinion-writing stage is only completed when all the justices have decided which opinion they support. When this has happened, the Court judgement is announced.

Role

The Supreme Court stands at the apex of the federal court system and is the only one specifically created by the Constitution. A decision of the Supreme Court cannot be appealed to any other court. Congress has the power to fix the number of judges sitting on the Court and, within limits, decide what kind of cases it may hear – but it cannot change the powers given to the Supreme Court by the Constitution itself.

The Supreme Court has original jurisdiction in only two kinds of cases – those involving foreign dignitaries, and those in which a state is a party. In all other cases, the Court is involved on appeal from lower courts or from the supreme courts of the 50 states. It decides on around 160–70 cases a year, although thousands are filed annually. Most of them are concerned with the interpretation of a particular law, or the intentions of Congress in passing it.

Cases in American courts

10,000 cases are tried annually by the American courts, 2 per cent of them by federal ones. Of these, around 7,000 reach the Supreme Court.

In an average year, around 90 are the subject of oral argument, and 70 or 80 are decided by a signed, written opinion.

However, an important part of the work of the Supreme Court involves the determination of whether executive acts or legislation conform to the Constitution. This is the power of **judicial review**, which is not specifically referred to in the original document. However, it is a doctrine inferred by the Court from its reading of the Constitution, and it

> **judicial review**
> The power of any federal court to refuse to enforce a law or official act based on law, because in the view of the judges it conflicts with the Constitution.

was propounded very clearly in the *Marbury v Madison* case (1803):

> A legislative act contrary to the Constitution is not law ... it is emphatically the province and duty of the judicial department to say what the law is.

Judicial review is necessary because the Constitution provides only broad and rather vague principles for the organisation and operation of government. It establishes three branches based on the principle of the Separation of Powers, and it sets out a federal structure and guarantees certain individual rights. These rules have remained largely unaltered, but they require elaboration and interpretation. Somebody has to decide what the Constitution actually means, and then interpret its relevance to specific cases. The Supreme Court acts as the arbiter of the constitutionality of the acts of the legislature and the executive. In the words of Alexander Hamilton in *The Federalist Papers* (no. 78) the duty of the Court 'must be to declare all acts contrary to the manifest tenor of the Constitution void'.

After the 1803 case, the authority of the courts to act as the final arbiter on constitutional matters was confirmed in other cases in 1810 and 1821, and it has been accepted ever since. Maidment and McGrew[7] have calculated that some 80 federal statutes and more than 700 pieces of state legislation have been struck down in the subsequent period as 'unconstitutional'. The frequency of such rulings may be an indication that the federal and state governments have too often acted without due recognition of the constitutional proprieties involved, or of the assertive stance taken by Supreme Court justices. But two other possible explanations are:

1 that the Constitution has not proved to be a straightforward document to interpret. Maidment and McGrew ask whether the First Amendment ('Congress shall make no law ... abridging the freedom of speech, or of the press') literally means that Congress cannot legislate on matters such as libel or pornography. Was the intention of those who devised the Constitution really to prevent Congress from passing any legislation at all in such areas, or was it really meant to be a safeguard of political liberty, to prevent undue exercise of governmental power which might curb beliefs and the expression of ideas on matters political, social and economic?
2 that the courts have had to deal with a changing country. Even if the intention of the framers of the Constitution was to create a system that

would last indefinitely, a society in rapid development clearly needs some machinery to accommodate the pace of change. The Court has had to be faithful to the original document, yet seek to interpret its provisions in a way relevant to the times. The increased role of government in the social and economic lives of the people has posed a clear challenge to those on the bench. From after the Civil War through to the Great Depression of the early 1930s, the regulation of economic activity by the government became a key issue. From the presidency of Franklin D. Roosevelt, the scale of federal intervention has grown dramatically, and the Supreme Court found much of the New Deal legislation unacceptable in its original form.

The Supreme Court has made decisions affecting every aspect of American life, decisions which have shaped the course of development in every sphere of governmental activity. The earliest ones were often concerned with the division of responsibility between the federal and state governments at a time when the nation was rapidly expanding in size. The question of slavery was relevant to that discussion. Thereafter, the degree of economic regulation by the government was a controversial subject, as was later the massive expansion of federal activity in the New Deal in the 1930s. Since World War II, the issues tackled by the Court have often been of a different type, for by then the debates over the degree of economic regulation and intervention had been resolved. The issues of the postwar era have been ones of civil liberties and rights.

The Court and political controversy

The Supreme Court is a complex body, for it is neither a completely judicial nor a completely political/policy-making body. As Grant[3] observes: 'Politics play a crucial role in the appointment, working and decision-making of the … Court, and many of its judgements have broad policy implications'. Yet if its work and personnel are involved in political controversy at various times, it is also supposed to interpret the Constitution, a function which places it above the everyday political fray.

The Court has constantly been involved in political matters, even though in theory it has generally stayed clear of questions of direct political controversy. Its rulings can and often have had political implications, so that when in *Dred Scott v Sandford* (1857), the Court declared that a slave was a property and had no rights this was a serious blow to those campaigning for an end to slavery. In other words, a judicial judgement had impacted on the political process.

In the 1930s, a Court reflecting the conservatism of the 1920s overturned programmes aimed at fighting the economic devastation of the Great Depression. Roosevelt was dissatisfied with the Court's performance, for its members posed a threat to the New Deal by their willingness to strike down key measures as 'unconstitutional'. The broad objection raised was that the federal government was exceeding its authority, and that the President and his advisers were too willing to downplay constitutional considerations. Since then, there has been much debate about the rights and wrongs of the issue, some writers believing that legislation should have been more carefully drafted whilst others taking the view that political malice was involved. Four of the nine justices were hostile to the New Deal, seeing it as a threat to property rights and the powers of the states. Several of them were elderly and conservative.

As a result, FDR came up with a Court-packing scheme, which would have enlarged its size and curtailed the power of older members. The plan ran into opposition, for it seemed to some Americans to be a bending of the rules. However, in the end Roosevelt got his way, for after 1937 the President had no further problems with the Court, as its members – reinforced by new appointments – began to allow legislation to pass onto the statute book ('a switch in time, saved nine').

In the 1950s and 1960s, the judgements of the Warren Court (see pp. 148–9) ushered in one of the most liberal periods in the history of the Supreme Court. Some of its decisions aroused intense controversy, as indicated by the abortive movement at one time during his stewardship to replace the existing Court with a new Constitutional Court of fifty members.

The decisions of the Court are not mere exercises in constitutional exegesis interpretation. They are related to the great questions of the day, and the verdicts delivered impinge upon the nation's economic, political and social life. Can a tax be levied? Can an abortion be performed? If so, under what conditions? Can pornography be banned? Can races be segregated? These are all issues of primary concern to many Americans, and decisions broadly seen as liberal or conservative can greatly affect the tone of political debate. On some controversial questions, such as church–state relations, **affirmative action** programmes and abortion, the Court was evenly balanced, often voting 5–4 one way or the other, until the early 1980s. The choice of justices was therefore a highly significant one. It had political, as much as judicial, implications.

> **affirmative action**
> Policies and actions designed to remove the effects of past discrimination by promoting and expanding minority job and promotion opportunities.

The political role of the Court is well established, and the justices play an important part in the political process. They are appointed for political reasons, and after their appointment they inhabit an intensely political atmosphere. It may seem strange to many people that matters affecting the fate of society are ultimately decided by nine unelected justices who, once on the bench, have no direct contact with public opinion. But as has often been pointed out, 'they read the election returns, too'. In other words, they understand prevailing pressures, and react to changing moods among the population, as in their decisions on affirmative action in recent years.

At various times, the Court runs into difficulties with the Left and the Right, for both liberals and conservatives sometimes find its decisions controversial and unacceptable. This is because it is charged with handling issues which are of vital importance to democracy and society at large. Yet justices use their powers sparingly, for they realise that if they allow themselves to become out of step with popular opinion for too long then the reputation of the Court will be damaged. They also wish to avoid open confrontation with the other branches of government. They understand the need to interpret the Constitution in the light of the requirements of today's industrialised society, and thus ensure that it remains a living document which continues to command general assent. The Court has performed its role rather well, and Professor Archibald Cox,[4] the Watergate Special Prosecutor, has explained the reasons for this success:

> The Court must know us better than we know ourselves ... the roots of its decisions must already be in the nation. The aspirations voiced by the Court must be those the community is willing not only to avow but in the end to live by, for the power of the constitutional decisions rests upon the accuracy of the Court's perceptions of this kind of common will and upon the Court's ability, by expressing its perception, ultimately to command a consensus.

Three Chief Justices and their Courts

Earl Warren, 1953–69

At the time of his appointment, Warren was not thought of as being progressive. He was widely expected to be a consolidator, so Eisenhower could feel comfortable with his choice. Yet the Warren Court was to be noted for its judicial activism. Decisions taken in that era were of fundamental importance, and concerned such things as the rights of individuals, especially minorities, equal representation and equality before the law. This was an innovative Court, one of the most liberal in its history. It made a huge impact on many aspects of American life, so that the years 1953–69 witnessed what has widely been seen as a constitutional revolution.

It was in the field of civil rights that Warren made his greatest impact. Segregation had developed in the United States under the constitutional doctrine laid down in *Plessey v Ferguson* (1896), when it was decided that it was constitutional to segregate people according to colour on the railways, as long as the separate facilities were equal in quality. In the landmark judgement in *Brown v the Board of Education in Topeka, Kansas* (1954), it was declared that segregation in schools was unconstitutional, for separate facilities were seen as inherently unequal, and thus a breach of the 14th Amendment which declared that no state could 'deny to any person within its jurisdiction the equal protection of the laws'. The verdict applied only to segregation in schools, but it soon became apparent in other judgements that no service offered by the state could be provided on a segregated basis. The Court later ruled that it was constitutional to bus children across school district lines to achieve racial equality, a decision which upset many Northerners, just as the 1954 ruling was greeted with dismay in the South.

The Warren Court also:

1 produced what was criticised as the 'criminals' charter'. Justices took the view that, in criminal cases, the balance of opinion had swung too much in the direction of the prosecution rather than those on trial. New guidelines were imposed upon the police, especially over powers of search and detention, and in interrogations a code of conduct limited the possibility of unfair behaviour by those in charge of the case. Those opposed to such measures were often moved to outrage, as indicated by the posters which appeared – 'Impeach Earl Warren'. Some used 'Hang' instead of impeach!
2 was willing to show a new spirit of tolerance on other issues of civil liberty. The press was rendered less vulnerable to prosecutions for libel, and the state of New York was prevented from allowing a prayer to be recited in schools, as this was deemed to be a violation of the First Amendment.

Such judgements aroused dismay and opposition, and many felt that via the new liberal line the Court was becoming too immersed in political controversy. In the 1968 election, the performance of the Warren Court came under much scrutiny, and Richard Nixon promised to appoint 'strict constructionists': those who would confine themselves to the task of interpretation, rather than engage in 'political meddling'. When Warren resigned shortly afterwards, Nixon (as President) had his opportunity. He nominated Warren Burger as his successor.

The Burger Court

The Burger Court was again intended to be a consolidating one, but the counter-revolution which Nixon favoured never really took place, for although the new nominees made in this period were generally conservative they did not seek to undo the work of the Warren Court in their decisions. The Court may not have been as innovative as its predecessor, but it produced some surprisingly bold judgements. If its decisions on the criminal law were more cautious than those of the Warren era, none the less on racial matters, abortion and over Watergate it acted adventurously.

In matters of criminal justice, the approach leaned more towards police powers, although there was no attempt to return to the pre-Warren era, but on civil rights and abortion, the stand was adventurous. The Court decided that affirmative action could be constitutional (e.g. the Baake case of 1978 – see p. 33), and in favour of abortion. In *Roe v Wade* (1973), it struck down state anti-abortion laws, and ruled in favour of the right of women to control what happened to their own bodies – in the words of Gillian Peele,[5] 'a liberal interpretation of the Constitution, based on a right to privacy which is not to be found in the text of the document'.

Finally, it was the Burger Court which ruled against President Nixon in the matter of the Watergate tapes, recordings made by those around the President to provide him with a clear record of conversations which had taken place in the Oval Office. As the scandal unfolded, with its allegations of a massive cover-up and obstruction of justice following the break-in of the Watergate building, a federal District Court judge issued a subpoena, ordering the President to release 64 tapes. The President claimed Executive Privilege, and refused to release them to the Special Prosecutor. The Supreme Court insisted unanimously that the tapes must be handed over, and Nixon complied with the decision – an illustration of the status of the Supreme Court. The executive and legislative branches of government abide by its decisions, even though it

---

The Supreme Court and the 2000 presidential election

The final decision of the Court in the *George W. Bush v Albert Gore Jnr* case was among the most momentous of its history. In addition to deciding this particular presidency, it could have the effect in future of pushing the nation's highest court into more election battles – an area it has traditionally avoided.

The Court was dealing with an appeal by George Bush Jnr against a ruling in the Florida Supreme Court to order a manual recount in the state. The nine justices basically had three options:

1 It could have found for Bush on the grounds that the only votes usually counted in Florida are those clearly marked, so that the state's Supreme Court decision to allow other votes to be included was a departure from normal practice. Justices Rehnquist, Scalia and Thomas were supporters of this viewpoint which, if handed down, would have been final and stopped all recounts without qualification.

2 It could have ruled clearly for Gore, deferring – as federal courts normally would do – to state courts on matters of state law. This might have involved issuing guidance to the Florida Supreme court on how the recount should proceed. Justices Breyer and Ginsburg wanted to do this. To do so would have made the process more lengthy, but would have meant that ultimately the choice lay with the voters.

3 The third option, which it actually took, was to seem to do the second, whilst actually doing something akin to the first. By 7–2, it sent the case back to the Florida Supreme Court (FSC) 'for further proceedings not inconsistent with this opinion'. In practice, as the various dissenting opinions made clear, this meant that by 5–4 the FSC had to have the votes counted, allow sufficient time for judicial review of these proceedings and do it all by midnight, 12 December two hours after the Supreme Court issued its ruling (the

lacks any direct means of enforcement. The impact of the 'tapes issue' was enormous, and within a fortnight Nixon had resigned. The action of the Court had again been of momentous consequence.

The Rehnquist Court

Given the disappointment felt by many conservatives over the performance of the Burger Court, President Reagan was determined to appoint Justices of conservative persuasion. As Chief Justice, he opted for Rehnquist on Burger's retirement, and it is the Rehnquist Court which is still in place in 2001. The intellect and diplomatic skill of the new incumbent were not doubted, but those of more liberal leanings saw Rehnquist as the most conservative member of the existing nine. Even though justices sometimes act in unpredictable ways – contrary to the expectations of those who appoint them – there has certainly been a markedly less liberal tone in the judgements delivered in recent years.

---

date when the Electoral College votes were supposed to be over). By opting for the impossible, this meant that the Court effectively handed victory to Bush.

In its defence, seven justices had found serious constitutional violations in the way that the manual recounts had been conducted. Even Associate Justice Ginsburg, a Democrat appointment, called the process 'flawed'. They were uneasy about the way in which decisions on vote-counting were being taken away from the officials whom the legislature had appointed for the task of managing the election, and handing them over to the judiciary. Neither was the recount to include 'all ballots', a requirement of state law. All in all, the Court had brought finality to a messy business and produced a result.

To Gore sympathisers, any outcome of the Court's deliberations would have been questionable, but the final decision seemed to be intellectually less than rigorous. Doubts were expressed about the reasoning and remedy that led to the verdict. The verdict expressed implied that the Supreme Court knew better than the Florida Supreme Court what was meant by Florida state law, a strange judgement from a generally constructionist court which has generally been very sympathetic to states' rights. As Justice Breyer pointed out, the Florida Supreme Court would have preferred a recount finished on 18 December (when Electoral College votes were due to be certified), for it had stressed 'the will of the voters' and its willingness to recount ballots in its decision.

By rejecting some ballots as it effectively did and acting in a way which seemed to reflect its Republican majority, the Supreme Court has involved itself in controversy. The case created intense excitement and partisan feeling, and Americans and observers world-wide were waiting to see how the verdict would go. By its judgement, it has risked eroding public confidence in its collective wisdom and fairness, what Justice Breyer called 'a public treasure that has been built up over many years'.

Presidents Reagan and Bush had the opportunity to tilt the balance of the Court, and seized it. President Clinton was able to make two appointments, so that the reaction of the nine on controversial matters such as abortion and affirmative action is not entirely predictable. But his are the only Democrat members and although there are two other moderates the conservative cause can muster a majority if Sandra Day O'Connor votes with it. She is the least predictable justice and her reaction in the controversies surrounding the 2000 election was watched with interest (see pp. 150–1 and also pp. 195–8).

In general, the Rehnquist Court has taken a notably less progressive line than its predecessor, its judgements being cautious and less spectacular than some earlier ones. The broad approach has been to nibble away at the edges of

---

Judges and their role in Britain and the United States: a comparison

One of the most significant political developments in Britain in recent decades has been the growing importance of judges and the courts. Previously, the role of the courts in British politics had been restricted and sporadic, whereas it is now often said to be central and constant. Today, the power of judges to review the legality of governmental action has become an important stage in the public policy process. Its increased relevance was apparent when in 1987 government lawyers produced a document for civil servants, entitled *The Judge over your Shoulder*. It showed them how to avoid the pitfalls into which they might tumble.

Between 1981 and 1996, the number of applications for judicial review rose from just over 500 to nearly 4000; in the latter year alone, there were 1748 immigration applications and 340 concerning homelessness. The increasing resort to review and the decisions which judges reached in several cases ranging from criminal injuries to deportation caused resentment under the Major government. Tension became acute, for ministers were overtly critical of judges and complained about judicial activism, whilst some judges felt there was a campaign to discredit them. The tabloid press joined in the 'judge-bashing', complaining of the 'galloping arrogance' of the judiciary.

Opponents of a British Bill of Rights – many of whom are Conservatives – often claim that it would remove power from the hands of elected MPs and give it to the judges. Similar fears about the transfer of power to the judiciary are at the heart of much anxiety about the 1998 Human Rights Act which incorporated the European Convention on Human Rights into British law. If today that suspicion is often voiced on the political Right, in the past it was the Labour Movement which felt uneasy about judicial power. Its suspicion was not based solely on a number of well-documented and unfavourable verdicts. It had much to do with a feeling that these judgements derived from problems about the selection, backgrounds and attitudes of those 'on the bench'.

Many British judges have formerly practised at the bar, membership of which has long been thought to be elitist and unrepresentative. Members tend to have professional,

contentious issues, rather than make a direct challenge to the whole direction of past policy in areas such as abortion and affirmative action. This failure to reverse many liberal judgements of an earlier era has disappointed many conservatives, but none the less Schwartz[6] has detected in the Rehnquist a series of cumulative decisions 'limiting the use of habeas corpus by prisoners, broadening the power of the police to search automobiles, applying the harmless error doctrine to a constitutional error committed at the trial, and upholding regulations prohibiting abortion counselling, referrals or advocacy by federally funded clinics'. Many observers from the Left and the Right have praised Rehnquist for improving the Court's efficiency and for his effectiveness in dealing with colleagues.

middle-class backgrounds, and have often been educated at public school before attending Oxbridge. In other words, they are said to be conservative, wealthy and out of touch. A privileged lifestyle might not by itself render judges unsuitable to exercise greater political influence. But – it is alleged – the nature of their training, and the character of the job they do, tends to give them a preference for traditional standards of behaviour and make them particularly impressed by traditional values in matters of behaviour, family life and respect for the law. They are unlikely to be overly sympathetic to demonstrators, minority activists and those who are strident in seeking justice for their cause.

Courts of law are part of the political process in most democratic countries, for governmental decisions and acts passed by the legislature may require judicial decisions to be implemented. Courts need to be independent to be respected, but in practice this is difficult to achieve. There is rarely full independence as far as appointment is concerned, though in America the process is more overtly political.

As a broad trend the role of judges in the political system has increased in liberal democracies. Some fear that this political involvement has gone too far, and that there are dangers for the standing of judges if this is unchecked. Others worry less about the damage which may be done to their reputation, but instead place their emphasis upon fear of judicial power. In both countries, alarm is sometimes raised about the politicisation of the judiciary and interest centres on the character and leanings of those who are appointed judges.

Nowadays, to see the judiciary purely as being pre-occupied with the legal system would be to ignore its key political role. As Chief Justice Holmes once put it: 'We are under the Constitution, but the Constitution is what the judges say it is'. In Britain too, judges are now much more willing to step into the political arena, an area long inhabited by justices of the Supreme Court. The same fear about their activities is voiced in both countries: those on the bench are unelected, unaccountable and invariably rather elderly.

The Rehnquist Court in 2001

	Year of birth	Year of appointment	President who made appointment
Chief Justice			
William Rehnquist	1924	1986	Reagan
Associate Justices			
John Stevens	1920	1975	Ford
Sandra Day O'Connor	1930	1981	Reagan
Antonin Scalia	1936	1986	Reagan
Anthony Kennedy	1936	1988	Reagan
David Souter	1939	1990	Bush
Clarence Thomas	1948	1991	Bush
Ruth Ginsburg	1933	1993	Clinton
Stephen Breyer	1938	1994	Clinton

Much interest – particularly in the *Bush v Gore* case, but also on matters such as abortion – centres on the composition of the Court at any time, with the past records of the nine coming under much scrutiny.

Broadly (perhaps crudely), Breyer, Ginsburg and Stevens are liberal, O'Connor and Souter are right-centre, and Kennedy, Rehnquist, Scalia and Thomas conservative. Clinton's two appointments have made the Court a moderate one, much depending on the reactions of O'Connor and Souter, who have both sometimes been joined by Kennedy in taking a more liberal line on matters of civil liberties.

CONCLUSION

Those who serve on the Supreme Court invariably survive those who put them there. This means that there is a thread of judicial continuity from one presidential administration to another and that the Court can act as a powerful counter to the other two branches of government. The situation was summed up by an early twentieth-century President, William Taft. He observed that: 'Presidents come and go, but the Supreme Court goes on forever'. True enough, but the fact that the nine justices and those who serve as judges across the country are political appointments does help to shape the development of public policy. On occasion, as in the 2000 election, it may be thought to play too large a role when the justices reach their verdicts.

Because the courts have so much power, the role they play in addressing important social issues is much discussed. Dispute centres on whether judges should confine themselves to interpreting the Constitution, implementing the letter of the existing law, or whether they should actively seek to broaden the nature of justice by identifying and redressing grievances. On occasion, as with the Warren Court, judicial activism is triumphant. Usually, and certainly more recently, judicial restraint is the norm.

REFERENCES

1 M. Vile, *Politics in the USA*, Hutchinson, 1978.
2 R. Maidment and D. McGrew, *The American Political Process*, Sage/Open University, 1992.
3 A. Grant, *The American Political Process*, Dartmouth, 1994.
4 A. Cox, *The Court and the Constitution*, Houghton Mifflin (New York), 1987.
5 G. Peele (ed.), *Developments in American Politics*, Macmillan, 1998.
6 B. Schwartz, *A History of the Supreme Court*, Oxford University Press, 1993.

USEFUL WEB SITES

www.uscourts.gov Federal Judiciary Home Page. Comprehensive guide to federal court system, with court statistics, answers to frequently asked questions etc.

www.law.cornell.edu/supct/ Cornell Law School. Provides a diverse array of legal sources and full text of Supreme Court judgements.

SAMPLE QUESTIONS

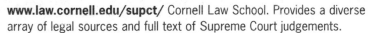

1 How 'supreme' is the Supreme Court within the American political system? Would the Founding Fathers be troubled by the way in which its role has evolved?

2 'A judicial body certainly, but its decisions often have a major impact on the political scene'. Discuss this verdict on the Supreme Court.

3 Do Supreme Court judgements follow popular opinion? Should they?

4 Is it true that the judgements of the Supreme Court have a greater impact on American society than the actions of the President or Congress?

5 To what extent are the decisions of the Supreme Court influenced by its changing membership?

6 'Legislatures may make laws by passing statutes, but judges have to apply them in particular situations'. To what extent do judges in Britain and the United States make the law?

Elections and voting

7

Elections, campaigns and voting are central features of democratic life. America has more elections than other democracies and voters are faced with alternative visions, programmes and personalities at all levels of administration. Many of them decline the opportunity to make up their minds about their preferred choice, even in the four-yearly presidential contests.

In this chapter we are concerned to find out why elections are so basic to thinking about democracy in the United States and to see how the various types of election are conducted, particularly that for the presidency. We ask why so many Americans do not turn out to vote and what influences those who do so. We also consider the use of 'direct democracy', examining the growth in the popularity of initiatives and referendums in recent years.

POINTS TO CONSIDER

➤ Why are there so many elections in US politics?

➤ In what ways has television changed the nature of election campaigns?

➤ How is the President elected? Could the system be improved? Does it need to be improved?

➤ Why do so many Americans not vote in important elections such as those for President, Congress or governors?

➤ What changes have occurred in voting behaviour since the 1980s?

➤ Why might Americans 'split the ticket' when they vote?

➤ What similarities and differences are there between voting behaviour in Britain and the United States?

➤ Is direct legislation a good thing?

GENERAL FEATURES OF ELECTIONS AND ELECTIONEERING

The importance of elections to American democracy

Elections are basic to the American democratic process. At every tier of political life, the incumbent (occupant) is selected by election. In some states, even such offices as the Municipal Judge and the Registrar of Wills are contested. Americans who turn out to vote have the chance to choose the President (via the electoral college), a representative, a senator, state legislators, a governor, state administrative officials, local councillors, local administrative officials, mayors and county officials. They might also help to choose judges and party officials, and take part in referendums (votes on single issues). There are in excess of a million elected offices, though because many of these are local they fail to make headline news. When allowance is made for the primary elections which are held to determine who will represent the parties in the main contests, it is obvious that elections in America occur with considerable frequency.

The vast number of elections is a reflection of the general growth of the democratic principle since the eighteenth century. Americans have long believed that the greater the direct involvement of the citizen, the better the likely outcome in terms of the quality of output. More participation is thought to lead to superior government. But it has another explanation: the belief in limited government. From the days of the Founding Fathers, Americans have always had a fear of too much power residing in one pair of hands. Elected officers should not be trusted too much or for too long. It is desirable for citizens to retain as much power as possible under their own control.

How people get elected

The selection of elected representatives is done via a two-part process, comprising the nomination stage which is carried out by the party, and the final stage (polling day) which is done by all the voters in a particular town or state.

The method of selecting candidates has evolved over the 200-year history of the United States. In colonial times, the method adopted was the **caucus** (literally, 'a meeting of wire-pullers'), an informal meeting of party leaders at which agreement was reached on the individuals who merited support. As the country evolved, different forms of political organisation developed, and the various local caucuses began to delegate representatives to meet with representatives from other local caucuses to form county and then state groups, which finally selected candidates. These enlarged bodies were known as **conventions**, the early prototypes of the presidential nominating conventions used today. The third development was the use of the

> **primaries**
> Preliminary elections held within a party to choose the candidate for that party in the general election.

primary election. **Primaries** are statewide intraparty elections. Their basic purpose is to give voters the opportunity to select directly their party's candidates for various offices.

In general elections, the candidates of the political parties for all positions are pitted against each other. Usually, the party candidates for all offices – federal, state and local – run as a block or 'slate'. In addition each party draws up a statement of its position on various issues, called a **platform**. Voters thus make

THE USE OF PRIMARIES

At the beginning of the twentieth century, many 'progressives' were concerned at the power exercised by party bosses and their political organisations. They wanted to curb the corruption felt to be endemic in public life, and pressed for reforms to break the control of the party machines and the 'bosses' who ran them. In this spirit, they urged the use of primary elections which would transfer power away from the party regulars meeting in smoke-filled rooms to the interested ordinary voter. This was seen as a significant step towards greater democracy.

The use of primaries gradually spread, although for many years the system was still not widely used for choosing presidential candidates. By the 1970s they had become nationwide for almost all forms of election, local, state and federal. It was not only the large city machines which lost power with the advent of primaries – party organisations everywhere lost their hold. Even where there was no suspicion of doubtful propriety, they lost a key function, that of nomination – for any candidate could stand for election, whether or not he or she had rendered some service in the local party.

Types of primary

Practice varies from the restrictive to the generous. In some states everyone can vote, whereas in others only those who are registered as members of the party who have the right. Where only registered members can vote, this is a **closed primary**. Where anyone, regardless of party affiliation can vote, then this is an **open primary**. In Connecticut and Delaware in the Northeast, only party members are eligible. In the same region, Vermont holds open primaries. So does Rhode Island, which none the less requires a voter to state his or her affiliation. By contrast, Alaska in the northwest uses open primaries, allowing voters to vote in both parties, should they wish to so do.

their decisions not only for or against persons who run for office, but also on the political, economic and social philosophies of the parties they represent.

Candidates may run for office without the support of a political party, as Independents. To do so, they must present a petition, signed by a specified number of voters (varying from state to state) who support the candidacy. Another device is the write-in vote: a candidate's name does not appear on the ballot, but is 'written' in by voters in a space left blank for this purpose.

The timing of elections and the voting system

Most issues relating to elections are decided within the states, although the Constitution lays down the general requirements on how often they are to take place for each institution.

Open and closed primaries: the procedure

As we can see, the exact procedure for use in primary contests varies between different states, each of which makes it own regulations for the conduct of the election. Broadly, the position is that:

1 In **open primaries**, the elector is given two ballots, one for each party. He or she fills in one to go in the ballot box, and the unused one is discarded in a sealed container. He or she cannot use both, and there is no way of knowing which one has been filled in. Some object to this process on the grounds that it is possible for the voter to use their vote not to distinguish between the candidates in his or her favoured party, but rather to seek to 'wreck' the chances of the other party by voting for its least impressive candidate. If that weak person were to be chosen, this might increase the chances of the voter's preferred party.

2 In **closed primaries**, this 'wrecking' cannot occur, but neither is the process so secret for, on entering the polling station, the voter must express his or her affiliation. The appropriate ballot paper is then handed over, and if the party officers of one side question the allegiance it can be challenged.

The merits and disadvantages of primaries

There are obvious benefits in the use of primaries: they are more democratic than the system they replaced, they emphasise the personal qualities of the candidates rather than their party label, and they sometimes produce good candidates who would otherwise not have been chosen. They can provide a chance for the different wings of the parties to air their viewpoints, and so indicate where the preferences of members really lay. They have drawbacks, in that they are an additional expense – often the machine still fights hard to ensure victory for its favoured candidate – and they demand that the voter turns out for yet another election: the frequency of elections is one reason sometimes given for low turn-outs, for many ordinary voters lack the stamina or interest.

American elections are used to choose representatives for a fixed-term period of office, so that the date of future elections is known in advance. They are scheduled in such a way that every fourth year (1992, 1996, 2000 and 2004) there is a presidential election. They are always held on the Tuesday after the first Monday in November, in an even year. This contrasts with the situation in countries such as Britain and Canada, where an election can be called at any time as long as there is at least one every five years.

According to the Constitution, two years is the fixed period served by a member of the House of Representatives. The election occurs on the day of the presidential election and two years later (e.g. November 2000 and November 2002). For the Senate, the period is considerably longer – six years – and the election again occurs in November. Whereas members of the House are all elected together, this is not so with the Senate: senators are elected on a staggered basis, one-third at a time.

The method employed

For all elections, the method employed is the one used in Britain and Canada, the 'first past the post' or simple majority system. In other words, the candidate with the most votes in the single-member constituency is elected. This method is widely seen as making it more likely that a two-party system will result, for third parties are discouraged; they may win many votes in an area, but unless they can win in an individual constituency they get no tangible reward. By comparison, proportional methods of voting, such as those used in most of continental Europe, are said to encourage the formation and development of small parties. They have a chance of gaining representation in the legislature, even on the basis of relatively small support.

Election campaigns

In past generations, speakers have needed to be effective 'on the stump', addressing a gathering in the local market-place or school hall. Sometimes those running for office addressed electors from a platform at the back of a train, most famously Harry Truman whose 'whistle-stop' tours involved the train pulling up at every local station. He was the last campaigner to deploy this method of electioneering on such a scale, though others subsequently (e.g. John F. Kennedy) conducted very active speech-making tours and sometimes spoke from the rear of a railway carriage.

Today, television has taken over campaigning, but the purpose remains the same, to encourage the electorate to support the personality and policy platform on polling day. Reaching the maximum number of them has always been a priority, but whereas at one time an audience could be counted in tens or hundreds, now it can be counted in millions for a single programme. The whistle-stop tour could last weeks and the candidate might see a hundred thousand altogether.

Candidate-centred campaigning

The process of electioneering has always demanded certain qualities from the person chosen – a pleasing voice, a gift for public speaking, the ability to sell one's personality and to persuade people of the merits of a particular case. However, today, deficiencies in any of these aspects can be a serious liability exposed before the whole nation, whereas previously many voters did not know about them. Other personal failings are also highlighted in the blaze of publicity surrounding a modern election campaign.

Elections are nowadays far more focused on the candidate and his or her positive qualities and/or failings than on party labels. What candidates must do is to put together a winning coalition of support – they do this by making sure that there are sufficient funds to allow them to get the message across as widely as possible, so that everyone knows who they are and what they stand for.

Whether the election is for Congress, for the presidency or for some other position, the trend has been towards far greater professionalism than ever before. Those who run them are skilled in the new campaign technology. They use the direct mail-shot – targeted to individual voters – to arouse interest and obtain funding. They use computers to analyse the voters of a particular precinct. They employ professional opinion pollsters and media gurus – specialists who are able to advise on the best means of exploiting the potential of the candidate and downplaying or destroying the qualities and reputation of an opponent.

Once candidates are chosen, parties are obviously concerned to help them to sell themselves and their message. They send out their voluntary workers to canvass on the doorstep, they use the phone to call possible voters, they arrange lifts for those who otherwise might not make it to the polling booth, as well as involving themselves in fundraising, commissioning and studying opinion polls and advertising. However, the role of parties in electioneering has been downgraded, for increasingly – with the breakdown of the party machines, after the reform of the arrangements for financial contributions in the early 1970s – it is the individual candidate and the team of supporters he or she puts together which has become important. With the backing of Political Action Committees (whose primary function is to help finance election contests), candidates now tend to run their own campaigning.

The purpose of the campaign is not only to reach as many people as possible, but to ensure that those who are sympathetically disposed actually turn out

Electioneering in Britain and the United States: a comparison

British election campaigns are much shorter than American ones. Even though there is much speculation and a pre-election atmosphere in the third or fourth year of the lifetime of a Parliament, the campaign proper lasts only three to four weeks. Campaigns for all elective offices in America are longer, but this is especially true of presidential ones.

Despite the increasing personalisation of British politics, for example the emphasis on the gladiatorial aspect of the Blair versus Hague contest, it remains the case that the voter is still voting for a party rather than just one person: other key figures in the Cabinet or Shadow Cabinet play a significant role in the campaign, as do the local and national party organisations. By contrast, the American experience is more candidate-centred. More stress is placed upon the personal qualities of the candidates than on their party allegiance. 'Personal qualities' can include many things, from the superficial such as looks and friendliness to others including character, temperament and outlook. As the person, once elected, will make up his or her own mind on political issues, personality and views can be very significant.

The organisations which provide the contestants with support (parties and PACs) have more of a personal than a party loyalty. They are concerned especially with the funding of the campaign and political advertising, aspects which are still more developed on the other side of the Atlantic – though Britain is moving in the American direction, with increased use of public relations advisers, negative advertising on posters and via the style of some Party Election Broadcasts.

Britain does not allow unlimited access by the parties to television time, which is strictly regulated. America does not have the British-style election broadcast, but candidate-centred structures make extensive use of the media – their access is only limited by the funds they have available.

and vote. Given the relatively low turnouts in the United States, it is important for the parties and PACs to do anything they can to assist in the process of voter registration and to encourage those who are registered to go to the polls.

The role of money in American elections

The role of money in American elections has long been controversial, as have been the sources of funding. Several sources exist. Money can come from the individual candidate, interested individuals, interest groups operating through Political Action Committees and political parties. There are also several purposes for which the money is made available. It may derive from the generosity of a benefactor, it may be given out of idealistic support for a particular individual, idea or set of principles, or it may be offered in the hope of securing some goal of personal or group benefit.

Whatever the motive of the donor, what is important is that the representative – once elected to public office – does not feel unduly beholden to those who have financed the campaign, at the expense of the general public who they are there to represent. The fear is that money given is 'interested money', in that those who donate it are looking for favours from the persons they back.

Given the new technology and methods of electioneering, national elections have become very costly, whether for Congress or for the presidency. An individual is – in most cases – unlikely to be able to meet those costs on his or her own. The difficulty is all the greater if the candidate is not an incumbent Congressman, for incumbents find it easier to raise money from affluent individuals and from PACs, which prefer to contribute to sitting tenants than to challengers.

There are then problems surrounding the sources of money and the unequal distribution of the money available. Attempts have been made to regulate political money, for by the 1960s many commentators were concerned at the escalating costs of election campaigns, the incidence of very rich candidates who could easily outspend their rivals and the possibility of undue influence being exercised by those who handed over money.

The first significant piece of legislation was the **Federal Election Campaign Act (FECA) of 1971**, which replaced all earlier laws on the subject. All candidates for political office, as well as the individuals, campaign committees, parties and PACs which backed them, were made to declare their contributions. As a result of evidence heard in the Watergate hearings, it was felt necessary to tighten up on violations of the 1971 measure – hence the 1974 Act, which was designed to reduce further the impact of money on the democratic process.

Two main themes were tackled in the second measure: the importance of tough limits on contributions and the need for public funding of election campaigning (see p. 164). The new legislation tightened up the rules for disclosure of campaign income, and restricted the influence of wealthy individuals. Strict limits were imposed. Donations of more than $100 had to be disclosed. Individuals could pay up to $1000 towards a single campaign, with primaries and general elections being counted as separate entities; a maximum expenditure of $25,000 per year was permitted. There was no overall limit on the amount which PACs could provide in a single year, but they were restricted to $5000 per campaign. PACs were thus placed at an advantage over other donors, so that, as Grant[1] has pointed out, 'the law effectively increased candidates' reliance on them'.

The Federal Election Commission which oversees the statute is seen as ineffectual and lacking 'teeth'. But as a result of its passage, we now have a

State funding for candidates

A scheme of public financing for presidential candidates was introduced in 1971, and subsequently substantially amended in 1974, 1976 and 1979. It provided, *inter alia*, for funding of the primary contests and for the main election. For every candidate who could raise $5000 across 20 states from small individual contributions (under $250), there was to be a matching sum available from the federal government. State aid was not, then, unconditional, but triggered by the decisions of private individuals.

Funds are provided for candidates by means of a tax check-off box on the declaration of income from individual income tax returns. The money collected is then distributed to those candidates who have chosen to opt for public funding. They must accept stringent restrictions upon the raising or spending of corporate money. Most accept the offer of financial assistance, even wealthy candidates such as Ronald Reagan and the two George Bushes.

clearer idea of where politicians get their money from and how they use it. Voters and interested commentators can check the disclosures made, and see the resources available to candidates; they have to declare their personal wealth, their property and their debts. This means that there is greater transparency, and people can assess the impact of any financial considerations which may influence the policy pursued by those who rule.

The scale and control of spending in presidential elections

The costs of presidential elections have risen dramatically in recent years. Figures from the Federal Election Commission suggest that in the 2000 contest, Al Gore spent $117.1 million on his primary and general election campaigns, George Bush $168.4 million.

Money is crucially important in American elections, making the US distinctive both in the amount raised and the range of sources from which it is collected. The law has been used to regulate the raising and spending of money, but there remains a significant difference in the actual provisions of the law and current practice. There are ways in which the regulations can be evaded, particularly by the collection of so-called **soft money**. An amendment to FECA in 1979 allowed parties to raise and spend money to be used on party-building and get-out-the-vote activities, a purpose which is not easy to distinguish from supporting party candidates. As the amount of spending on these activities has significantly

soft money
Money contributed in ways and for purposes (such as registration and mass-mailing) which do not infringe the law, as opposed to 'hard money' contributions, which are strictly regulated. Soft money is collected at state and local level, but is often used for national purposes.

increased of late, there are grounds for suspicion about the ways in which money is used.

More could be done to control the influence of wealth in American politics. For instance, airtime could be made available freely to each party for a fixed period, so that no longer would being poor or modestly well-off be a disadvantage. This might have the effect of encouraging more blacks and other minority candidates to come forward, as well as introducing an element of greater fairness. Candidates could still be expected to pay for the making of their own advertisements, but this is not the problem. It is the frequency with which advertisements are repeated which makes election campaigns so expensive, for what happens is that at present one candidate with greater means available can outgun his or her opponent simply by reiterating the message over and over again.

Participation in American politics

Democracy implies participation, by which we mean that people should be able to take part in the formulation, passage or implementation of policies. Democratic standards are more likely to prevail where people are well informed and willing to get involved. In the *polis*, the city state of Ancient Greece, it was considered natural that people would take part in politics; then, to be able to do so was the privilege of a few.

The United States has always attached great importance to the ideas and values of democracy. Although the founders of the American Republic were wary of majority rule, they none the less believed that most people would be able to take part in the electoral process and thus be able to play a key role in determining the direction which government policy should take. Yet at a time when the electorate is more informed about politics than ever before in its history, we find that turnout in elections is lower than it has been for many years and involvement in party activity is on a downward slide.

Turnout in presidential and congressional elections

In much of the twentieth century, the successful presidential candidate has won an election in which less than half of the eligible electorate turn out to vote, so that the decisions about who should govern the country and the direction in which it should be led are in the hands of a minority of the population. The 1960 presidential contest had a better turnout than usual, but since then the percentage voting has declined more or less continuously as the figures indicate.

Turnout in presidential elections since 1960

Year	Percentage of people voting
1960	63.8
1968	61.0
1976	54.4
1984	53.0
1992	53.0
2000	51.2

The figures are unimpressive by European standards, and the table below suggests that the US lags well behind Britain, which itself has a smaller turnout than most other countries. Whereas Britain has usually achieved a turnout of almost 75 per cent in general elections (a figure that dropped decisively in 2001, however), 55 per cent is good by American standards. The comparison is not, however, an entirely appropriate one, for British figures relate to the number registered who vote whereas American ones are based upon the number of Americans over the minimum voting age who actually do so. According to V. O. Key[2] the difference may be worth as many as six or seven percentage points.

Turnout in some of the main democracies
(figures based on the general election most recent to 2001)

	Turnout %	Compulsion?
Australia	95.3	Yes
Austria	80.4	No
Finland	80.1	No
India	60.0	No
South Africa	89.0	No
United Kingdom	59.3*	No

*71.3% in 1997

The US presidential campaign certainly gets massive television exposure, for it dominates the media from the time of the first primaries through to November. This might have been expected to generate interest and excitement, but yet in the media age we are faced by decline. The drop in turnout rates is the more notable if we bear in mind the increase in the size of the potential electorate since the 1970s. The passage of the 1965 Voting Rights Act added many black voters to the list of those eligible to vote. Moreover, women have become more politically involved in that period, and their turnout levels have risen to such an extent that more women turned out than men in the 1996 and 2000 elections. Finally, given the overall increase in education and living standards one might have expected that more would be inspired to vote, the more so as it is traditionally the least well-off who are the category the most reluctant to vote.

Yet some half the registered electorate does not turn out even in presidential contests, and for other elections the number is considerably greater still. In an off-year (when there is no presidential contest), the average figure for turnout is 35–40 per cent in congressional elections, and in primaries the figure is often below 30 per cent.

Why are turnouts so low?

Several reasons for low turnouts have been given, but among them **registration** arrangements have always been seen as important

Registration emerges as a key issue. In most states it is up to individuals to register themselves as qualified voters before election day. Failure to do so disqualifies anyone from using their right, even if in other respects they are eligible to do so. Registration involves either meeting a registrar or filling out a form at the county courthouse. When allowance is made for this responsibility and for age and residential qualifications, it is evident that there is built-in discouragement to voting.

A change was introduced in 1993 when President Clinton signed the so-called **motor voter** bill designed to ease the process of registration. Citizens are now able to register when they apply for a driving licence (hence the name) or some other form of public document. Furthermore, states must designate a public office concerned with providing help to the public, a place where assistance is also available with voter registration – e.g. a state welfare agency. The effects should have been to enable and encourage more people to turn out on election day, for it has long been the case that in those states with same-day or no registration, turnout is considerably above the national average.

The new legislation operated from 1995, and within eight months some 5,000,000 new voters registered. Some commentators predicted that if this momentum was maintained, almost four out of every five voters would be registered by the end of the century. It was not and today some 66 per cent of Americans are registered to vote, a few percentage points up on the situation before 'motor voting' was introduced. Yet in 1996 and 2000, the turnout figures were disappointingly low. As President, George Bush Snr had vetoed such a measure, perhaps in the belief that the Democrats would benefit more from a higher turnout. His fears seem to have been largely unjustified.

Alternative explanations include the following.

1 Apathy

Some have used apathy as an explanation, but surveys of political interest suggest that if anything Americans are rather more politically interested than people in many other democracies. Voting does, however, require more personal effort than elsewhere for the reasons we have given, and the frequency of elections could result in voter fatigue and a loss of interest.

2 Lack of a meaningful choice between the parties

Some commentators would suggest that voters who are registered fail to detect any real difference between the parties, and that the electors feel that a choice between tweedledum and tweedledee is not one worth attempting to make. They say 'a plague on both your houses', and see parties as increasingly irrelevant to their lives. No party really addresses their concerns.

3 The lack of an inspiring choice of candidates

Others say that the quality of political leaders fails to inspire, and there are too many unattractive personalities who become candidates. Discontent with the available choice was a much discussed feature of the Bush v Dukakis contest, the 'Wimp' v 'the Shrimp' (1988), the Clinton v Dole contest in 1996 and the Bush v Gore contest in 2000.

4 The composition of the electorate

Broadly-speaking, middle-class people, those with a professional education and with a college education, are more likely to turn out than unskilled working people or those whose qualifications are only a high-school diploma or less. Again, family influence may be significant. In those homes where there is a tradition of participation, it is more likely that future generations will turn out to vote and become more generally involved in political life.

Certain groups have persistently been more reluctant to vote. Non-voting is greater in the South and in rural areas, among the young, the less educated and among the minorities such as the black population and Hispanics. Young people (under 24) have regularly been less disposed to involve themselves in the electoral process, although those who claim a clear allegiance towards one of the main parties are markedly more willing to vote than those who are apathetic about politics and current affairs. Whites are more likely to vote than blacks, blacks than Hispanics.

An important consideration is that the groups which shun the democratic process are ones that make up an increasing proportion of the electorate.

5 The nature of electioneering

It may be that negative advertising produces disillusion with the Washington politicians and the political system in general, and that this contributes to the falling turnouts of the last generation. In the 1994 elections, it was suggested that one of the most toxic campaigns in living memory had left many people turned off politicians. American voters have become more disengaged from political strategy, as the style of advertising increasingly antagonises them. Overall, they are seen in Hames' words as 'over-long, over-slick and dominated by the mass media with a premium on character attacks on political opponents'.[3]

6 *Other factors*

The theory has been advanced[4] that America is now in a post-electoral era. More and more voters see parties and elections as no longer very significant. Now, major decisions are made by investigating committees and the courts, and through media revelations. The traditional processes have had their day.

Another idea is that non-voting is broadly a sign of contentment with the political system. If Americans felt worried, because their country was in crisis, they might feel inclined to turn out to avert a national catastrophe. But in times of peace and prosperity, most Americans are happy to leave the politicians to get on with their task; there is less need to vote.

Alternative forms of participation

Political issues are not the be-all and end-all of most peoples' lives, and – like most people – Americans are concerned with bread-and-butter matters such as making a living, improving their family position and enjoying their leisure. The level of interest varies sharply between different groups of the community, but the findings of the 1992 *American National Election Study*, conducted by the University of Michigan, show that only 26 per cent were interested for 'most of the time', 41 per cent for 'some of the time' and 21 per cent 'only now and then'; 11 per cent were 'hardly at all' committed.

Many people may find politics a complicated process, and certainly surveys of political knowledge and understanding reveal widespread public ignorance. According to a survey by the **American Political Science Review** (September 1980), 40 per cent of those interviewed could not name one of their state's senators. Ignorance covers personalities and policies. Given such a lack of interest and information, participation in the political process is inevitably unlikely to be very high.

Those who possess knowledge and understanding tend to participate more. They are often the better-educated people who read a newspaper, watch current affairs programmes and engage in political discourse with their relatives and friends. At the other end, are those who participate very little, the least educated who may feel isolated from the political world which they may see as having let them down. Many of those who are somewhere in between, having sporadic interest in politics, will join in from time to time.

Town meetings in New England: direct democracy in action

The purest form of direct democracy was to be found in ancient Greece. All qualified citizens were allowed to participate in the government of their city-state. They were encouraged/expected to play a positive role in controlling their own life, rather than leaving the task for others to act on their behalf. Such direct democracy is no longer seen as possible in large, modern industrial societies and the nearest approximation in most countries is the use of the referendum and/or initiative. However, in New England, town meetings have operated ever since the first British settlements.

The experience of meetings in the six states of that region has been variously described as 'the Secret Flame of democracy'[5] and 'a bedrock form of democratic expression'.[6] Of Maine's 493 incorporated municipalities, 440 have a town meeting form of government, in which residents attend for a morning or a day to chart their communal course. Topics debated range widely, from property taxes to budgets for administration, from same-sex marriages to nuts-and-bolts issues concerning local facilities.

Town meetings are not without their critics and there are problems with the way they function today. In particular:

- Often meetings are not well attended. Rarely do more than 10 per cent of registered voters turn out to participate, and the trend has been consistently downwards in recent years. In a recent study, Joseph Zimmerman[7] has examined figures collected for the last three decades and finds the trend is common to all six states. He sees declining attendance as a parallel to the downward trend in voter turnout in state and national elections and as correlating with towns' increasing difficulties finding candidates to run for local office and volunteers to run fire departments.
- Those who can attend are often self-employed, retired or otherwise not working at regular daytime jobs and therefore cannot accurately reflect the opinions of local

They will vote in certain elections which seem relevant or interesting to them – as we have seen, more often in presidential ones than the rest. They will occasionally discuss political issues at times of peak media attention, but for much of the time choose not to read about or view what is going on.

Of course, there are more opportunities for participation than voting alone. Americans can involve themselves in election campaigns, join political parties and pressure groups, and take part in protest marches and forms of direct action (see p. 243). The American system also offers the citizens of some states an opportunity for direct participation in decision-making which is generally denied to the British electorate except on rare constitutional issues. This is done via the **town meeting** (see pp. 170–1) in New England, and via the initiative and **referendum** (see pp. 190–4) in many areas of the country.

citizens. An article in a local newspaper in Maine[8] carried a report that in Kingfield '65 people are calling the shots for the entire town', and that reports from officials in Eustis and Strong also reported low, unrepresentative turnouts: 'in Farmington, a town of 7,600, only 80 people attended the annual meeting'.

Several reasons have been advanced for declining turnout. For instance, it is sometimes claimed that:

- Even at the level of a small New England town, society is now too large and complex for direct democracy to be a complete success. Towns used to be smaller, with more of a sense of community. Urbanisation has affected even New England, and people are now too busy, often travelling some distance to work. Meetings take too long for those with little time available. They can spend their spare time on various forms of entertainment.
- Voters are frustrated and disenchanted with government at all levels.
- Many people are better off than ever before and therefore feel that it is not a matter of serious personal self-interest whether they attend.
- There are fewer stress factors (i.e. no burning issues) in municipal government.

Town meetings have been described[9] as 'alive, but troubled'. In some towns they have actually ceased to exist, ten out of the 31 towns in Rhode Island having abandoned them; turnout in the remaining towns in that state is often exceptionally low, at four to five per cent. Voters are experimenting with alternatives to the traditional open town meeting, some opting for meetings where the time is spent in directly voting on a series of referendum questions, others preferring either representative town meetings for which residents elected representatives to vote on their behalf (anyone can stand and speak, but only the representatives can vote), straightforward town councils or citizen-initiated referendums. It is in the smaller towns and more rural areas of northern New England that town meetings continue to function best.

Participation in various forms of electoral activity, 1968–88 (% of total US population)

Type of activity	1968	1978	1988
Persuading others	33	22	29
Attending meetings	9	10	7
Working for party/candidate	6	6	3
Wearing buttons/sporting car stickers	15	9	3
Giving money to party/candidates	9	13	8
Writing to public officials on key issues	20	n/a	n/a

Adapted from M. Conway, *Political Participation in the United States*, Congressional Quarterly Press, 1991.

THE MEDIA AND ELECTIONS

Democracy requires the free flow of ideas, information and comment, and the role of the mass media is central in influencing public opinion; they both reflect it and help to mould it. For many people, it is through the media that they become acquainted with what is happening in the world and their own viewpoint on issues, and there is much academic debate as to whether television in particular actually creates opinions or reinforces them.

The media are sometimes described as 'the fourth branch of government', rivalling the three main official branches in their political influence and power. Here we are concerned to examine the ways in which they influence modern electioneering.

THE TERMINOLOGY OF MODERN ELECTIONS

Photo-opportunities

Carefully stage-managed episodes in which the leading figure is set against a particular background – perhaps to demonstrate concern for the area or its industry: e.g. Ronald Reagan favoured the image of the all-American cowboy, riding on horseback into the sunset, thereby conjuring in the mind of the electors an image of the great outdoors as part of the wholesome American dream.

Sound-bites

Short sayings, full of concentrated meaning, which consist of a few easily remembered words, and yet convey a particular message: e.g. Reagan's 'You ain't seen nothin' yet' and George Bush Snr's 'Read my lips. No new taxes', a slogan which backfired when, as President, he found himself supporting higher taxation.

The Rev. Jesse Jackson is a master of 'soundbitese'. Recognising that he will get perhaps 15 seconds on a news bulletin, he can summarise his argument in an exciting epigram. His rhyming sound-bite 'we're going to have demonstrations without hesitation and jail without bail' was a more memorable and catchy way of saying that 'we are not going to spend a long time deciding whether to have a demonstration. We are willing to go to jail for our cause and will not accept bail'.

Spin-doctors

Spin-doctors are part of the media team, their task being to change the way the public perceive some happening, or to alter their expectations of what might occur. They try to put a favourable gloss on information and events. Spin has become an accepted feature of campaigns in the US. The term derives from the spin given to a ball in various sports, to make it go in a direction which confuses the opponent.

By the media, we mean the various forms of communication available; by the mass media those which in the modern day are available on a large scale. All are concerned with the dissemination of ideas in the form of information, entertainment and persuasion. However, if the term is all-embracing, in popular usage it is applied particularly to television and the press.

Television has now become the most important of the ways via which the candidates seek to gain popular approval and support. Although party managers may still be interviewed and seek to use the medium to promote the party cause, it is the candidate who is the focus of media attention. He and his team of consultants are constantly on the look out for opportunities to ensure that they gain favourable coverage and are vigilant in watching out for any signs of bias against them. They attempt to 'manage the news' and arrange appearances on chat-shows. Presidential candidates also take part in presidential debates.

Managing the media involves ensuring that journalist get the right stories (information slanted to their particular viewpoint) backed up with good pictures. It can range from crude political arm-twisting to more subtle means. Advisers dream up sound-bites and photo-opportunities, and use their spin-doctors to put across an appropriate line (see opposite). They try to book interviews with 'softer' interviewers, rather than undergo a potentially damaging interrogation. They seek to control the agenda, sticking to themes on which they are strong and avoiding (or downplaying) embarrassing issues.

Presidential debates

The presidential and vice-presidential debates have been of varying quality, and the rules of engagement have differed from election to election. The one which has been endlessly quoted was that held in 1960 between Kennedy and Nixon. Kennedy looked handsome, impressive and youthful, whereas his opponent looked unshaven and untrustworthy. The debate was broadcast on radio and television and, significantly, whereas polling showed that a majority of listeners thought that Nixon had emerged on top, a majority of viewers was in no doubt that Kennedy had won. When he did win, it was by the narrowest of margins, by 0.5 per cent of the popular vote; it may well be that television swung the outcome.

Debates have almost certainly made a difference to the outcome of some elections, for in a close-run contest the importance of appearing steady and in control is supreme. If you cannot win, it is crucial to avoid mistakes. Errors have been made and some have been costly. Apart from the Nixon performance in 1960, the other famous or infamous gaffe was the moment in 1976 when Jimmy Carter benefited from a fatal howler committed by his opponent, Gerald Ford, the Republican President. At a time when the Cold War was still a determining factor in international diplomacy, Ford said that Poland was not then under Eastern European domination!

Presidential debates have become the pre-eminent media event of the campaign, and they attract a vast audience of approaching 100 million. At their best, they are a useful means of providing each candidate with an opportunity to reach a mass audience. Their impact is unlikely to change the allegiances of the committed voters, more to confirm them in their predisposition. However, on the increasing number of non-aligned voters, a strong or weak performance may be all-important. They help viewers to assess character and ability, and may also increase their knowledge and understanding of politics. This is why media advisers are so concerned to get the details right.

THE MEDIA IN BRITAIN AND THE UNITED STATES: A COMPARISON

In both countries, the media fulfil similar functions of entertaining and informing the public. Both have a privately owned press which is often accused of political bias, and there are similar worries about concentration of ownership in too few hands and a consequent lack of diversity of opinion. In Britain, there is a much more vigorous national press, whereas in the US many people read a more local paper; in both countries, newspaper readership is in decline.

Television has come to dominate political coverage, especially at election time. It has tended to personalise politics, so that there is now more emphasis on the qualities of those who lead and less on serious discussion of issues. American campaigns are more candidate-centred (see pp. 161–2), but in recent years commentators have frequently portrayed British party conflict in terms of the Blair–Major, Blair–Hague, or Blair–Duncan Smith conflict. Similar allegations of trivialisation are made on both sides of the Atlantic, a recognition of the fact that television is primarily a means of entertainment.

The Americanisation of British politics?

Britain has in many ways learnt from the American experience. Campaigners have visited the United States and sometimes participated in elections there. Inevitably, their findings have been relayed to their colleagues back home. In addition, people in Britain see pictures of presidential electioneering, and there has often been discussion in the media of the techniques employed. As a result, America has been a useful source of innovation in British campaign techniques. Just as the Conservatives under Margaret Thatcher absorbed a lot from the Reagan experience in the mid–late 1980s, so too the Labour Party was keen to derive insights from the success of the Democrat, Bill Clinton, in 1992 and again in 1996.

In recent years, there has been an increasing British obsession with walkabouts, photo-opportunities and other pseudo-events created for the media. In the 1980s and 1990s,

Political advertising

The quality of individuals and the image they present is also important in political advertising. Here, the emphasis is often less upon the assets of the candidate, more upon the deficiencies of the opponent. Advertising can be blatantly unfair.

The scale of such advertising has significantly increased in recent years, although the advertisements have become much shorter. Advertisers know that the public can only take in so much information at any one time. During the vice-presidential race in 1952, Richard Nixon took 30 minutes of paid television time to answer charges of corruption in front of 58 million viewers. Nowadays, advertisers specialise in the 60- or (more often) the 30- or even 15-second commercial which makes a point briefly, yet dramatically.

there have been several examples of the americanisation of politics at work, not least in the style of some party broadcasts (*Kinnock – the Movie*, 1987), and in the Sheffield Rally of 1992, a triumphalist occasion very reminiscent of the American convention.

Yet there are differences and some safeguards from the British point of view. In Britain, we are electing a party rather than just one person, and politics is not about personality alone. The in-depth interview provides a kind of antidote to the dangers of shallow but media-friendly leaders being chosen, for their personal qualities come under heavy scrutiny and in the in-depth Sunday-lunch time type of programme policy deficiencies can be much exposed. We also can now see our representatives in action in the House of Commons, and Question Time at least is an institution which shows those in power being forced to defend their position, even if it does little to inform people of the issues. The interviews conducted in the election in *Election Call* are a reminder of how leading figures can be put on the spot by skilful members of the public who can unsettle their composure.

But most people do not watch such encounters, and the likelihood is that those people who use television the most to obtain their information may be the very people who are least discerning and able to come to a reasonable conclusion based on knowledge. They probably don't read other sources and therefore what they see and hear has a potent effect on the least sophisticated electors.

Party broadcasts instead of political advertisements, free air-time, vigilant journalists, in-depth political interviews and politicians more prepared to answer questions about their proposals, help to differentiate us from US experience in certain respects, and are some kind of protection against our adopting the worst aspects of American electioneering methods into Britain. Yet as we have seen, the party broadcasts themselves have to some degree 'gone American' in style and form.

It may be that on this side of the Atlantic we are less susceptible to the excesses of emotionalism and negative campaigning that beset American politics.

Americans have often used advertisements which are autobiographical in style. Television is good at handling personalities and stories, and some of the most effective advertisements judiciously combine the two elements. Not all advertisements are of this type. It is overwhelmingly negative, and goes for the jugular. Often, it pinpoints alleged deficiencies in the moral character of an opponent. Examples range from the candidate in Tennessee who was congratulated by his opponents for 'kicking [his] chemical dependency' to stories concerning marital infidelity.

Bill Schneider, an American political scientist,[10] sees negative advertising as a very efficient tool: 'For one thing, it's easier in 30 seconds to turn people off your opponent than to build a positive case for yourself – especially since television is a medium particularly suited for carrying negative, warning-style messages … you get more bang for the buck by running negative ads'.

ELECTING THE PRESIDENT:
A CHOICE BY ELECTORAL COLLEGE

Running for the presidency involves three stages:
- winning the support of delegates to the party convention;
- winning the approval of the convention itself;
- winning in the presidential race following the autumn campaign.

Winning delegates to the convention

The first stage in the process of choosing a new President is for the parties to choose their nominee, and this consumes several months of the election year. Any person who hopes to become a presidential candidate has to decide when to launch his or her bid for the White House. Some make a decision to stand soon after the last election is over, but any announcement of the intention is not usually made until the year before the election at the earliest, even if campaign planning is already actively underway. Candidates and those who manage their campaigns know the importance of lining up support and raising funds before their declaration.

Candidates have to decide how to navigate the primaries and caucuses which take place in the early months of the presidential year, and this decision involves a number of considerations. Until the 1970s, it was not common for candidates to take the primary route but this has become the accepted procedure for any 'hopeful' to adopt. A decision not to stand entails the risk of losing momentum whilst others secure the support of party delegations.

The arrangements vary in detail from state to state, and in some cases the parties in a particular state employ different approaches. But today the use of primaries is the accepted method by both parties in most of them. Eight states use a caucus and/or convention system, the details of which are laid down by its legislature. In those using caucuses, the party organisation is still important, whereas in those using conventions the choice of national delegates is made by people who are themselves delegates from local meetings.

The primary route

More than 80 per cent of the delegates in 1992 were chosen as a result of primary contests, and most candidates now take the primary route. They need to decide which primaries to enter, but whereas it was once common for a candidate to miss some of the early ones this is now seen as a high-risk strategy. Jimmy Carter decided to seek the Democratic nomination by staging a nationwide primary campaign and involved himself in the early contests and as many as he could thereafter. This is now the usual policy, and most commentators believe that it is wise to enter as many as possible. Candidates tend to choose contests where they are likely to make a good showing. The number of rivals, their personal standing in the opinion polls, local interests, the timing of the contest and their level of financial backing – all these play a part in the decisions made.

The first primary takes place in New Hampshire, and a strong performance in the early contests can lend a useful momentum to the campaign and help to demoralise other rivals who do less well. Many states have now brought their primaries forward, hoping that this will give their voters a greater influence on the final choice of candidates. As a result of this 'front-loading', some 70 per cent of the delegates to the convention have been selected by the end of March.

To do well in the primaries, candidates need to manoeuvre with some skill. The opposition in each primary will vary, and tactics used to defeat a strong rival in one state may not work in another. Media coverage, as well as financial and human resources, are also relevant to the outcome, and candidates looking for good coverage will spend heavily on the early contests in their bid to gain popular momentum. It is important for the candidates and those who support them to use the media wisely and to downplay the expectations of what they might achieve. If they then do well, this gives their campaign a boost. If it is widely expected that they will perform well as the frontrunner, then a disappointing outcome (even though it is a technical victory) can cost valuable momentum.

The presidential primaries are the arena in which lively personal battles are fought, and they are conducted under intense public scrutiny by the media and commentators. Sometimes, the battles have been so savage at this stage that great damage is done to party unity.

Winning support at the convention

The national nominating conventions are held over a four-day period in July and August. By then, the outcome is usually a foregone conclusion, and normally the successful candidate is chosen on the first ballot. Delegates are now forced to pledge themselves to a definite candidate for at least the first two ballots, although in the past this was not the case and delegates arrived with varying degrees of commitment.

Once the candidate has been chosen, the nominee makes an acceptance speech and receives homage as the party's standard-bearer for the forthcoming struggle. At this point, the intraparty battle which has dominated the political scene for so many months, becomes unimportant, and the concentration of those present has to be on the contest with the other party. As Malcolm Vile[11] has observed: 'This switch from the bitterness of internal conflict to the competition between parties is one of the perennial wonders of the American political scene'.

The convention comprises those delegates elected in primaries, caucuses or state conventions. Their task is to choose the presidential candidate (in effect, already done) and the vice-presidential nominee – a choice actually made by the presidential candidate and invariably ratified by those assembled. Delegates also help to write the party platform, and at this stage there is often a tussle between different factions who seek to move the party in their direction. The policy statement is not binding on the two people chosen to run for the White House, but as it indicates prevalent feeling in the party candidates do not usually ignore such an expression of the mood of the faithful.

The conclusion of the national convention season brings to an end a long-drawn-out process for which the candidates have been planning and working for many months – if not years. As a result, the two main presidential candidates have been chosen and are ready for the main battle ahead. But there is an alternative way by which presidential candidates can be placed on the ballot for the November election, one which shuns the primary/convention route. This involves a would-be challenger complying with the petition requirements in each individual state (difficult in Maryland, where 3 per cent – approximately 60,000 signatures – are required, simple in Louisiana, where payment of a filing fee of $500 is sufficient).

Ross Perot fulfilled these requirements in each individual state, for his funding and voluntary support enabled his cause to be well represented across the nation. Once on the ballot paper, it is these days much more possible to achieve national prominence without the backing of a political party, as the candidacy of Perot has shown. Television can provide ample exposure, via chat show and other appearances. It was a matter of some pride to Perot that he was able to run an efficient and effective campaign without dipping too heavily into his own substantial private fortune. Without any established party organisation, he was able to launch a highly successful bid in 1992 and eventually win 19 per cent of the popular vote in November.

Winning the presidential race

There is only a short pause between the end of the convention and the beginning of the campaign, and in this time the parties are concerned to pull together again after what can be a wounding primary process. They also devise their strategy for the final stage – the bid for the White House.

The campaign, and in particular the ever-growing importance of television, are discussed on pp. 160–2 and 171–6. Some of the important features include:
- the growing use of market research;
- the use of professional consultants and assorted media gurus;
- the increasing attention to the importance of photo-opportunities, to provide the media with pictures as well as words;
- a concentration on themes which appear appropriate for the national mood;
- the use of television opportunities, ranging from chat shows to interviews and, of course, the presidential debates.

Much depends on creating the right image for the candidate who at this stage needs to adopt a stance which can appeal to many Americans of all social groups, well beyond the confines of traditional party support. The candidate needs to be attuned to the mood of the hour. Franklin Roosevelt caught the popular imagination in 1932 with his promise of dynamic action; John F. Kennedy seemed to embody the hopes of those who wanted to see America move forward to the challenge of New Frontiers, in 1960; Bill Clinton was presented as a man who might get America moving again in 1992, after a period in which domestic policy had been neglected.

Of course, doubts about a candidate's personal standards of behaviour can throw the strategy off course. But in Clinton's case in 1992, he was able to keep the economy in the forefront despite the attempt of the Bush team to portray him in a negative way – just as it had successfully painted a picture of Dukakis as 'soft' on issues of public concern, such as crime. In 1992, it was perhaps easier for the Democrat to stick to his emphasis on the pivotal role of the economy, for Ross Perot was also making this the central element in his campaign.

The election takes place on the first Tuesday after the first Monday in November.

The Electoral College and how it works

The method of becoming President in the United States is in many ways a clumsy and protracted process. A candidate needs to acquire 270 votes in the Electoral College, out of the 538 available. Each state is apportioned a number of votes according to the number of seats it possesses in Congress: two for the Senate and a variable number for the House of Representatives. Thus, in 2000, California had 54, Pennsylvania 23 and New York State 33.

Because of the equal representation of each state in the Senate, the smaller states are over-represented in the Electoral College, so that Delaware and Vermont, with well under a million people each, still have three votes. The electors in the College formally make the choice of the person to become president, just as they separately decide on the vice-presidency also. The choice is not made by the ordinary voter, who when he or she went to the polling station actually voted for electors who were pledged to Gore/Lieberman or Bush/Cheney. In each state, the candidate who received the largest popular vote won all of the electoral vote, though Maine and Nebraska have a slightly different procedure.

If when the electors in the College are making their choice, no candidate gains a majority, then the choice is thrown open to the House of Representatives, which chooses from among the top three candidates. If there is no majority for the position of Vice-President, then the choice goes to the Senate, which chooses between the first two candidates. If it became necessary to use this process, then it is the new Congress just elected (e.g. November 2000) rather than the old one which makes the choice. Theoretically, it would be possible for the two houses to choose candidates from different parties, so that under the procedure the House could have opted for Gore, the Senate for Cheney.

From this short account, it becomes apparent that it is essential for any presidential candidate to win in the Electoral College. To achieve this, he or she needs to perform strongly in the large urban and suburban states which have so much influence. Indeed, it has often been said that to become President it is necessary to win in California; its 54 votes are a greater number than the 14 least populated states and the District of Columbia all combined. New York, Texas and Pennsylvania have a significant number of votes and – as the 2000 result indicated – so does Florida. The candidate is likely to focus attention particularly on such large states and on those where he or she can expect to fare well.

The importance of certain individual states dictates the strategy of any would-be contender. A candidate who can win in California or New York is more important than one who can do fairly well in every state, for most candidates do not aim to win across the nation and often fight less than enthusiastically in some hostile territory. For this reason, it is important for the main parties to have a candidate of wide appeal in the states which are liable to go one way or the other. If you choose a candidate from a safe state, then this wastes the possible bonus of choosing a local person in a state or region in which there is a chance of success. For the Democrats in 1992, the choice of Clinton was a useful way of trying to restore the party's fortunes in a region where its support had been eroded over the Reagan years.

Such considerations are in the mind of the parties and commentators as they ponder the campaign scene in a presidential year. But the other factor of great significance is television, the impact of which is enormous. It has made the country one vast constituency, and concentrated attention on the personal appeal and overall abilities of the candidate. Because of this, the campaign is increasingly in the hands of the advisers and gurus who collectively enjoy the label of 'political consultants'.

Yet as we have seen, this is not the end of the process. The result of the contest may be known within a few hours of the close of polling, but it is another month before the actual election of the president takes place – when the members of the Electoral College cast their votes. The event is largely unnoticed in the outside world, yet it is of profound importance even if the actual outcome is a formality in almost every case.

Because the smaller states are proportionally over-represented in the College, it is possible for a candidate to win the most popular votes in the country but not the majority of the votes in the Electoral College. This has happened in the past – in 1824, in 1876 and in 1888 – and it happened again in 2000. It nearly happened in 1960 and 1976, elections which were closely contested. Neither of the men elected in those years, Kennedy or Carter, received a popular majority of the votes cast, and neither did Bill Clinton in either of his two victories.

The method of choosing the President assessed

The process of choosing an American President is long, complex and expensive in the eyes of many outside observers. It certainly tests the mettle of any candidate for the highest office, and particularly in an age of television any contender who can emerge relatively unscathed after such a prolonged procedure must have considerable powers of endurance and stamina. Hence Vile's reference to 'almost lethal' demands.

The system enables the person chosen to become established as a national figure. In the case of someone such as General Eisenhower, his reputation was already well known. This is not the case with many of the persons who seek to win the presidency via the primary route. Jimmy Carter was an 'outsider' from Georgia, unknown to the Washington elite in 1975, a year before he was elected to the White House. Others may be more familiar, but the way in which a presidential candidate emerges does ensure that he or she becomes a national figure by when the time comes to take office. Either by travel in the past or especially via television today, he or she has been exposed to the critical gaze of millions of American voters, has been forced to sell his or her personality, and to demonstrate an understanding of the needs and wishes of the voters, and is worthy of their respect, trust and that he or she support as the country's leader.

Yet there are many criticisms which can be made of the way in which the US chooses its national leader. Some concern the primaries, some the Electoral College and others the system of election and the nature of the campaign – with its heavy reliance on the media, its increasing professionalism and expense, yet low turnouts and mounting public cynicism.

The primary system is often criticised because of the number and timing of the various contests, a situation which forces a candidate to navigate the primary season with some dexterity. He or she needs to stand in as many contests as possible, although this can be very costly and involves putting one's name down in several states which ballot on the same day; for instance, several primaries in the South are held on Super Tuesday, in early March. This makes a campaign difficult to organise and conduct.

A possible improvement would be to hold a national presidential primary, an election on a single day across the whole country, in the late spring or autumn. As an alternative, the separate state primaries could all be held on the same day. Such a one-off election would reduce the demands on the candidate, attract much media publicity (and therefore a higher turnout?) and produce a fair and representative verdict. But would it increase the role of television and emphasise the professionalism of the modern campaign, with all of its advisers, consultants and preoccupation with image-building? Would it not favour the wealthy or well-resourced candidate who could afford to advertise his cause in every state?

It would, of course, be possible to revert back to the older system, and rely more on caucuses to make the choice. We have examined the reasons for the greater use of primaries (see pp. 158–9 and 176). It is unlikely that there would be any strong support for scrapping their use today, although for those who wish to strengthen the role of political parties in the American system of government there could be a benefit in so doing.

Most of the anxiety about the American system relates to the use of the Electoral College, for it is from the use of this approach that several potential problems derive. Criticism centres on several aspects, notably:

- the over-representation of very small states and the excessive concentration on those which have many College votes;
- the use of the simple plurality method of voting;
- the possibility that members of the College may vote for a person other than the one to whom they were pledged;
- the fact that it is possible to win the popular vote and yet lose the election;
- the fact that there may be no clear victor in the College, if no one emerges with a majority. This could have happened in 1992, if Ross Perot had actually managed to carry some states. It was the strategy of George Wallace in 1968 to aim for deadlock, and thereby throw the decision into the House. A choice made in Congress could be contrary to the people's will as expressed in the ballot box in November.

Why have an Electoral College?
Does the system work well?

The Founding Fathers wanted a method of choosing their President which would shun 'mob politics'. Democracy was then not yet in fashion, and as they were creating an elected office they wanted to ensure that they were not handing power to demagogues who could manipulate popular opinion. They were suspicious of the mass of the people. Choice by college, after the voters had expressed their feelings, could be conducted in a more leisurely and rational manner. As Hamilton put it in *The Federalist Papers*: 'The immediate election [of the President] should be made by men most capable of analysing the qualities needed for the office'. In this spirit, the Founding Fathers set up a system in which the electorate actually chooses between two competing lists or 'slates' of Electoral College candidates, although on the ballot papers it is the names of the candidates for the presidential office which are actually given.

There was never any serious likelihood that members of the Electoral College meeting in December would ignore the expression of public feeling in early November, and candidates for the College soon became pledged to cast their vote for one of the presidential challengers. In other words, they do not use their individual discretion, but reflect the feelings of voters in their state. In fact, the college does not even meet as one deliberating body. Members meet in their state capitals, and their choices are conveyed to Washington. Very rarely, an elector in the Electoral College has changed his or her mind and not voted for the person to whom he or she was pledged. In 1948 a Tennessee elector did not vote for Truman who had carried the state, but opted instead for the States Rights candidate. Twenty years later, an elector in North Carolina switched from Richard Nixon to the Third Party candidature of George Wallace. In 1988, a Democrat voted for Lloyd Bentsen, the vice-presidential nominee, rather than Michael Dukakis, the candidate for the presidency.

Some writers have also drawn attention to the way in which balloting takes place. Instead of there being a proportional split in the Electoral College vote of a particular state to reflect the division of the popular vote, the candidate who gets the most votes carries the whole state allocation. This simple plurality or 'winner takes all' method may seem unfair, especially when the result is very close. In 1960, Kennedy obtained all of New York's 45 College votes, despite the fact that he only obtained 52.5 per cent support; a proportional split would have given him 24 votes, to 21 for his opponent. This method makes the impact of geography very important on the outcome, for as we have seen a candidate who can carry California and other populous states has an enormous advantage. This would not be the case if the College vote was divided. The importance of urban states with dense populations is unduly emphasised under this process.

For all of its disadvantages, the system has so far worked tolerably well. When there is a close popular vote, as in 1960, the outcome in the College makes the result clear-cut. Until 2000, the same has been true in other contests where the gap between the main candidates is a narrow one.

Is there a better alternative to the Electoral College?

There have been many suggestions for the use of an amended college system, and others for its total abolition. Modifications could take the form of using a different electoral system other than 'winner takes all'. A proportional division of the College votes is an alternative to the simple plurality.

The most obvious change would be to jettison the Electoral College and opt for a straight popular election of the President by the voters, instead of using the present indirect process of election. If it proved to be the case that no candidate could overcome a 40 per cent hurdle on the first round of voting, then there could be a replay, a run-off between the two candidates who had scored most successfully. The person elected could then claim to have wide national backing, and not be unduly beholden to the voters in especially populous states. No longer is there the same apprehension about democracy as prevailed when the Founding Fathers made their choice.

It is true that such a method could further enhance the power of television, for few candidates could ever get across the nation to tour every state to encourage popular support. Yet effectively this is what happens now; the campaign is already organised for its television impact. More seriously for some critics of reform along these lines, it might weaken further the two main parties and encourage the candidature of third party nominees.

For defenders of states rights, such a proposal might seem to be a threat to the federal system for it undermines the importance of each state and region in the contest. In particular, the smaller states may feel uneasy, for their influence in deciding the outcome would be diminished compared with the current situation.

Is change likely?

It is far more likely that the present system will continue indefinitely, for although there is periodic unease about the Electoral College this mainly coincides with the prospect of an indecisive outcome in the next presidential election. When a clear winner emerges, as eventually happened in 1992, much of the earlier talk of change vanishes.

There is no agreement on any alternative. Direct election was supported by Jimmy Carter early in the life of his presidency, when he described the existing arrangements as 'archaic'. Many analysts might concur with such a view, but there are strong forces ranged against it. The federal system was designed to protect the influence of the states, especially small ones, and they would not readily vote for a change, either via their Congressmen or in their state legislatures. For the Dakotas or Vermont, the Electoral College gives them an influence beyond their size, and why should they wish to surrender it?

HOW AMERICANS VOTE
AND WHY THEY VOTE AS THEY DO

The traditional picture of voting behaviour

Ever since the time of the New Deal, there has been a marked trend for urban workers with low incomes, who generally live in the poorest districts and have a lower level of formal educational qualification, to vote Democrat. In contrast, well-to-do voters, often with a higher level of educational attainment and living in suburban areas, have usually inclined to the Republican side.

The Democrats have had the support of minority groups such as blacks who suffered in the Great Depression and regarded the party as the one which conferred benefits and was more likely to be interested in advancing their economic interests. The majority of Catholics, mainly of Irish immigrant stock, have inclined to the same party, and so have groups such as the Jews and other minorities who participated. However, just as white southern Democrats were often noted for their deeply ingrained Protestant fundamentalism, so Republicans always had some voters who were poor whites, Catholics, Jewish or black. There was never a complete racial, religious or socio-economic divide.

A changed picture in recent years

The pattern of voting behaviour in Britain and America has changed over the last generation, and some of the broad generalisations were found to be inadequate by the 1980s and 1990s. The changing class structure, with fewer people working in manufacturing industry, greater prosperity for most classes in the population and more upward social mobility challenged some previous assumptions about the way Americans vote. Voting behaviour has become more volatile and as Stephen Wayne[12] has written:

> While class, religion and geography are still related to party identification and voting behaviour, they are not as strongly related as they were in the past. Voters are less influenced by group cues. They exercise a more independent judgement on election day, a judgement that is less predictable and more subject to be influenced by the campaign itself.

Political scientists today talk more about party identification, the appeal of the candidate and issues than they did in the past. There is, of course, no clear-cut division between them, for the party one associates oneself with will often help to determine what one thinks about the candidate and the topic under discussion.

By **partisan identification**, we mean the long-standing identification that a person has for a particular party, a preference which will have often been formed over many years. It will have been influenced by family background, education and the influence of peers in the early years, and this sense of attachment stays with people for much of their lives, modified by life experience, especially economic considerations and impressions formed of the effectiveness of particular administrations in delivering the goods and making people feel content.

The idea is that most Americans will stick by their normal party affiliation unless there are seemingly good reasons for not doing so. The affiliation may be a strong or a weak one, and research carried out by the *American National Election Study* team has divided responses into seven categories: Strong Democrats, Weak Democrats, Independent-Leaning Democrats, the same three categories for the Republican Party, and the Independents, who really show no obvious affiliation at all. The apolitical, the two to four per cent who normally would not vote and show little interest in the subject, are not included for our purpose.

The studies have shown that whereas at the 1960 election when Kennedy was successful, 51 per cent could be described as Democrats of one variety or the other and 37 per cent Republican, in 1980, when Ronald Reagan gained the Presidency, the figures were 52 per cent and 33 per cent. In other words, comparing a good year for the Democrats in the presidential contest with a bad year, shows no significant difference. Indeed, in 1992 the figures remained fairly stable, 50 per cent and 37 per cent. It may be that party identification is the best guide to voting behaviour over the long term, but clearly in the shorter term there must be other factors which are more important, for otherwise the Democrats would be regularly more successful than their opponents.

Less stable factors, ones which fluctuate from election to election, include the attractiveness of the individual candidate and the issues which are in the forefront of people's minds. Martin Wattenberg[13] has argued that what has happened is that there has been a change of focus in recent years from party allegiance to concentration on the merits of the nominee: 'The change … is an important historical trend, which has been gradually taking place over the last several decades'. Voters now seem to be more interested in the qualities the candidate possesses, not surprisingly as these are now featured in the media more than ever before. Via television, they can assess their leadership ability and charisma, their honesty and experience, their knowledge or their ignorance. 'Strength' and 'leadership' are much-admired qualities, as is what George Bush Snr called 'the vision thing'; many people like to be led by a person who knows where he or she wishes to lead them.

The trend to split-ticket voting

Since the days of Democratic ascendancy, which ended in 1968, there has been a clear reduction in voter loyalty. Voters are more willing to vote differently between elections and within them – by **split-ticket voting**. The trend to split-ticket voting actually has a longer history, going back to 1952, but it has intensified in recent years. Whereas in 1952, 12 per cent voted differently in their choice of party for the President and their member of the House of Representatives, by 1968 26 per cent did so, and in 1980 the figure was 34 per cent. Voters were enthusiastic about electing Ronald Reagan, but less willing to vote for his party in the congressional elections.

The trend is notable at all levels, with more voters behaving differently in choosing a candidate for the White House and ones for Capitol Hill, more voting one way for the Senate and a different way for the House, and – particularly marked – a larger number voting differently in their choice for state and for local representatives.

Issues are also important, but rather less so than party identification and candidate-appeal. Voters are often ambiguous about where a contender stands on a particular issue, for politicians realise that clarity can sometimes antagonise people and groups whom the candidate hopes to attract. If they have taken the trouble to find out rival policy positions and understand them clearly, then it may be that they incline to one side on one issue, the other on a different one.

More broadly, voters think in terms of what the last administration has done for them (**retrospective** issue voting) and what the candidates are offering for the next four years (**prospective** issue voting). In 1992, many were unimpressed by the domestic performance of the Bush presidency, particularly his handling of the economy. They felt that Bill Clinton offered a better future

---

Voting behaviour in Britain and the United States: a comparison

The academic study of voting behaviour became popular in the 1960s on either side of the Atlantic. Early studies such as *The American Voter* and *Political Change in Britain*[14] showed how voting was influenced by long- and short-term influences. Since those early days, theories of voting behaviour have undergone substantial modification. Social changes have occurred in all developed countries and as a result the old certainties have vanished. Voting is now less predictable than in the past. In an age of greater volatility, short-term influences are likely to be more significant, and parties cannot count on traditional loyalties to provide them with mass support.

Short-term influences relate to a particular election, and include:
- the state of the economy;
- the personality and performance of political leaders;
- the nature of the campaign;
- the mass media;
- events leading up to the election.

Long-term influences include:
- party loyalty;
- social class;
- factors relating to the social structure such as age, gender, occupation, race and religion.

In Britain, the features most noted in the post-war years up to 1970 were:
- the stability of voting patterns, as people stayed loyal to the party they had always supported;
- the relevance of social class (Pulzer[16] could once memorably write that: 'Class is the basis of British politics; all else is embellishment and detail');
- the recognition that elections were determined by a body of floating voters in key marginal constituencies;
- the uniform nature of the swing across the United Kingdom;
- the domination of the two main parties which between them could count on the support of the majority of the electorate.

Since the 1970s many of these assumptions have lost their validity. The main parties can no longer anticipate the degree of support they once enjoyed, and the rise of third parties has made inroads into the share of the vote the two parties can command. In 1994,

– reform of health care, and a new emphasis on recovering from the recession and creating jobs ('It's the economy, stupid!'). However much Bush might try to stress the 'character-issue', by suggesting that his opponent was untruthful, evasive and not to be trusted, this appeared to matter less on this occasion than the promise of movement on the domestic front.

Madgwick concluded[17] that: 'Voting is still related to social class, but the relationship is complex, and there is less confidence about the significance of the term'. His conclusion was heavily influenced by Ivor Crewe whose researches showed that not only was class identification weakening, but so was party identification generally.

The publication of *Decade of De-alignment*[18] was a psephological milestone. Bo Sarlvik and Crewe showed the extent to which the two parties had steadily lost their once reliable supporters. They found that the bulk of the electorate was now liable to switch votes, and become actual or potential floating voters. In particular, they discovered that demographic changes were taking their toll of Labour, for the old working-class communities were being destroyed by redevelopment schemes and the inner cities were emptying. Labour's traditional electoral base was being eroded, a point which led Peter Kellner to write[19] that the 'sense of class solidarity which propelled Labour to power in 1945 has all but evaporated'. Tony Blair's New Labour party recognised that Labour needed to extend its appeal, particularly in Middle England. In 1997 and 2001, Labour gained broad support from across the ages, sexes and social classes.

In the US broad trends in voting behaviour in recent years are that:
* Party identification means less today than was once the case.
* Voting has become more candidate-centred. In a television age, voters know much more about the candidates, and considerations of perceived competence, integrity and visual appeal matter more than ever before. In presidential debates, these qualities can be easily assessed by the electorate.
* Policy issues may play a greater role than in the past. Today, those who stand for office are regularly grilled about how they respond to particular issues and events.

In both countries, voters are now less committed to their long-term allegiances. Partisan de-alignment has occurred, and this means that there has been a weakening of the old loyalties, and a new volatility among the electorate. Other key points of comparison are that:
* social class, once a key determinant of voting especially in Britain, has lost much of its impact;
* the personality of the candidate has assumed greater importance in a media age, particularly in America where the party label anyway counts for less;
* issues and the election campaign become more significant as there are today more votes 'up for grabs'.

DIRECT LEGISLATION

The referendum and other devices

The United States is one of only five democracies which have never held a nationwide **referendum**. However, in 46 states and many cities there is provision for direct legislation (the initiative and the referendum), and the facility has been more widely used in several of them in the last generation.

> **referendum**
> A vote on a single issue in which all registered electors are eligible to take part. Instead of being asked to give a verdict on the administration as a whole – as in a general election – they are asked their opinion on one measure or act presented to them by the legislature.

Early twentieth-century progressives supported the use of direct democracy and many states where it is now employed adopted it around that time, originally South Dakota in 1898 and Oregon in 1902. Most of the 'early' ones opted for the **initiative** and referendum, but as David Magleby[19] points out, the states which have incorporated direct legislation since World War I decided in several cases not to go for the whole package:

> In short, in the early going, states were much more likely to embrace all aspects of direct legislation, and provide the most direct forms of the process ... While many states permit both the initiative and the popular referendum, it is the initiative that is much more frequently used. Since 1980, there have been roughly five initiatives for every popular referendum.

Direct democracy is most commonly used in the western states. Their political systems were still relatively undeveloped at the turn of the twentiethcentury so that they were much more open to the arguments of the progressive movement. Progressivism was firmly entrenched in the region, supporters urging anti-institutional reforms which allowed for popular involvement. It never took root in the same way in the older south and northeast, which provide less opportunity for this form of direct democracy. (NB:

> **initiative**
> A device by which an individual citizen (or group of citizens) can – if they collect a given number of signatures on a petition – have a proposal placed directly on the ballot in a statewide election. As such, the initiative is particularly useful in cases where law-makers refuse to enact or even consider a law that the people want.

some towns in New England have a different form of direct democracy, the town meeting – see pp. 170–1).

Frequency

There were 204 ballots in 42 states in the 2000 elections. They offered Americans tough choices on a wide array of subjects, from animal welfare to gay rights, from abortion to firearms purchases. The number of such initiatives has been on the rise in recent years, a symptom of increased turbulence in state politics and government. They were used in several western states in the 1990s, among other things to:

- test how many terms a person could serve in a state legislature or on Capitol Hill;
- restrict (or enhance) personal liberty;
- reduce (or hike) taxes;
- decide fishing rights;
- prohibit the trapping of black bears out of season.

The state most frequently associated with the use of initiatives and referendums is California. There can be as many as 30 propositions on the biennial November ballot paper, where they are placed alongside the contests for federal and state offices. The protagonists on either side are allowed to draw up statements of the pro and anti cases; these are freely distributed to the voters, in weighty booklets. In 1998, topics ranged from tribal gaming to an animal trap ban, from air quality to the sale of horsemeat. In 2000, they covered the treatment of non-violent drug offenders, the use of school vouchers and the issuing of bonds as a means of raising money for schools.

Why has direct democracy become more popular?

There are several explanations for the upsurge in the popularity of initiatives and referendums in the last two decades. Key factors include:

1 Activists have discovered their value as a means of advancing particular interests – for liberals, this might be an issue such as environmental protection and for conservatives tax-cutting or curbing abortion.
2 Some politicians have been keen to associate themselves with initiative proposals as a useful means of raising public awareness of particular subjects and their own profile. This can win them the backing – and finance – of issue activists.
3 An industry has developed to professionalise the use of initiatives and popular referendums. Pollsters, media consultants, petition circulators and others have brought their expertise into the field and thereby made it easier to get an issue 'off the ground'. The 'initiative industry' operates not just in getting measures onto the ballot, but in challenging or defending measures which have been approved by voters, in the courts.
4 The news media particularly thrive on initiatives, for the attempts to raise or block contentious issues provide good stories, often with a strong human interest and great headline potential.

Participation and turnout

Citizens are involved in direct democracy in a number of activities. For the more active this may involve organising and circulating petitions, campaigning to maximise support or seeking/providing lunch. For most people, the limit of their involvement is voting.

Sometimes a contentious issue may provoke an enthusiastic response, but usually turnout is only high if the initiative is being held at the same time as a general election. Magleby quotes[20] the example of Maine which stages initiatives in general election years and in the odd-numbered years in between when there is no other vote. Far more people take part in the years when

---

Direct democracy in Britain, Europe and the United States: a comparison

Referendums are a means of giving the electorate a chance to have a direct influence over the decision-makers on specific policies. In recent years they have been much more widely used in many parts of the world. As we have seen, a growing number of American states have used them to decide on contentious moral, social issues and constitutional issues. Some member states of the European Union have used them to confirm their membership of the EU or to ratify important constitutional developments. The new democracies of Central and Eastern Europe, particularly the 15 republics of the former USSR, have used them to decide a range of issues relating to the form of their new governments.

In the past, referendums were often associated with dictatorial systems such as that of Nazi Germany or democratic ones with authoritarian overtones such as the Fifth French Republic of Charles de Gaulle. Often they were then known as plebiscites. It is the memory of such past experience which troubles some democrats who fear the purpose and management of such means of consultation with the public. Hence the attitude of British Prime Minister Clement Attlee after World War II. Worried about the countries which had practised 'direct democracy', he described referendums as 'devices alien to our traditions' and saw them as instruments of 'demagogues and dictators'. He pointed to their often suspiciously high turnouts. Such overtones have largely disappeared and initiatives and referendums are now used with increasing regularity in countries and states which have impeccable democratic credentials.

In some countries, the outcome of such referendums is binding, in others it is advisory. In Britain, with its commitment to the idea of Parliamentary Sovereignty, only Parliament can cast a decisive vote on any issue, but it is unlikely that a majority of legislators would make a habit of casting their parliamentary vote in defiance of the popular will as expressed in a referendum. Ministers have accepted that to consult and then to ignore the verdict is worse than never to have sought an opinion. In 1975, Prime Minister Wilson accepted that a majority of even a single vote against so doing would be enough to take Britain out of the European Community. In other words, both governments and MPs

offices are being contested then when there is just an issue(s) up for election. Also, in general election years, he detects a mean drop-off of 15 per cent in the number who cast a vote on the propositions, compared with the number who cast a vote for the candidates.

When there is a general election, the task for the voter can be lengthy. A long ballot paper is sometimes needed, as when in 1988 the voters of San Francisco were asked to decide on 52 separate questions. The 1990 Arizona ballot pamphlet ran to 224 pages! Voter weariness means that even some of the more enthusiastic citizens do not answer every question, although the fewer the questions the better the response.

accept that they should treat the popular verdict as mandatory, in the sense that it is morally and politically binding.

Britain has until recently had very little experience of voting on a single issue, even though the case has often been canvassed in the twentieth century. A Conservative leader and former Prime Minister, Arthur Balfour, told the House of Commons back in 1911 that 'so far from corrupting the sources of democratic life [they] would only be a great education for political people'. The Conservatives held a referendum on the border issue in Northern Ireland in 1973, and the Scottish and Welsh electorates were allowed to vote on whether they wanted devolution in 1979. Yet the only occasion when all of the voters have been allowed to vote on a key national issues was four years earlier, when they were asked whether or not they wished the country to remain in the European Economic Community. There have been local votes on the future status of schools and the ownership of council estates, and in Wales the issue of 'local option' on the Sunday opening of pubs has been decided in this way. Some councils are now consulting their electorates as to whether they should preserve public services by raising the level of Council Tax.

Since May 1997 referendums have already been used to resolve the issue of devolution, and the future shape of London's government. Also, in concurrent votes, popular approval of the Good Friday Agreement was supported by electors on both sides of the border in Ireland. Ministers have promised a vote on electoral reform at some time in the near future, and should there be a decision for Britain to join the single currency then this too will be submitted to the people for popular backing.

Whereas the British have embraced the referendum slowly and with some reluctance, Americans have been more enthusiastic about direct legislation though not at the national level. In a country in which the proper role of government is much discussed, issues of public spending and taxation, matters of public morality and governmental or political reform, have all been seen as suitable subjects for popular consultation, whereas the British have been wary of resolving controversial matters such as drug use or abortion in this way.

Are initiatives and referendums a good thing?

There has been some discussion of the idea of initiatives for the federal government, but as yet no national vote has taken place. Many who exercise power are reluctant to opt for more direct democracy and argue that whilst it may be appropriate for deciding local and state issues it has disadvantages in national politics. Conservatives tend to fear its use on key questions of defence and foreign affairs. Liberals worry about the repercussions for minority groups. Many members of both categories feel safer with traditional methods of representative democracy.

In Favour of votes on single issues, it may be said that:
1 They give people a chance to take decisions which affect their lives, whereas in a general election they can only offer a general verdict.
2 They stimulate interest and involvement in public policy.
3 They may exert pressure on the legislature to act responsibly and in the public interest.
4 They help counter the special interests to which legislators can be beholden.
5 They help overcome the obstructionism of out-of-touch legislators and therefore make reform more likely.

Against:
1 Proposals can be ill thought-out and badly drafted.
2 Campaigns can be expensive and therefore to the advantage of well-funded groups. Money is too dominant in the process. Business interests have far more scope to influence the outcome
3 There are too many issues for voters to handle – they elect representatives to decide. This is what representative democracy is all about. If the voter dislikes the decisions made, he or she can turn against the controlling party in the next election
4 Initiatives and allied devices undermine political parties and therefore weaken the democratic process
5 They encourage single issue politics, rather than debate based on a conflict of broad principles.
6 They can work to the disadvantage of minorities who can be persecuted by the majority – e.g. blacks and gays.

Despite all of the reasons that may be used to oppose direct democracy, no state which possesses the provision for initiatives and/or referendums has ever repealed it. The process is likely to continue to be a major factor in the political life of many states.

ELECTION 2000: A CASE STUDY

The outcome

Result of the presidential contest on 7 November 2000 (turnout estimated at 51.2%)

Candidate	Popular vote	Electoral college
Albert Gore (Democrat)	50,996,039 (48.5%)	266*
George Bush (Republican)	50,456,141 (48.0%)	271
Ralph Nader (Green)	2,878,157 (2.7%)	0
Pat Buchanan (Reform)	448,868 (0.4%)	0
Harry Browne (Libertarian)	386,035 (0.4%)	0

* One blank vote was cast in the Electoral College, by a Gore supporter from the District of Columbia who wished to protest against the city's lack of representation in Congress.

In 2000, the voters unknowingly opened a legal can of worms when they recorded their votes on 7 November. The outcome of the election was not finally known until 13 December, because of the various legal challenges to the result mounted initially by Al Gore and then by George Bush. The key dates in the long battle for the White House were as follows.

- **7 November**   Election day. The TV networks declared Florida for Gore, then Bush. Gore conceded, but Florida declared an automatic recount and he retracted his concession.
- **14 November**   Florida Secretary of State Katherine Harris declared Bush the winner in the state, but overseas votes were still to be counted. Four days later, the official count, including overseas votes, gave Bush a lead of 930 votes.
- **21 November**   Florida Supreme Court ruled that recounts could go ahead in three of the state's 67 counties, but must be completed by November 26. Recounts in these heavily democratic counties could turn up enough Gore votes to make him the winner.
- **22 November**   Election officials in Miami-Dade suspended the recount, but there was hope for Gore when Palm Beach County decided to include dimpled ballots as well as properly punched ballots in the recount.
- **26 November**   Bush was again declared the winner in Florida after a recount, but by only 537 votes. Gore wanted the votes counted in Miami-Dade county.
- **8 December**   Florida Supreme Court ordered a manual recount of votes as demanded by Gore. But Florida's legislature threatened to override the courts and name 25 Republican nominees to the Electoral College: that would have handed the election to Bush.

- **9 December**   The US Supreme Court, the highest court in America, suspended recounts across Florida pending a hearing on 11 December.
- **13 December**   After the Supreme Court ruling by a 5–4 majority that Florida recounts would be unconstitutional, Gore took advice from his lawyers and Democratic Party chiefs and admitted defeat. Bush became the President-elect, ready to take over on January 20.

The Bush victory

Only one thing seems clear after the miasma of the presidential election and that is we will probably never know for absolute who won it. The margin in Florida was so infinitesimal, a few hundred out of some six million cast, that it will always be open to doubt. It would have only taken three 'faithless electors' to swap allegiance in the Electoral College, as most were free to do, to have swung the result back to Gore, but of course this did not happen. The last time the nation was so divided was in 1960, when John F. Kennedy defeated Richard Nixon by only 100,000 votes.

If Gore had won, he would have had the narrowest of victories with his opponents just clinging on to the control of Congress. Now that Bush has emerged victorious, it means that for the first time since Eisenhower's victory in 1952, the Republicans are in control of the presidency and Congress, although in the Senate their dominance is nominal, dependent upon the casting vote of the Vice-President, Dick Cheney. As it is, George Bush has won, but without the legitimacy of achieving a majority in the popular vote. He and his party have the trappings of control, without the legitimacy of a popular mandate. There have only been two minority presidents before and the earlier one, Rutherford B. Hayes in 1876, was mocked as 'His Fraudulency'. (It is interesting that it was in Florida on that occasion too that the four disputed Electoral College votes made all the difference.)

The aggrieved Gore camp has reason to believe that the election was stolen, in error if not by fraud. Many Democrats see themselves as the moral victors, even if their candidate didn't win in the way that he had every chance of doing. Some among them would have liked to see the contest re-run, at least in some counties in Florida. They will always be able to point to the people unable to cast their vote or whose votes did not count or were not even counted. The claims of racial discrimination in voting are especially troublesome. People will wonder what strings Jeb Bush, as Governor of Florida, was able to pull in order to deliver for his brother.

The Bush team, in contrast, consider the Florida result to have been fair and as for their lower popular vote they respond that the rules of the game have always allowed for this possibility. The Democrats knew the rules when the campaign opened, and indeed in the days immediately before 7 November it seemed possible that Al Gore might snatch a last-minute victory by winning enough of the large states to win in the Electoral College but not command a majority of the popular vote. Would he have complained if he had won?

Why did Bush win?

This was an election which the Democrats should have won. They had presided over a successful economy and many Americans were enjoying a better standard of living than ever before. Yet in the end, there was a nail-biting finish which was resolved in favour of George Bush Junior only after an agonising delay during which the battleground moved from the polling stations to the courts. The close result reflects the nation's indecision about who they wanted in office over the coming years.

Gore's decline in the later stages of the campaign was remarkable. In September, following the national conventions, it seemed as though he was about to soar ahead, his party gaining the credit for its economic legacy. *So what went wrong?*

1   On the night of the election, when it was apparent that the Democrats had failed to win in the way they might have hoped, it was easy for some of them to blame the intervention of the Green candidate Ralph Nader, for their fall, for they claimed that his vote was the deciding factor in narrowly contested states such as Florida and Oregon: 'a vote for Nader was a vote for Bush'. Yet Nader fell far short of the five per cent target he had set himself and can hardly be held responsible for Gore's failure to enthuse the American electorate.

2   Some Democrats blamed Al Gore's decision to distance himself from Bill Clinton. They wondered why the President had not been allowed to go to Arkansas, his home state and one which the party lost. Certainly, in detaching himself from Bill Clinton to avoid being besmirched by the 'Clinton Scandals', it made it more difficult for Gore to identify himself with the Clinton successes, the widespread sense of economic well-being. He also missed out on the campaigning skills of the President, who might have been able to rally doubting Democrats to turn out and vote.

3   Probably the main reason why the Vice-President did not run away with victory was that at a time of unprecedented prosperity it was unwise to run as a populist, left-of-centre candidate. He appealed more to traditional Democratic voters such as car workers, teachers and blacks, but this limited his attraction for broader groups, so that the result was a mandate for continuity and moderation, rather than for populism. By abandoning the Third Way, Gore let compassionate conservatism slip in.

4 Personal factors played a part. At a time of broad national contentment in which the country seemed recession-proof, George Bush best represented continuity but without the scandals. He also came across as genial and likeable. He had no major issue on which to galvanise support, but he survived the character test. On the campaign trail, Gore was often wooden and ill at ease. In the presidential debates, he was more hostile and combative, even aggressive. He was also unable to demonstrate the benefits of his superior experience, knowledge and subtlety. His performance gave his challenger undeserved legitimacy, somehow making Bush seem better than he was.

CONCLUSION

There are various ways in which Americans can participate in political life. Many choose not to do so, having only a limited interest in politics. The vast majority never engage in any political activity between elections and pay little attention to what is going on.

Elections and election campaigns are the processes by which voters in any democracy choose the direction they wish to take in the future. They are the opportunity for voters to have their say. Americans are called upon to participate with great frequency, for there is a theoretical enthusiasm for the ballot box in public life. Yet many of them choose not to take advantage.

Those who do vote, do so in the light of various influences, of which their long-term party identification has traditionally been the most important. However, in a television age, in which campaigning is conducted in a more visible way than ever before and in which the amount of information available has dramatically increased, the merits of the candidate and issues of the time have become particularly relevant.

REFERENCES

1 A. Grant, *Contemporary American Politics*, Dartmouth, 1995.
2 V. O. Key, *Politics, Parties and Pressure Groups*, Crowell, 1964.
3 T. Hames and N. Rae, *Governing America*, MUP, 1996.
4 B. Ginsberg and M. Shefter, *Politics by Other Means*, WW Norton, 1999.
5 Prof. F. Bryan (University of Vermont), as quoted in a Vermont Public Television video entitled 'Town Meeting: A Day in the Life', 2000.
6 Joe Rankin, *Morning Sentinel* (Maine), 26 March 2000.
7 J. Zimmerman, *The New England Town Meeting: Democracy in Action*, McGraw-Hill, 1999.

8 J. Rankin, *Morning Sentinel* (Maine), 26 March 2000.

9 Prof. F. Bryan (University of Vermont), as quoted in a Vermont Public Television video entitled 'Town Meeting: A Day in the Life', 2000.

10 B. Schneider, as quoted in L. Rees, *Selling Politics*, BBC Books, 1992.

11 M. Vile, *Politics in the US*, Hutchinson, 1978.

12 S. Wayne, *The Road to the White House 1996*, St Martin's Press, 1996.

13 M. Wattenberg, *The Rise of Candidate-Centred Politics*, Harvard University Press, 1991.

14 A. Campbell *et al.*, *The American Voter*, John Wiley, 1960; D. Butler and D. Stokes, *Political Change in Britain*, Macmillan, 1966.

15 P. Pulzer, *Political Representation and Elections in Britain*, Allen and Unwin, 1968.

16 P. Madgwick, *A New Introduction to British Politics*, Thorne, 1994.

17 B. Sarlvik and I. Crewe, *Decade of Dealignment*, Cambridge University Press, 1983.

18 P. Kellner, *New Society*, 2 June 1983.

19 D. Butler and D. Magleby, *Referendums around the World*, Macmillan, 1994.

20 D. Butler and D. Magleby, *Referendums around the World*, Macmillan, 1994.

USEFUL WEB SITES

On elections

www.fec.gov The Federal Election Commission. Provides data on the financing of election campaigns.

http://pollingreport.com The Polling Report. Gives data on elections and campaigning events.

On the media

www.appcpenn.org The Annenburg Policy Center. Provides analyses of television coverage of politics.

www.neeewsuem.org The Freedom Forum; museum of journalism. Provides insight into changes in the reporting of news over the years.

In addition, most newspapers and television channels have web sites, for example:

www.washingtonpost.com The Washington Post.

www.cnn.com CNN cable network.

SAMPLE QUESTIONS

1 'Vast amounts of money are spent on elections and electioneering in the US, more than in any other democracy'. Are the elections better for all this expenditure?

2 Why does America have so many elections and why are many Americans so unwilling to vote in them?

3 'Nowadays, American election campaigns are geared to the requirements of television.' Discuss.

4 Evaluate the strengths and weaknesses of the way in which presidential candidates are chosen.

5 Should the Electoral College now be abolished?

6 Account for the growth in popularity of methods of direct legisation in recent decades. Are initiatives and referendums a reliable guide to what Americans think?

7 Account for the changes in American voting behaviour since the 1980s.

8 Compare the conduct of elections and the methods of electioneering in Britain and the United States.

Political parties

8

In any democracy, political parties play an important role. They are basic to democracy, in that they organise elections and provide voters with a choice of ideas and personalities. American parties play a significant role, though not a comparable one to those in Britain. American constitutional arrangements impede the development of strong parties and were designed to do so. Many academics and commentators see their role as less important now than it was in the past. This has led to talk of 'the decline of American parties'. Other commentators detect signs of a resurgence.

Here, we are concerned with the development of parties, how the party system operates today, what the main parties stand for and whether there are substantial differences between them, and the ways in which they are organised. We can then decide whether or not their role has diminished in recent years.

POINTS TO CONSIDER

➤ Why were the Founding Fathers suspicious of political parties?

➤ Can America be said to have a two-party system?

➤ What are the main ideas and beliefs associated with the two main parties?

➤ How might the emergence of a successful national third party change the nature and role of the two main political parties? Is such a development likely?

➤ How are American parties structured? In what respects does their structure differ from that of British parties?

➤ Are American parties in decline or undergoing a resurgence?

The role and value of parties

American history reveals a long-standing distrust of **parties**, which have been portrayed as factions by some writers ever since the days of the Founding Fathers. James Madison (the fourth President) defined a faction in unflattering terms:

> By a faction, I mean a number of citizens, whether amounting to a majority or a minority of the whole, who are united and actuated by some common impulse or passion, or of interest, adverse to the rights of other citizens or to the permanent aggregate interest of the community.

political party

A group of people of broadly similar views who organise themselves and recruit candidates for election, with a view to achieving office so that they can carry out their ideas and programme. They are not people with identical attitudes and interests, for parties are inevitably coalitions of individuals whose approach on some issues can be widely divergent.

George Washington too made clear his anxieties about 'the baneful effects of the spirit of party generally [with] its alternate domination of one faction over another, sharpened by the spirit of revenge natural to party dissension'. For him, parties 'kindle[d] the animosities of one part against another'. But his warnings were delivered too late to influence the course of events. Since his time, they have been accepted as a 'necessary evil', in that they help to organise the democratic process and present Americans with a choice of candidates and policies.

The main functions of parties are concerned with fighting and winning elections.

1 **They arrange for the choice of candidates**. This was once done in 'smoke-filled rooms' by party bosses who selected their preferred choice, but in the US today it is in most states the voters who choose their preferred candidate in primary elections. By the time of the party nominating conventions the choice is normally clear-cut.

2 **Supporting the candidates**. Once chosen, by whatever method, candidates need to have a supporting organisation to handle their campaign. Traditionally, the parties have arranged door-to-door canvassing to put their candidate's message across; they also establish phone-banks, arrange lifts to the polling station, assist in fund-raising and advertising, and commission the carrying out of private polls. Again this role has been downgraded in recent years, for with the decline in influence of the 'party machines' candidates have increasingly organised the running of their own campaign. Moreover, the growth of Political Action Committees has meant that parties have a lower profile in fundraising and advertising than was formerly the case. The 'supportive' function has its uses, however, and at the national conventions the parties are keen to ensure that the presidential campaign attracts the maximum of favourable publicity. They attempt to 'sell' their chosen candi-

dates for the presidency and vice-presidency, and may arrange for 'endorsements' of the ticket by well-respected party dignitaries.

3 **Organising the contest**. Throughout the nation, parties at every level conduct the useful tasks of helping to register voters and arouse their enthusiasm for the contest. They help arrange candidate-training, research into policy issues and the publicity which is so helpful in getting the name and message across.

4 **Clarifying the issues**. Parties help to simplify the choice which is offered to the voter, for they provide them with information and help to organise the discussion of issues into a 'for' and 'against' format. The arguments on either side are reduced to an appropriate level of public comprehension

5 **Involving the electorate in the democratic process**. Parties give the individual American a chance to participate in the democratic process. A relative few work as party activists; others who are party members have a chance to vote in primary elections and attend any local meetings. This enables the voter to rally around the party which best fits his or her vision of how American life should be organised. In other words, parties are an outlet for people's interests and enthusiasms, a focal point for their allegiances and loyalties. In providing this outlet, parties are a useful intermediary between the governed and the government – for through parties, the individuals can make their views known and conveyed to those who seek to win and retain their support.

The two-party system

America is a country of great diversity, with marked ethnic, social and regional differences, which one might expect to see represented by parties concerned with their specific interests. Yet it has a two-party system, in which only two main parties seriously compete for political influence and in particular every four years seek to capture the presidency. This has always been the case except for rare moments in the country's history. As V. O. Key[1] put it:

> While minor parties have arisen from time to time and exerted influence on governmental policy, the two major parties have been the only serious contenders for the presidency. On occasion, a major party has disintegrated, but in due course the bi-party system has reasserted itself.

A two-party system does not preclude the existence of other parties, and in the United States as in most other western democracies several other third and minor parties continue to operate. What it does mean is that only the main parties, the Republicans and Democrats, have a meaningful chance of achieving the highest office or gaining a majority in Congress. In a two-party system, the two parties may change or adapt; the American Republican Party replaced an established one, as did the British Labour Party. But although there may be transitional phases in which one party is giving way to another, usually within a generation there is a return to normality. In the United States, small parties find it difficult to achieve a breakthrough nationally, although in various states some are well-established (see pp. 208–13).

The phrase 'two-party system' is misleading in some respects, for the American pattern of party activity could also be viewed as an 'agglomeration of many parties centred around the governments of the 50 states and their subdivisions', whilst from another point of view it is a four-party system based upon Congress and the presidency. Writers such as Vile[2] have stressed that although the system nominally operates via two parties, this obscures the fact that for most purposes 'America operates under a multi-party system which coalesces into two great coalitions for strictly limited purposes'. As he puts it:

> The nature of the Constitution, spreading power as it does to different levels of government, tends to have a disintegrating effect on party structure so that national parties tend to be **coalitions** of state and local parties forming and reforming every four years, so that what we have is not a single party system. We have 50 state party systems. Politics operate in a framework of 50 systems, for much decentralisation has occurred.

There is a variety of forms of party competition throughout the country. Politics in Minnesota are different to politics in New York, for inevitably, given the size of the country and the constitutional arrangements, political life varies from state to state. In most, two parties compete for

electoral coalitions
Groups of loyal supporters who agree with the party's stand on most issues and vote for its candidates for office.

power, although the intensity and effectiveness of competition depends on the custom in the individual case. There may well be a genuine alternation of power, with both Republicans and Democrats having a chance to capture the Governorship and control of the legislative chamber. In others, only one party normally ever wins, and there is never the prospect of a change of control. A number of major cities – such as Chicago and Detroit – are regular strongholds of the Democrats, just as Kansas, Utah and Wyoming are traditionally loyal to the Republicans. There are also still several non-competitive congressional districts in which one of the two major parties always wins. In 1992, twelve candidates for the House were elected without opposition, and several others faced only a token battle. The same is true of several state legislatures, a number of which have regularly been controlled by the Democrats. Where one party dominates, the battle is between different factions and individuals within the organisation.

By contrast with the one-party dominance we have been discussing, the New York scene is very different. It is not unusual for several parties to take part in any contest. When there is a multi-party situation, there are often candidates from the two regular parties, and also from the American Labour Party and the Liberal Party.

If federalism is one reason why use of the term 'a two-party system' can be misleading, so too is the Separation of Powers another. The strict division of constitutional responsibility means that the two parties each have a congressional and a presidential wing. This led James MacGregor Burns[3] to describe the American scene as a 'four-party system' with 'separate though overlapping parties', each with their own distinctive style.

> Presidential Democrats are seen as different from congressional ones, in that they have a different electoral base and appeal to different sections of the people. The presidential party seeks its major support in the urban areas of large industrialised states, whilst the majority of Democratic Senators and Congressmen are responsive to rural and suburban influences.

Congressmen are inevitably concerned with the narrow interests of the locality they represent, whereas presidential candidates must appeal in a much wider constituency. The presidential party is either in office (having captured the presidency), or else it is in a state of oblivion for much of the intervening period between elections, whereas the congressional party, Republican or Democrat, is permanently active. The presidential wings of both parties tend to be closer together doctrinally than they are to the respective congressional wings of their own parties.

All of these considerations make it difficult to label the American system straightforwardly as a two-party one, but for most observers it remains meaningful to talk in such language. When people think of the parties in America, they think of the battle between the Democrats and the Republicans, and (especially on this side of the Atlantic) they think primarily of the contest for the presidency.

Why does America have a two-party system?

Several factors may be advanced to explain the American system, some institutional, some cultural or historical. Key[4] has suggested that once the basis of the two-party divide had come about at the time of the formation of the Republic, then it was always likely that it would be retained for 'there is a tendency in human institutions for a persistence of [the] initial form'. Discussion of the form of the Constitution resolved itself into a battle between two opposing viewpoints, and events thereafter in American history – such as slavery and the Civil War – perpetuated this pattern. Once the two-party system was established, the parties did all that they could to keep it that way and prevent a fractious section of the party from breaking away. In other words, a two-party system tends to be self-perpetuating.

Some would stress the natural tendency for opinion on issues to divide into a 'for' and 'against' position which often follows the basic distinction between people who generally favour retaining the status quo (the conservatives) and those who wish to see innovation and a quicker pace of change (the progressives). Duverger[5] long ago argued that a two-party system conformed to the basis division in society between those who wish to keep society broadly unchanged, and those who wish to see change and improvement. However, the liberal–conservative, progressive–stand-pat distinction has not always been appropriate to American politics, and in either party there have always been those who are more forward-looking and those who oppose social advance.

Neither has the approach based on social class fitted the picture accurately – the idea that one party represents the working class and the other the middle and upper class (as in the traditional view of the Labour and Conservative clash in Britain) has never had much relevance as an explanation in a country where class plays a less significant part in the political process. In several countries, there is a clear conflict between a socialist and an anti-socialist party, but in the United States there is no large party committed to transforming the social and economic order.

There are more fundamental explanations of the continued dominance of two parties at national and state level:

1 A single executive

There is only one vacancy at the highest level, the presidency. The nature of the position means that it is not possible for coalitions of more than one party to share it, as can happen with a cabinet system. To win the presidency is the focus of a party's aspirations, for the office is the focal point of all national political life. The campaigning involved is costly and needs to be planned over a long haul, as today candidates seek to make progress and win support via the primary system. It requires substantial organisational and financial backing. In these circumstances, the best means of winning is to create a coalition behind one man, for any splintering of support makes success unlikely. The method of election makes a two-party system more desirable, for to win a majority of votes in the Electoral College it is necessary to avoid divisions. As Vile[6] has argued: 'The ability of a party to master the technique of coalition-building is the measure of its ability to command the presidency'.

2 The broad appeal of the existing parties

As there is only one supreme prize, it is necessary for any party to appeal as widely as possible. Once the presidential candidate is chosen, the leading parties seek to show that they are attractive to many interests in the country, and this makes it difficult for any smaller party to carve out a distinctive identity which is not already catered for. Both the Republican and Democratic parties are essentially coalitions: large organisations under which umbrella a variety of groupings can more or less comfortably co-exist. Between them, they cater for all sections of society, being sufficiently flexible to assimilate new ideas which come along and assume importance.

The reasons advanced above (1 and 2) explain why there are only two main parties at the presidential level. They do not entirely explain why it is that in the battle for Congress the various states tend to have two-party competitions.

3 The mechanics of the electoral system

The electoral system discourages the formation of third or minor parties. For presidential, congressional and other elections, the British Simple Plurality or 'first past the post' ('winner takes all') method is employed. Candidates need more votes than their rivals, not an overall majority of the votes cast in any state. A candidate carries any state on election night in which he or she has the highest number of votes. Small parties may total a considerable number of votes nationally or within the region, but it is winning in individual constituencies which counts. Under a proportional electoral system, they would have more chance of gaining some representation in the legislature.

4 Barriers to third or minor party advancement

In many states, there are real barriers to the formation, progress and survival of third parties. The US is the only nation in which the rules for ballot access in national elections – for Congress as well as the presidency – are not written by the national government but by the states. In several states, legal hurdles have been constructed by the major parties which place third groupings at a serious disadvantage. Many either prohibit 'subversive' ones altogether or make life difficult for them.

Where there is no ban on particular parties, states may require that they have to be of a certain size to get their name on the ballot paper. In a few states, the hurdle is so small that it becomes a formality, so that in Arkansas a grouping of at least 50 only needs to hold a convention to qualify. In others, the barrier is so large that it poses a totally unrealistic obstacle. In certain states, there is no procedure whatever for enthusiasts to qualify to get on a ballot under their own party label. They must either run as Independents or not at all. Georgia and Texas made it very difficult for the veteran consumer rights and environ-mental campaigner Ralph Nader to get on the ballot paper in 2000.

These statutes have often been challenged in the court as a denial of 'equal protection' under the law, and as a violation of the general right of a party to exist. But it has been consistently upheld that restrictions are constitutional, and that there is no requirement to extend to small or new parties the same privileges that are granted to others.

5 *Fear of a wasted vote*

Even if they get off the ground, it is difficult for third parties to sustain any momentum over a period, for to stay in business a party needs to be able to raise funds, maintain an organisation and reward its supporters with the prospect of office or influence. As voters know that small parties will have difficulty in gaining power, they tend to regard a vote for them as a 'wasted vote'. If they cannot eventually win a majority of the votes, they are devoid of real influence; they will not get that majority if people think that they have little chance of achieving it and accordingly fail to vote for them.

Third parties

The late Clinton Rossiter[7] referred to the 'persistent, obdurate two party system', and went on to note that:

> There exists in this country today the materials – substantial materials in the form of potential leaders, followers, funds, interests and ideological commitments – for at least three important third parties, any one of which could, under the rules of some other system, cut heavily and permanently into the historic Democrat-Republican monopoly. There is no reasonable expectancy, under the rules of our system, that any such party could make a respectable showing in two successive elections. Indeed, if a new party were to make such a showing in just one election, the majority party closest to it would move awkwardly but effectively to absorb it.

Types of third party

Although the American political system is basically a two-party one, at various times third parties have had a significant impact. Many have existed throughout American history. In recent years, some third-party candidates win election to public office, and in 1990 Alaska and Connecticut both elected Independents in the battle for the state governorships. Vermont re-elected a socialist to the House in the same year. In 1996, Jesse Ventura, a former professional wrestler known as 'the body', was elected as Governor for Minnesota, on behalf of the Reform Party (see opposite).

By a third party, we usually mean one that is capable of gathering a sizeable percentage of popular support and regularly gains seats in the legislature. On occasion, it may win – or threaten to win – enough support to influence the outcome of an election and the control of government, and in particular regions or constituencies it may break consistently through the usual two-party system. We do not usually refer to one which polls only a tiny percentage of the vote and almost never gains representation as a third party. Such organisations are really minor parties.

Most small parties in America are minor ones which may or may not be permanent; they rarely gain more than a minute percentage of the popular vote. From time to time, however, there are those which do erupt on to the national scene, and make headline news as they bid for the presidency. These are truly third parties. The terms are often used interchangeably in textbooks, and whether we describe them as third parties, minor parties or small parties we are here concerned with all of those bodies which are parties, but which operate outside the mainstream of the two party battle.

These small parties differ considerably in type and permanence. They range from those formed to propagate a particular doctrine over a long duration, to those which are more or less transient. The Prohibition and Socialist parties have over long periods been kept alive by bands of dedicated enthusiasts, and regularly contest elections of all types and in several states. But American party history is noted for the turbulence generated by the rapid rise and equally rapid decline of minor parties; they may play a significant role at a particular time, and then become extinct.

In the 2000 batch of elections, some 50 minor parties had candidates standing in one or more states.

Third parties in presidential campaigns

Some third parties arise during presidential elections and continue to have an impact. Often they are based largely around a single person, as with Theodore Roosevelt (Bull Moose) and Perot (United We Stand, America in 1992, the Reform Party in 1996). In 1992, Perot created a high-profile campaign, and won the support of activists normally associated with the two main parties. Given his substantial wealth, he could afford to buy extensive advertising on television. For all of the resources at his disposal, he did not win a single state, although he gained an impressive 19 per cent of the popular vote and a couple of good seconds, in Maine and Utah. Perot's was at first more a personal movement than a formal political grouping, but by 1996 it had been transformed into the Reform Party.

Some third parties break away from one of the main parties because of disagreement over aspects of the **platform** which the party currently adopts. John Anderson stood aside from the

> **platform**
> A statement of party goals and specific policy agendas, similar to the British manifesto.

Republicans in 1980 because he disagreed with the conservative line taken on social issues by the Reaganites, even though he liked the economic approach of the Republican candidate.

Other such parties are more long-standing, such as the Libertarians and the Greens. In 2000, the highly visible consumerist Ralph Nader was the Green candidate. He managed to win three per cent of the vote.

The role and importance of third parties

A source of new ideas

Third parties can think more of principles than power, for they are unlikely ever to have to implement their proposals. They can 'think the unthinkable', before it later becomes the fashion of the day. Through them, ideas and interests that are not catered for within the main parties may find expression politically. They can handle contentious issues on which neither party can take or is willing to take a clear and decisive line. They provide new ideas and issues for the voters to consider. They are not faced with the difficulty of reconciling several views under one umbrella; they can be clear-cut in the solutions they offer. They suffer no particularly serious consequences if their solutions are, on analysis, found to be wanting, for they are not putting them into effect. If the ideas do capture the public imagination, then they may well be adopted by one or other of the main parties. The policy is then translated into established public practice.

At various times the Socialists, Prohibitionists and Progressives have taken up controversial matters, and thereby acted as vehicles for the expression of political discontent. Some of the best ideas have been originally advanced by those outside the political mainstream. The point was well-made by the historian, Richard Hofstadter.[8] Writing of third parties, he observed that their function

> has not been to win or govern, but to agitate, educate [and] generate new ideas. When a third party's demands become popular enough, they are appropriated by one or both of the major parties and the third party disappears ... [They] are like bees; once they have stung, they die.

A healthy democratic outlet

Even if they do not see their ideas adopted and rarely or never win a congressional seat (let alone the ultimate prize of the presidency), small parties have at the very least drawn attention to the way people feel. They form an outlet for those who dislike the character and attitudes of both the main parties, and for those who reject the party battle they provide a haven. They articulate the thoughts of a section of society, and represent a segment of public sentiment. However incoherent or impractical their view may at times be, they have something to say which needs to be considered if only to be rejected. In a democracy, they have a right to exist and put forward their ideas, however weird they may seem to the majority of people.

Holding the balance

At rare times, a third party can be in an influential position, holding the balance of power and/or affecting the outcome of an election. This is unusual, but in 1992 the Perot intervention probably cost George Bush Senior the presidency just as the votes won by Ralph Nader in states such as Florida kept Al Gore out of the White House in 2000.

A case study of two third parties, their outlook and impact

The Libertarian Party

Americans are deeply attached to the ideas of personal liberty and limited government. Some of them are attracted to the Libertarian Party, formed in 1972. Libertarians are wary of both parties and feel that neither of them can be trusted to defend the rights of individuals. They wish to see most services run on a private basis, and disapprove of federal and state welfare programmes, and policies which offer subsidies to any group, farmers, businessmen and others. They dislike any regulatory bodies of a federal nature such as the FBI or CIA, and laws which curb individual freedom such as those on the wearing of seat-belts and helmets.

Whereas most conservatives take a socially restrictive view and wish to limit the sale of marijuana and other soft drugs, gambling, prostitution and pornography, Libertarians would leave such things unrestricted. They would abolish all legislation designed to promote a particular view of morality. On abortion, there is some division, though the founders of the party were more committed to allowing free choice.

The New York Liberal Party

The Liberal Party of New York state claims to be the longest-existing third party in the history of the United States. It was founded in 1944 as an alternative to a state Democratic Party dominated by local party machines which were rife with corruption and a Republican Party controlled by special interests. It has a history of nominating candidates on the basis of independence, merit and a progressive viewpoint, regardless of party affiliations; it is interested primarily in whether they are likely to provide good, effective and forward-looking government. Past nominees have included Governor Mario Cuomo, Senator Robert Kennedy and New York City Mayors Fiorello LaGuardia and John Wagner.

The Liberal Party remains an influential force in New York politics, campaigning on such things as:

- reproductive freedom – a woman's right to choose abortion;
- health care – the need for a system which is well run and affordable;
- democracy involvement – encouraging popular participation in civic life;
- environmental progress – a serious attempt to place environmental considerations at the forefront of policy-making;
- civil rights – comprehensive legislation to ensure that discrimination on grounds of race, ethnicity, religion, gender, sexual orientation, disability and economic class do not restrict people's lives.

Socialism in America: its failure to take root

America has not proved to be fertile ground for socialist thinkers and their ideas. The main writers and philosophers of socialism have been Europeans, and their ideas and their approach has been developed from European experience. Perhaps because of the influence of German and Jewish believers, Socialism has often been regarded as an alien import unsuited to the conditions of American life.

Socialism in its various forms is traditionally associated with the wish to replace private ownership of the means of production, distribution and exchange with a system of greater public ownership. In the ultimate socialist utopia, property is owned by the state on behalf of the people, and in Marx's phrase, each receives what is necessary for his needs: 'From each according to his ability, to each according to his needs'. In America, there is more discussion of the rights of private property than interest in public ownership.

American socialists of whatever disposition broadly favour an increased role for government, and wish to place a greater burden on the rich by higher taxation. They would use the revenue thereby obtained to introduce more redistributive policies, including public works schemes to offer work for the unemployed, and more aid to the least well-off.

Socialist doctrine has gained a small but influential following among a section of middle-class intellectuals, but the working classes have never taken up the cause with much enthusiasm or in any significant numbers. Groups have developed to represent the various shades of socialism, most notably the American Socialist Party, but as in Europe left-wing organisations groups have been prone to internal schism, factional strife and secession.

Why has socialism failed to make headway in America?

1 The American Dream. Most Americans see capitalism as basic to the American way of life, for it promotes enterprise and initiative. It is part of the American Dream that a person, given the right encouragement and incentives, can strike out on his or her own and make a fortune. Working hard, earning their reward,

being able to keep most of what they earn, passing on their fortune – whatever its size – to their offspring: these are features of life in which there is much faith. The belief is that people should be able to keep what they earn, use it to buy property of their choice, be it a dream home or a more humble shack, a factory or a farm.

Fundamental to all of this is a belief in free enterprise, and this means that doctrines such as communism and socialism are seen as un-American by most voters. They don't want to see a redistribution of other people's wealth, they are more interested in having the freedom to go ahead and make their own. Neither do they like the state to take their money via excessive taxation and spend it on costly welfare programmes which discourage other people from being as self-reliant as they are themselves.

2 **The relative absence of class antagonism.** There was never any feudal system in the United States, no society with a hierarchy of lords and ladies at the top, peasants at the bottom. Americans were, in the words of de Tocqueville, 'born equal'. There was never an American class struggle as one group sought to displace the influence of another. There are objective class divisions, but there has rarely been any sense of class consciousness or worker solidarity as seen in Western Europe. The principle of equality is little disputed, even though there are differences of opinion over exactly what it means in policy implementation.

3 **Over-riding social factors more significant than class.** Class solidarity is less important than other social distinctions; racial and religious attachments are strong, with distinctive groups such as the Jews in New York, the Irish, the Europeans and so many others. America has a very heterogeneous population, and the massive wave of early twentieth-century immigration has created an ethnic mosaic which is matched by the religious diversity of these peoples. These groups have continued to exist in their social enclaves, though many have moved from inner cities to the outer suburbs. Americans have traditionally been conscious of their roots, even if they also wish to develop an American identity, learn the language and be naturalised as citizens. There is no sense of social solidarity, such as exists in parts of Europe. In particular, race and ethnicity cut across divisions based on other economic and social considerations.

4 **The absence of a tradition of strong, left-wing trade unionism.** Trade unionism has never been particularly attractive to many Americans, and unions have consequently never gained great influence. Those that did develop rarely based their ideas on socialism as a means of overthrowing the established economic order, and inclined to individualist rather than collectivist ideas. Any attempts to foment industrial strife by militant, left-wing trade unionists have met a hostile response. Such groups have sometimes been banned or in other ways actively discouraged.

The two main parties, the Democrats and the Republicans

Policy attitudes: similarities and differences between the Democrats and the Republicans

To non-Americans, the policy differences between the two main parties may seem modest, if at times almost non-existent. Lord Bryce[9] once suggested that they were 'two bottles, each having a label denoting the kind of liquor it contains, but each being empty'. The parties have certainly often seemed to have much in common in their policy attitudes.

Areas of agreement

The rhetoric of politicians in both parties suggests greater dissimilarity than actually exists. They wish to emphasise the differences and thereby clarify the choice for the voters, but if one looks beyond the speeches and the party literature and examines the record of the parties when they have won the presidency in recent years, then often there has been a broad acceptance of much that has been accomplished by their opponents.

Both parties agree about far more things than they disagree about. Both attach great importance to the Constitution and are committed to maintaining America's present form of government. Both accept the pioneering American values of free enterprise and individualism, on which there is little discord in society. Neither favours root-and-branch change in the economic system. There is certainly no deep ideological divide, and in particular no contest between socialism in its various Western European forms and those who oppose it.

Each party's candidates always closely resemble the others and few contests between them ever present the electorate with a clear-cut choice. Many years ago, one commentator, D. W. Brogan, observed[10] that: 'The fact that all Republicans claim to be democrats and all Democrats to be republicans makes the confusion of party names nearly complete'. Both parties recognise the need to appeal to a wide spectrum of groups and interests, and this generally keeps them near to the political centre; they have tended to offer a broad range of rather similar programmes. It is rarely the case for one party ever to be wholly united against the other. This is particularly true when the two parties are in a broadly consensual mould, less so when, as in the early Reagan years, one party veers off on a more distinctive ideological route.

Even when differences are more discernible, it is important to realise that the differences within parties can be more significant than those between them. A Massachusetts Democrat such as Edward Kennedy may be a very different political animal from a colleague from Arkansas or the Deep South, as is often an east-coast Republican from one out in the Midwest. However, there are differences of emphasis and style, degree and method, and distinct bases of support. It is to the differences which we now turn.

Party differences (see also pp. 219–20 and 223) for a listing of party policies in the 2000 election)

Each party has its own character and image. A 'typical Democrat' might be a member of an ethnic minority, belong to a trade union and the working class, non-Protestant and an urban dweller. He or she would support measures of social welfare to assist the poor and needy, favour regulation of big business and a fairer distribution of wealth and support the global role of America as leader of the free world. A 'typical Republican' might be white, male, middle class, college-educated and Protestant. He would support law and order, believe in limited government and individualism, support big business and free enterprise, be wary of American involvement overseas and see himself as a conservative.

Yet this is too simplistic, as generalisations invariably are. The Democrats have supporters who are white and black, working class and middle class, urban and rural dwellers, combining as they do workers in the northern industrial cities and more wealthy farmers in the West. The Republicans have within their ranks business, professional and working people, many who are small-town religious fundamentalists and some who are city agnostics, many who support curbs on abortion, others who believe in free choice.

If we look at specific issues, there tend to be divergent positions on such contentious matters as:
- abortion;
- civil rights for blacks and other disadvantaged groups;
- affirmative action;
- the role of the federal government in education;
- anti-poverty policies and welfare reform;
- the provision of medical care;
- the problems of urban renewal;
- defence spending and the role of America in the post-Cold-War era.

One way of distinguishing the parties has in the past been to categorise them as 'liberal' or 'conservative' in tone and outlook, depending on how they view such controversies. Since 1932 the Democrats have generally taken a liberal position, whereas the Republicans have adopted a more conservative stance. The distinction is not always an effective one, for as we can see from the discussion on p. 217 the 'l' word is one that has gone out of fashion in American politics. In recent years, the centre of gravity has moved well to the right. Nevertheless, for a long while after 1932 the division had some validity and there are some party supporters who remain proud to be a liberal or conservative.

Examples of the likely beliefs of liberals and conservatives

Policy: economic/social	Liberals	Conservatives
Role of government	Important as regulator in public interest	Distrust, preference for free-market solutions
Spending	Spend more on disadvantaged	Keep spending down
Taxes	Tax the rich more	Keep taxes down
Abortion	Emphasise freedom of choice	Support right to life
Affirmative action	In favour	Wary, wish to make inroads
Crime	Look for causes of crime, respect rights of accused	Be tough on criminals, stress rights of victims
School prayer	Opposed	In favour

American liberalism

Classical liberalism emphasised liberty and individual rights, and a minimal role for state intervention. But by the twentieth century, liberalism became associated with protecting the individual by a regulatory action. Today's liberals see government as having a positive role to promote greater justice in society and more equality of opportunity. They talk of individual rights, including the right to own private property, but they also see a need for measures to control the defects of a market economy. Most accept that inequalities of wealth are inevitable and even desirable, but they wish to ensure that everyone has a certain minimum level of wealth, so that they can enjoy life and have a fair deal.

Franklin Roosevelt was the model for American liberals with his attempt to steer America out of the depression, via the New Deal. The problems of the twenty-first century are different, for the country operates in a more prosperous climate, but there are still those who are left behind. Modern liberals want to provide better education and housing, are alarmed by inadequate and costly health care, and support progressive taxation graduated according to the individual's ability to pay. They are committed to civil rights and affirmative action to overcome the effects of past discrimination against minorities and women; many activists involved in areas ranging from women's liberation and the pro-abortion campaign to the gay and the disabled movements come within the liberal fold. These are all examples of the positive use of government to improve society and remove its defects.

Neo-liberalism and the passing of Rooseveltian liberalism

In the last few years there has been talk of neo-liberals, who are willing to argue the case for traditional liberal beliefs of justice and liberty, and the need for government intervention, but who do not endorse the whole liberal agenda. Neo-liberals are more suspicious of union power, welfare provision and big government with its large, Washington-based bureaucracies. Some also doubt the increasing concern for minority causes. In the words of Irving Kristol,[11] a leading proponent of the idea, they are 'liberals mugged by reality'.

The growth of neo-liberalism reflects the fact that liberalism has rather gone out of fashion, and even those who believe in it are aware of its allegedly adverse effects. Critics, mainly Republicans and southern Democrats, have portrayed liberalism as being too concerned with federal action by the government, with costly programmes which require huge bureaucracies to run them, and with penal taxation which hits the voter in his pocket and tends to destroy his incentive for individual effort. Welfare is seen as damaging to the qualities which made America what it is; it undermines the work ethic and the entrepreneurial spirit. Neo-liberalism has more in common with classical liberalism – *laissez-faire*, the minimal state and a strong commitment to economic freedom which is interpreted in a different way from what FDR meant by the term.

In 1992 Clinton was concerned to show himself as a new type of Democrat. In the more conservative climate of that decade, he and others were anxious to show that they too believed in the virtues of free enterprise, the perils of communism, the need for tough action against criminals, strong defence and a new emphasis upon traditional patriotism. 'Liberalism' has increasingly became a term of abuse used by those on the political right

Liberalism still has its advocates and at a time when politicians are reluctant to use the word there have been academics and journalists who see merit in what it stands for. Thus Arthur Schlesinger could write an article entitled 'Hurray for the L-Word', in which he claimed:[12]

> The presidents we admire and celebrate most – Jefferson, Jackson, Lincoln, Theodore Roosevelt, Wilson, FDR, Harry Truman and JFK – were all, in the context of their times, vigorous and unashamed liberals. They were all pioneers of new frontiers, seeking out the ways of the future, meeting new problems with new remedies, carrying the message of constructive change in a world that never stops changing. From the start of the Republic, liberalism has always blazed the trail into the future – and conservatism has always deployed all the weapons of caricature and calumny and irrelevance to conceal the historic conservative objective of unchecked rule by those who already have far more than their fair share of the nation's treasure.

The Democrats

Rossiter[13] was right in suggesting that a usual characteristic of Democratic rule has been a willingness to embrace change. The party accepts innovation, and has since the days of Woodrow Wilson been more willing to extend governmental intervention and welfare programmes. The very names given by presidential contenders for their party platform suggests an acceptance of the need to embrace innovation and move forward with the task of reform. Woodrow Wilson offered the 'New Freedom', Franklin Roosevelt the 'New Deal', Harry Truman the 'Fair Deal', John Kennedy the 'New Frontiers', Lyndon Johnson the 'Great Society', and Bill Clinton the 'New Covenant'.

Since the New Deal, the Democrats have been the party associated with more positive government action to promote social welfare and regulate business activity. They were seen as standing for some redistribution of income, the extension of welfare measures and increased governmental expenditure. Yet in the last decade or so, Democrats have gone some way to shed this image. Bill Clinton's programme in 1992 sounded a far cry from the more liberal ones of some of his party predecessors. It was notably more cautious than the platform adopted by Kennedy and Johnson.

Clinton attempted to blend features of the liberal tradition of positive government with elements of the traditional Republican programme such as controlling the budget deficit. He knew that Americans were growing weary of the problems posed by the urban centres, with such things as the breakdown of law and order, the preoccupation with civil rights and the use of affirmative action. Their anxieties about particular programmes combined with a feeling that government was growing 'too big'. They disliked the spiralling cost of welfare and other public spending, and warmed to promises to 'get Washington off their backs' and of lower taxes. In his New Covenant programme, Clinton was responding to profound changes in American attitudes.

Within the present Democratic Party, Nicol Rae has distinguished[14] several groupings:
1 The **New Left** is the most liberal faction and it represents the minorities who inhabit the party. It supports interventionist policies to help the disadvantaged – blacks, Latinos, gays and the disabled. It is generally pacific in its approach to foreign policy, and its attitudes are popular on university campuses. Rev. Jesse Jackson belongs in this camp.
2 **Neo-liberals** broke away from the New Left and therefore share the same ancestry. Supporters stress competence rather than traditional 'tax-and-spend' policies, and are generally sympathetic to civil liberties and minority rights. Their approach appeals to professional suburbanites.
3 **Regulars** represent the mainstream party tradition, with its emphasis on governmental intervention in economic and welfare matters; they also tend

to be more 'hawkish' on foreign policy. 'Regular' attitudes are more appealing to labour (unions) and to Catholics.

4 **Southerners** such as Bill Clinton and Al Gore tend to take a more conservative stance on a range of issues. They are less enthusiastic about government intervention and labour, pro-free-market in economics and tend to take a robust stance in foreign policy. Traditional liberal nostrums have little appeal, but on civil rights they are more sympathetic than Southern Democrats of the past; they rely heavily on black votes. They appeal otherwise to the white working class and rural voters. After the 1984 defeat, the **Democratic Leadership Council (DLC)** was formed, largely by Southern Democrats. It seeks to organise and co-ordinate the more centrist elements within the Democratic coalition. It serves as a forum for debate on policy, and has a Washington 'think tank' – the Progressive Policy Unit (PPU) – and a magazine, the *New Democrat*.

The platforms of Democrat parties in 2000

Main priorities as listed

Oregon:
- government is not the enemy, but a partner in bettering ourselves and our communities;
- the accessibility of excellent public education;
- the rights of workers to organise, bargain collectively and strike if necessary, as well as to earn sufficient wages to support their families;
- public safety, as part of a criminal justice system which protects the rights of victims and the accused; preventing crime;
- affordable, comprehensive and confidential health care;
- environmental programme to manage resources and provide for a sustainable economy;
- human rights and justice, enforcing anti-discrimination legislation and honouring Indian treaty rights.

Texas:
- equal opportunity for all citizens;
- rewards for honest, hard work, involving a living wage and a tax system that is fair;
- values that support and strengthen families;
- quality public education that gives all citizens the opportunity to reach their potential;
- freedom from government interference in private lives and personal decisions;
- separation of the Church and State to preserve the freedom to pursue beliefs;
- the strengths inherent in a diverse population;

- security in our homes and safety on our streets; criminals should face swift and certain punishment;
- the moral, economic, diplomatic and military strength of the United States.

The Republicans

Republicans have traditionally been more cautious than the Democrats in their approach. Sometimes they have been deeply conservative, their pro-business, pro-free-enterprise tendencies gaining the upper hand. At other times, in the years of the New Deal and after, party spokesman often sounded less hostile to government intervention, recognising the popularity of many Democratic initiatives. But there was always a general unease about the direction in which their opponents had taken the country. Many Republicans were lukewarm about the expanding role of the federal government in economic and social matters. These anxieties have developed since the 1980s, and the modern party wishes to curb the size and scale of governmental activity. It is more interested in economy in government, and the pursuit of the low taxation which reduced expenditure allows.

Some common Republican attitudes

- **Family** – support for conventional and God-fearing families.

- **Organised labour** – tendency to dislike union activity and resistance to the idea of industrial action.

- **Minorities** – many of its members are descendants of earlier settlers and pioneers (White, Anglo-Saxon Protestants: WASPs) and are suspicious of newer arrivals and of the countries from which they arrived.

- **Foreign policy** – members are often among the sharpest critics of active involvement overseas. Some are deeply isolationist, and even the east-coast establishment tends to be concerned about the scale of commitment made to Western Europe and the use of American troops abroad. There is a strong emphasis upon 'Americanism' and patriotic goals, involving protecting America's status in the world.

The New Right

In the 1980s, traditional conservatism – as described – increasingly gave way to a new variety of ultra-conservatism, its adherents often known collectively as the New or Radical Right. Ronald Reagan said that 'government is the problem'. True to this spirit, the Reagan years saw an emphasis upon the market economy, a relaxation of anti-business controls, hostility to organised trade unionism and low taxation. In as much as government was accepted as necessary, there was a move towards local or state governmental action over that of the federal government. Reagan's approach appealed to many conservatives in America.

Members of the New Right shared much of the ground occupied by other conservatives, but they became associated with particular causes which they wished to see become accepted as public policy. They sought to achieve their programme via greater representation in Congress, and in November 1994 the *Contract with America* was based upon the New Right's philosophical approach.

The New Right wrapped itself in the symbols of nationalism and patriotism, and supporters took a strong stand in favour of business, the death penalty and school prayer, issues which struck a chord with many voters. Today, it has a more distinctive social agenda than other conservative forbears, and its restrictive policies include strict control over abortion, drugs and pornography. It dislikes affirmative action and forced busing, and is lukewarm in its support for any legislation to advance civil rights.

This platform owes much to the outlook of the so-called 'Moral Majority', for the influence of Christian fundamentalists (often known as the Religious Right) is fast-growing in the United States. Its supporters have been successful at the local level in building a powerful base, and within the Republican Party their position is a strong one. They hold that religious values are the cement which holds the fabric of society together. They are therefore especially concerned with what is taught in schools for this will influence the attitudes and behaviour of coming generations.

The rise and continued rise of the Religious Right

Members of the Religious Right (also known as the Christian Coalition) are concerned to take the American nation back to its true heritage, and they believe that to do so they must restore the godly principles which made the nation great. The telegenic Pat Robertson is a leading spokesman who, via his daily talk show, the *700 Club* – a mixture of faith-healing, hymns and Christian-oriented news – informs his listeners that in the outlook of 'liberals' it is wrong to ridicule Hispanics, blacks, the disabled, women, the gays and lesbians, but it is 'open season' to ridicule and humiliate, denigrate and insult the Christians 'as it was with the Jews in Nazi Germany'. He portrays the women's movement as a 'socialist, anti-family, political movement that encourages women to leave their husbands, kill their children, practise witchcraft and become lesbians'. He thunders that: 'God does not want us to turn America over to radical feminists, militant homosexuals, profligate spenders, humanists or world communists'.

Since a loss of influence in the late 1980s, the Religious Right has rethought its strategy. Its approach has become more sophisticated. It is based on building up grassroots support, by involving people at the local level on the city council and the school board – as well aiming for the more obvious congressional targets. Evangelical Christians have directly involved themselves in the political process. They are encouraged to participate in Sunday evening sermons, with the advice usually pointing to the Republicans as the appropriate party for godly Christians to support. Support is made easy, for members of the congregation are often given sample ballot papers showing how and where to mark support for the required candidates.

Once in local office, Christian representatives on school boards seek to eliminate 'irreligious' material, particularly books which mention alternative lifestyles and such things as abortion or witchcraft: for example, Roald Dahl's *The Witches* has been banned from school library shelves by some boards. Teachers have been told that they should teach 'creation science' (the story of the world's creation as told in *Genesis*) as well as – or in some cases instead of – Darwinian theories of evolution. The Bible is seen as literally true and to be regarded as the prime resource of learning. Other books which do not meet the necessary criteria include works by Martin Luther King, C. S. Lewis, Rudyard Kipling and A. A. Milne. There are now some 2250 school boards in the United States, and the Religious Right reckons to control 15 per cent of them.

Among Republicans there is a schism, for more traditional party regulars fear a take-over of the party. The Christian Coalition is similarly contemptuous of what it portrays as 'country-club' Republicans of the old type, who somewhere along the way lost their conservative agenda and became 'me-tooists', too close to the Democrats. Its policies have much appeal in middle America, which has over the last generation had to come to grips with the sexual revolution and the rise of left-wing radical activism, and doesn't like what it sees. Members wish to stress pro-life policies, and take a firm line on issues such as capital punishment. Some even talk enthusiastically of a wish to export convicts to Mexico, which is prepared to take them for a price and incarcerate them more cheaply.

Among other Christian Coalition policies are:
- the abolition of federal endorsement for the arts;
- the elimination of the federal and state departments of education;
- a cap on spending on AIDS research and treatment;
- compulsory reporting of AIDS carriers;
- the mandatory teaching of creationism;
- the abolition of abortion;
- the restriction on pre-school education;
- the rejection of gun control.

The Religious Right has been in retreat since the failure of the Clinton Impeachment trial, which its supporters strongly backed. But it remains a potent electoral force on the American political scene.

Nicole Rae[15] has identified several key elements within the modern Republican Party:

1 **Economic conservatives**, who favour competition and free markets. On economic issues, they align with the Libertarian Right.
2 **The Libertarian Right**, which promotes a free market economy but criticises the growth of the role of government not just in economic, but in other aspects of life. Members stress the freedom of the individual, and see government as a threat to liberty.
3 **The Christian Right**, which represents the hopes, fears and prejudices of 'ordinary' white families from small-town or suburban America. Its supporters are distinguished by their moral fervour. Although they are broadly conservative in their outlook, they do not always see eye-to-eye with economic conservatives.

The platforms of Republican parties in 2000

Main priorities as listed

Arkansas:
- importance of respect for religion and a strong faith in God;
- no undue government intervention; more scope for individuals and families;
- making the state better serve the people;
- governments to pursue only those policies which encourage individual initiative and responsibility for economic, political and social well-being;
- basic functions of government are protection of life, liberty and property, and equal justice under the law;
- power to be exercised at the lowest possible level;
- freedom is inseparable from responsibilities to serve and participate in the life of the community, and work for preservation of our freedom.

Minnesota:
- cutting taxes and public spending;
- tackling crime;
- raising educational standards;
- family security and protecting life;
- property rights;
- government reform and ethics;
- health and welfare reform.

The voters and the parties: their perceptions

Ever since the New Deal, those with low incomes – particularly the urban working class, including the blacks and other racial minorities – have leaned strongly to the Democrats. More affluent suburban votes have traditionally been keen supporters of the Republicans, other than a liberal element in the middle class.

The voters seem to know how to tell the parties apart, and most Americans are quite capable of identifying particular attitudes and approaches within the two parties which are seen as standing for something distinctive. Most of the business and professional people, and large farmers, judge that the Republican party best serves their interests, while workers tend to look to the Democrats as being more helpful to them, 'the party of the little man'. This characterisation owes much to the New Deal, and the subsequent programmes of leading Democrats such as Truman, Kennedy and Johnson. Such an easy division into working and middle class is less clear-cut than it once was, and the union-oriented bias of the Democrats has become less apparent than in former years. But polls suggest that the instincts of many voters about the two main parties have not significantly changed.

The Republicans are widely seen as the party which does not wish to expand the role of government, especially in Washington. They are viewed as being more lukewarm about innovations whereas Democrats tend to see positive action as necessary to promote social welfare and control the worst operation of big business. Their opponents would call this traditional 'tax and spend' Democrat thinking.

The roll of interest groups that are broadly supportive of the main parties also tells us something about their respective leanings. Republicans have long been more associated with the American Farm Bureau Federation, the National Association of Manufacturers, and the American Medical Association (AMA). The Democrats are preferred by many members of the National Farmers Union (NFU), the American Federation of Labor and Congress of Industrial Organisations (AFL/CIO), and the American Political Science Association.

Party organisation

Mass organisation developed soon after the Constitution was designed and was underway in the 1790s. Since then, the grassroots has always been a significant source of power. Whereas in Britain the party headquarters has substantial control over the local party, in America it is the other way round. Indeed, at a national level, parties only come together four-yearly to bring about the election of the presidential candidate.

American parties are then, for most of the four-year cycle, loose alliances of state and local parties, and this **decentralisation** reflects the federal nature of the system of government. Indeed, parties are more decentralised than the system of government, which is why Malcolm Shaw[16] described the party system as 'confederal'.

> **decentralisation**
> Decision-making power is dispersed to local branches of the party organisation, so that the party is regulated at the state/local level rather than the national level.

There are so many offices for election in the United States at state and county level, and even lower, that the local party workers have many aspects on which to concentrate their attention. Their concern with Washington seems a far cry from this local preoccupation.

In the more centralised British system of party organisation, agents have a role at the constituency, regional and national level, all of them being trained in and supervised from London. In the US there is no comparable system. Local parties in America are not watched over in the same way. They have a free hand to choose the candidates of their choice, without any referral to headquarters. There is no list of 'approved' candidates provided from the centre, and it is highly unusual for there to be any attempt at influence or interference. The decision rests with the local party, though the system of primaries and the limitations on funding mean that the individual plays a substantial role in securing his or her own election.

The national role of parties is relatively small. Every four years, Democratic and Republican headquarters come to life; in between they contract. They do not have the powers to control local or state bodies, issue binding policy positions or censure members of elected representatives who stray from official party policy.

The national and local structure of the two main parties

Generalisation about the organisation of the two main parties is difficult, for the situation undergoes periodic change. For instance, the balance of power between minority activists and traditional party power brokers is liable to fluctuate. Similarly, because the party system is decentralised and the state parties can go their own way, the structural pattern is not identical throughout the nation. Nevertheless, it is broadly similar, even if it can vary in details from state to state.

The key functions of parties are concerned with choosing candidates for office, perhaps via the organisation of primaries, and especially with mobilising support behind the person who is chosen. Each tier of the party structure is therefore primarily concerned with elections in its own geographical area and is largely autonomous.

The Republican and Democratic National Committees (RNCs and DNCs) are the main national organisation in each party. The headquarters in Washington DC operates under the direction of the party's National Chairman, and is run day-to-day by a small paid office staff plus volunteers. Their job is to prevent the national party organisation fading away completely between presidential elections. Members meet a few times a year, survey the political scene and make pronouncements. The committees do some research work, produce occasional publications for party activists and are involved in raising money. But their main work is to clear up the finances of the party after the presidential election and plan for the next Convention four years hence, choosing the location and making organisational arrangements.

The National Convention in each party is held four yearly. Conventions are the arenas in which key players in the party seek to shape the future direction of their policy, and – if they are successful in capturing the presidency – of the nation as well. Their main task is to choose the presidential candidate. Effectively, candidates have usually already been chosen, having built up sufficient Convention votes via the primaries and party caucuses (held in states where there are no primaries). However, if there was to be any uncertainty, this is where the choice would be resolved. A vice-presidential candidate is also chosen, and a platform on policy agreed. The Convention then serves as the launching-pad for the bid to win the ultimate prize, the presidency itself.

Traditionally, the essential business at a Republican gathering was done behind closed doors whereas the Democrats have been more open about their dealings and more willing to have rows in public. Things have changed in recent decades. In 1976 the Reagan supporters staged a challenge to the incumbent Gerald Ford on the Convention floor and twelve years later the proceedings were again lively and acrimonious as six challengers pleaded for the nomination

At the state and local levels, organisation is carried out on the same lines. Each state has a state committee, headed by a state chair. Below state level, there are county committees, with varying functions and powers. At all levels, it is the choice and election of candidates for local office which is the key task. For winnable vacancies, there may be a primary contest. Where success is unlikely, it may be more a question of finding a candidate who will allow his or her name to go forward.

Recent trends

Traditionally, American parties have been decentralised coalitions of state and local parties, with a very limited role for the national organisations.

However, since the 1960s, there have been a number of contradictory trends in the development of parties. In general, there has been a weakening of their role in selecting candidates, making policy, raising funds, informing the voter and channelling the demands of groups in society. But at the same time, via party reforms, there has been a strengthening of national party organisations especially regarding the selection of delegates to the party Conventions.

The reforms in party organisations originally stemmed from a desire, especially among elements in the Democratic Party to reduce the power of party regulars from the states and increase participation by the voters in the process of choosing a Presidential candidate. The Democrats introduced changes along these lines in the early 1970s and the Republicans also tried to encourage participation by minority groups and ease access to selection meetings. These reforms strengthened the role of the national organisations, but two other developments weakened the power of national parties:

1 The increase in the number of presidential primaries which led to the growth of more candidate-oriented campaigns.
2 A change in the type of people who participated in the nomination of presidential candidates. Party leaders at state and local levels have less weight and the role of minority groups has increased.

The theses of party decline and of continued party vitality

The thesis of decline, as developed by several commentators, suggested that the two main parties had been overwhelmed by the range of challenges which confronted them; they were unable to adapt to the changing political environment. D. Broder, writing in 1972,[17] contended that national parties were in retreat in areas they had traditionally dominated, particularly in their most basic function, selecting and running candidates for public office. There was widespread agreement that parties, always weak, were in a seemingly irreversible cycle of decline, unable to respond effectively to changing circumstances.

Since 1980, this sombre view has been questioned. J. Bibby wrote on *Party Renewal in the Republican Party*[18] and A. J. Reichley on *The Rise of National Parties*.[19] They claimed that the evidence presented in the 1960s had been largely misinterpreted and that (certainly by the 1980s) parties had begun to adapt successfully. They saw evidence of party vitality, indeed of 'renewal'.

From this side of the Atlantic, Christopher Bailey[20] saw the 'most clear evidence of the continued vitality of the political parties ... in the Republican Party', but felt that by the mid-eighties the Democrats were also 'showing signs of continued vitality'. He quoted various commentators who believed that Parliamentary Action Committees (PACs), often seen as having 'rendered the parties obsolete', actually supplemented rather than challenged the work of parties; indeed, they 'often follow the party's lead when deciding which candidates to support. Moreover, many PACs have aligned themselves with either the Democratic Party or the Republican Party because of shared beliefs and values'.

There has been a modest resurgence of parties in recent years. They have shown that they can perform a useful, if limited, role. Partly, this has come about because the new issues of the 1960s and 1970s have lost some of their importance, but it is mainly connected with the new emphasis on strengthening party organisation at the federal level and reviving the party role in fund-raising. The Democrats weakened the power of party regulars and allowed minority activists a greater voice in party affairs. After the Watergate scandal, the Republicans too saw the need to clean up the party and make its organisation more professional and more appealing. Both parties have developed new techniques of fund-raising which make them useful and enable them to play once more a significant role in election campaigning. Candidates challenging for office have been keen to seek help from the increasingly more professional party associations, which can provide them with personal training, information networks, news clippings and research on their opponents, expertise in targeting particular precincts, as well as some financial help.

As Bailey has indicated, 'it is clear that attempts to characterise the developments of the last two decades are extremely problematic'. Because of the fact that different writers draw upon different evidence – or interpret the same evidence in a different manner – some portray a picture of party decline, others one of renewal.

Writing at the end of the 1980s, Paul Hernnson[21] developed a different model, stressing the 'primacy of the individual candidate in campaigning, and seeing parties as support agencies for candidate-centred campaign organisations'. Rather than parties running candidates for office, candidates run for office and seek to attract the resources of parties and other bodies for their own use. It is still 'easier for most candidates to obtain [resources] from the parties than from alternative sources'.

Party weakness and decline: a summary

American political parties are essentially weak and always have been, especially by comparison with parties in many other democracies.

Reasons for the historic weakness of parties include:
- The federal system places emphasis on the role of state rather than national parties.
- The concept of the Separation of Powers encourages members of a party in Congress to question even a President of his or her own party.
- The notion of broad consensus in American politics covers a range of fundamental issues.
- The ethos of individualism in American society is a feature of the widely shared American Dream.

Parties became weaker in the twentieth century because of:
- The growth of the system of primary elections made candidates less beholden to the parties.
- The development of the mass media led to more candidate-oriented electioneering.
- The 'new issues' which arrived on the political agenda often crossed party lines – e.g. feminism and environmentalism.
- The increasing importance of pressure groups and Political Action Committees (PACs) provided a new basis of support for candidates.

Parties enjoyed some resurgence in the late twentieth century because:
- Some of the new issues went off the agenda.
- PACs and groups began to work with parties, rather than as a replacement for them.
- Internal party reforms were carried out in the 1970s and thereafter.
- Parties have adapted to the role of working with and supporting candidates and been in the forefront of adopting new electioneering techniques.

Today, most people still think of politics in terms of the Democrat–Republican divide, and Congressmen are almost entirely elected according to their party label. Parties do matter, both for politicians and the electorate.

From a British perspective, it is easy to overstate the importance of parties at national level, and stress too much their decline or renewal. Commentators and academics on this side of the Atlantic sometimes place the emphasis on the national parties, especially their role in the nomination of presidential candidates, the most interesting and glamorous aspect of the process. But this is not the main arena for party activists and, as Alan Ware[23] has noted, 'in the federal structure it has always been at the local and state levels of politics that the parties have … had their main bases of power; contests for the presidency are merely the smallest but most highly visible apex of party politics'.

PARTIES IN BRITAIN AND THE UNITED STATES: A COMPARISON

In both democracies, parties fulfil some similar functions, notably clarifying the issues, stimulating public interest, supporting (in Britain choosing) candidates, organising the voters and providing an institutional framework for legislators. However, there are basic differences in the way in which parties operate in Britain and the United States.

Britain has party government. Under usual circumstances, a party wins an election and afterwards is in control of both the executive and the legislature. Having had its programme accepted by the electorate, it is expected to govern. To do so, it requires cohesive and disciplined parties if it is to act effectively. By contrast, America does not have party government in the same sense. Party allegiance is one factor born, in mind when decisions are made about public policy, but there is no similar expectation that the 'party line' will be followed. Often, key figures in American government are admired precisely because they do not adopt the party stance on issues of the day. Parties are less disciplined, although in Congress it is true that almost without exception members are identified as belonging to one of the two main parties.

The reasons for these differences have much to do with the American Constitution, which was designed to disperse power in two ways. Firstly, the Founding Fathers established a federal system across the country and secondly they were keen to create competitive institutions (the Separation of Powers). Both have the effect of making party government difficult and as we have seen do much to undermine tight discipline.

There are some similarities between the two systems. Both are often described as two-party systems, there being two main parties. Several small parties exist on either side of the Atlantic, but the electoral system ensures that in most situations they are unlikely to make a significant impact on the outcome of elections; there are formidable hurdles for them to overcome. There are difficulties with labelling the American system as a two-party system (see pp. 203–5), and in Britain the presence of a sizeable third party as well as nationalist parties in Scotland and Wales leads some commentators to talk not of a two-party system, but three- or four-party politics.

Policy attitudes

Of the two main British parties, one has traditionally been viewed as a socialist party whereas in America socialism has failed to take root. But in this respect, the two countries

CONCLUSION

Political parties provide an important link between the voters and their elected representatives. In the US, a two-party system has evolved, dominated by the Democrats and the Republicans. Other parties have been unable to make much

have moved closer. New Labour is not usually described as 'socialist' in any meaningful sense, other than by traditional party backers who cling to the party's past ethos. It has also gone some way to detach itself from the unions, making it more akin in style to the American Democrats. Significantly, both Bill Clinton (New Democrat) and Tony Blair (New Labour) have advocated similar 'third way' politics, shunning the old 'big government' and 'tax and spend' attitudes of bygone years and instead being willing to use the power of government yet also encourage personal responsibility.

Both countries have 'left' and 'right', progressive and conservative, parties. Labour and the Democrats are more willing to accept governmental intervention and expand social welfare; the Conservatives and the Republicans are attracted by less government and lower taxes. As we have seen, Labour has moved nearer to the Democrats than in the past, and both parties have had to accept that the centre of gravity in the political system moved to the right in the Thatcher–Reagan-dominated 1980s, and respond to this.

In the 1950s–1970s, party differences in both countries often seemed to be more concerned with degree, emphasis and timing. The Conservatives and the Republicans then tended towards consensual, 'me-tooist' policies. Both became more ideological in the 1980s, putting forward distinctive and highly partisan programmes of the type which their traditional supporters liked to see. In the 1990s and beyond, there has been less public appetite for overtly right-wing solutions. Divisions have been evident between those representatives who wish to pursue the preferences of party supporters and those who emphasise the need for a broad appeal to the wider electorate.

Organisation matters

British parties are not only more disciplined than American ones; they are also more centralised. Americans developed mass party organisations before Britain, partly because universal male franchise was introduced sooner than in this country. Grassroots organisation has long been well established and significant in the US and this – and the lack of strong leadership from Washington – makes for decentralisation. American state and local parties come together every four years to elect their president. At that time, the national headquarters plays an important role in electioneering, but in between presidential contests, its role is more modest. By contrast, British constituencies tend to be dominated by the party leadership and the controlling influence of central party headquarters.

headway, even if some have been on the political scene a long while. Many voters no longer feel the same loyalty towards the two parties which their parents and grandparents did and neither party can count on a permanent body of supporters. But most Americans still think in terms of the Democrat–Republican divide and are able to detect some difference between them. Parties remain important to candidates and office-holders, as well as to the voters.

Parties are essential in any democracy. They fulfil important functions such as organising the competition for public offices, simplifying the policy choices available and helping to translate those choices – once made – into effective action. They may often be written off as being in decline, if not dead. But in many ways, they exhibit signs of renewed vitality.

REFERENCES

1 V. O. Key, *Politics, Parties and Pressure Groups*, Crowel, 1964.
2 M. Vile, *Politics in the USA*, Hutchinson, 1978.
3 J. Burns *et al.*, *Government by the People*, Prentice-Hall, 1994.
4 V. O. Key, *Politics, Parties and Pressure Groups*, Crowell, 1964.
5 M. Duverger, *Political Parties*, Methuen, 1962.
6 M. Vile, *Politics in the USA*, Hutchingson, 1978.
7 C. Rossiter, *Parties and Politics in America*, Signet, 1960.
8 R. Hofstadter, *The Age of Reform: from Bryan to FDR*, Knopf, 1955.
9 Lord Bryce, *Modern Democracies*, Macmillan, 1921.
10 D. Brogan, *An Introduction to American Politics*, Hamish Hamilton, 1954.
11 I. Kristol, *Reflections of a Neoconservative*, Basic Books, 1983.
12 A. Schlesinger, *Cycles of American History*, Houghton Mifflin, 1986.
13 C. Rossiter, *Parties and Politics in America*, Signet, 1960.
14 T. Hames and N. Rae, *Governing America*, Manchester University Press, 1996.
15 T. Hames and N. Rae, *Governing America*, Manchester University Press, 1996.
16 M. Shaw, *Anglo-American Democracy*, Routledge and Kegan, 1968.
17 D. Broder, *The Party's Over*, Harper and Row, 1972.
18 J. Bibby, *Politics, Parties and Elections in America*, Wadsworth, 2000.
19 A Reichley, *The Life of the Parties: a History of American Political Parties*, Free Press, 1992.
20 C. Bailey, 'Political Parties', *Contemporary Record*, February 1990.
21 P. Hernnson, *Party Campaigning in the 1980s*, Harvard University Press, 1988.
22 A. Ware, 'Party Decline and Party Reform' in L. Robins (ed.) *The American Way*, Longman, 1985.

USEFUL WEB SITES

www.democrats.org Democratic National Committee. Details of many aspects of recent election campaign and party platform; issues of interest to the party.

www.rnc.org Republican National Committee. Details of many aspects of recent election campaign and party platform; issues of interest to the party.

Several third parties have interesting sites, explaining their histories and different policy positions:

www.lp.org Libertarian Party.

http://reformparty.org Reform Party.

www.greens.org Green Parties of North America.

www.dsausa.org Democratic Socialists of America.

http://ustaxpayers.org United States Taxpayers Party.

SAMPLE QUESTIONS

1 What are the distinctive features of American political parties?

2 In what sense does America have a two-party system?

3 Why are third parties unable to flourish in the US?

4 'Both American parties have a similar outlook on fundamental issues in American politics'. What are the main areas of agreement and disagreement in their ideologies and policies?

5 Assess the current state and prospects of either the Democratic or the Republican Party.

6 'Party decline' or 'party renewal'? Do parties still play an important part in American politics?

7 Compare the main British and American parties in respect of their ideas, sources of support and organisations.

Pressure groups: the lobby at work 9

In this chapter, we explore how individuals who share certain opinions come together to press their common outlook upon society and government. We have seen that this may be done via political parties. Here, we are concerned with the ways by which pressure groups lobby to propagate their views.

The leading groups are economic or occupational, but there is also a huge variety of civic, ethnic, ideological, racial and other bodies, which have memberships that cut across the large economic groupings. In recent decades, many of them have moved on from lobbying alone and have become far more involved and significant in the electoral process. Concern has been expressed about some of their activities, leading to calls for greater regulation and vigilance.

POINTS TO CONSIDER

➤ Which interests in American society are best represented by pressure groups?

➤ Does it matter that some sections of society are poorly represented?

➤ Should pressure groups be subjected to greater control?

➤ In what respects has the nature of group lobbying changed over recent decades?

➤ Is the influence of pressure groups generally benign or damaging to the workings of American democracy?

➤ Why is Congress more vulnerable to pressure group activity than the British Parliament?

The scale of lobbying

For many years, lobbyists have played a significant role in the legislative process, a role which has increased with the enlargement of governmental activity in the era since the New Deal. The term 'lobby' includes a vast array of groups, operating at several levels and covering commercial and industrial interests, labour unions, consumer associations, ethnic and racial groups. In the mid-1950s, the *Encyclopaedia of Associations* listed under 5000 of them; now it lists more than 20,000. Representation of companies in Washington has greatly increased, but more dramatic has been

> the explosion in the number of public-interest organisations and grassroots groups. These barely existed at all before the 1960s; today, they number in the tens of thousands and collect more than $4 billion per year from 40 million individuals.[1]

More than nine out of every ten Americans belong to at least one voluntary grouping, be it a church, civil rights organisation, social club of some kind or other public body. On average, Americans belong to four.

Under the **Legislative Reorganisation Act (1946)**, lobbyists were required to register with the relevant offices of the Senate and the House, and provide details of their work and funding. At that time, there were less than 2000 registered lobbyists with Congress, but in 2001 the number registered was approaching 9000. But this figure omits the vast array of individual corporations, state and local governments, universities, think tanks and other organisations in the private sector who engage in lobbying at some level, as well as the myriad of Washington representatives ranging from lawyers to public relations agencies which do similar work.

Organisations such as the Ford Motor Company not only belong to the appropriate interest group; they also maintain their own lobbying staff in Washington. Most other business corporations retain a sizeable lobby in the city, partly for reasons of prestige but also as a means of using any opportunity to influence laws and regulations. Similarly, labour unions and groups representing sections of society such as the elderly and causes such as the environment, maintain well-manned permanent offices. All wish to exert pressure at some level of government, many of them in Washington (either at the White House or on Capitol Hill). However, in recent years there has been a marked extension of lobbying activity within the states as well. The American political culture is tolerant of pressure group activity, and this encourages the creation of an array of organised interests. There are many access points for group representatives to explore. Because of their success, the average citizen looks as much to his voluntary groups for political satisfaction as to his elected representative.

Some relevant definitions

By the **lobby** we mean all those groups which seek to influence public policy, whether they are primarily promotional or propaganda bodies or those which seek to defend the interests of their group or organisation. The word 'lobby' originally derives from the location where the process occurred, the ante-room or lobby outside the chambers of Congress where representatives could be intercepted and urged to support a particular cause when they voted. Hotel lobbies have sometimes provided a similar venue, and lobbyists are those who wait there hoping for a chance meeting. To lobby is to seek to bring influence on legislators and officials. Lobbyists are therefore employees of associations who try to influence policy decisions, especially in the executive and legislative branches of government.

By **pressure groups** we mean associations of people who come together on the basis of shared attitudes to try to influence public policy. This may involve lobbying governmental institutions or their representatives or seeking to influence voters at election time. Such groups are different from political parties, which are also bodies that include within their membership people who share a broadly agreed approach to the conduct of affairs.

Pressure groups and political parties

Pressure groups are voluntary associations formed to advance or defend a common cause or interest. They are unlike political parties in that:
- they do not wish to assume responsibility for governing the country; rather, they seek to influence those who do so;
- they have a narrower range of concerns than parties which seek to draw together a variety of interests in order to broaden their appeal; pressure groups have a limited focus, many of their aspirations being non-political.

Because their concerns are liable to be affected by government decisions, they need to be organised in order to influence ministers and respond to what they propose.

Some writers dislike speaking of 'pressure groups', for the words may seem to imply the use of force rather than persuasion. American academics tend to use the term 'interest groups' instead. As we shall see, this label does not cover the whole range of associations with which we are concerned. Whichever term is used – and we will use the broader term pressure groups – there is a further distinction which can be made between **interest or protective groups** (e.g. the American Medical Association), which are primarily self-interested and seek to protect or defend the position of their members, and **promotional groups** (e.g. The American Civil Liberties Union (ACLU)) which are primarily concerned with propaganda.

The former category includes the most influential American associations which wield substantial economic power. The latter are usually less influential, promoting as they do some cause idea or issue not of direct benefit to themselves or to those who belong, but of general benefit to society. Promotional groups tend to be smaller than protective ones, and comprise dedicated people who commit themselves to what are sometimes minority concerns.

The distinction above is not adopted by all writers, some preferring to speak of the lobby, others just using the terms 'interest' or 'pressure groups', to cover every type of association involved in the process. Woll and Zimmerman,[2] employ the term 'interest groups' and defined interests as 'concerns, needs, benefits, or rights that groups or individuals have or would like to have'. The areas in which people have interests include, among other things, business, the workplace, education, the environment, health and religion. These interests are shared by a number of people who organise into groups to mobilise their common feelings. Hence, according to the two writers, interest groups are:

> Associations of persons who share common concerns, needs, benefits or rights and have as their purpose the satisfaction of claims to these. Usually, the claims are made on the government, and are met as a result of pressure.

Inevitably, there are some organisations which do not fit neatly into the division referred to. A number of them protect the interests of their members and also do a fair amount of promotional work which increases their acceptability to the community at large. One of the most prominent of these **hybrid** bodies is the **National Rifle Association (NRA)**. There are different motives for people who join together in this organisation. Some belong for reasons of commercial protection (they make or sell guns), and others for ideological or self-interested reasons (owners of guns who see it as their constitutional right to bear them or who simply feel that they are necessary).

Distinguishable from such groups, by whatever label we adopt, are **movements**. A movement is a wider and more all-embracing organisation, and it includes all those peoples and groups who are interested or involved in a particular cause. Movements often develop from local activity and become part of a larger national campaign – in the way that individual small groups of women in the United States took up particular concerns which then became national causes to which many more women were committed.

National Rifle Association (NRA)

The NRA is perhaps the best-known American pressure group. It has over three million members who are enthusiasts for shooting as both recreation and protection. It has successfully resisted most national attempts to limit the ownership of guns since the late 1960s, even though on occasion pressure for gun control has gained ground. At the turn of the twenty-first century, it has been paying more attention to state governments, for it is to that level that supporters of restriction have increasingly turned their attention. It is also seeking to widen its appeal, so that some of its recent propaganda has been targeted at minority groups and women.

Within the Women's Movement today, there are several groups which pursue their own distinctive agenda, whether it be peace, child welfare or low pay. They share some ideas and approaches, but may differ on controversial issues such as abortion, as well as over the tactics to adopt in seeking the fulfilment of their aims. The Civil Rights Movement for equal treatment for black Americans has similarly spanned several organisations, as do those on animal rights and the environment.

Categories of American pressure groups

It is convenient to classify the lobby into broad groups. This can be done either by opting for the protective/promotional typology, or by categorising organisations according to the sector they claim to represent. This is the approach we will adopt here.

Business groups

Business is the most effective area of group activity, because it has the advantages of expertise, organisation and resources. It includes organisations which speak up for small firms (e.g. the National Federation of Independent Business) and much larger bodies such as the National Association of Manufacturers, which represents large corporations. The Chamber of Commerce, with branches at state and local level, has a membership of more than 200,000 businesses. Such umbrella organisations have not tended to stress a Washington role, for their individual members often have representatives based in the capital. General Electric, Ford, General Motors and other industrial giants such as Union Carbide are well-represented in Washington. These corporations are so large and so vital in the American economy that politicians of all persuasions will listen to their concerns.

The business lobby is a powerful one though it would be wrong to assume that the large range of groups (about 20 per cent of all pressure groups) operate together as a powerful bargaining sector. 'Corporate America' is not a single entity with but one agreed objective. The interests of Amereia's fifteen million businesses diverge. In the 1980s, some leading manufacturers favoured high protective tariffs to fend off foreign competition. Others who operated more in the export market feared that such an approach would invite retaliation and damage their overseas prospects. Also, as we have seen, not all of these organisations focus on the same areas of decision-making. Some operate in Washington, others elsewhere; some favour one target, others another. Because of such considerations, umbrella or peak organisations have much less influence in the United States than does the Confederation of British Industry in Britain.

Labour groups

Unions have always been less prominent in American politics than in Britain and other European countries, for the US workforce is less unionised than in many democracies. Unions lack the clout of many large corporations and moreover they are numerically in decline, and suffer diminishing membership. They have more influence in the industrial areas such as the Northeast than in the South, which has traditionally been dominated by agrarian interests.

The largest umbrella body representing organised labour is the loose alliance known as the American Federation of Labour and the Congress of Industrial Organisations (AFL/CIO) to which 96 unions belong; it represents about 12 per cent of the workforce. In common with other union organisations, it lobbies government on workers' conditions and rights (e.g. the minimum wage and job security) and business/trade matters of concern to the workforce. Long-standing individual unions include the United Automobile Workers (UAW), the International Brotherhood of Teamsters (lorry drivers), the International Ladies Garment Workers Union (ILGWU) and the United Steelworkers of America.

Professional groups

Professional bodies cater for the needs of accountants, doctors, educators, lawyers, scientists and others, and those groups within this category often have no interests in common other than their status. They may, as with the doctors and the lawyers, sometimes come into conflict – as, for instance, in a case concerning medical malpractice. Among the foremost professional associations in Washington, the American Bar Association and the National Education Association have been notably influential, the former having a substantial voice in the selection of judges, the latter having forced education to the forefront of national debate – to such an extent that in 1988 George Bush promised to run as the 'education President'. Perhaps the most effective has been the American Medical Association, a federation of 50 state associations representing about two-thirds of the nation's doctors. In the early 1990s, it was much involved with other relevant interests in the struggle over the attempted reform of medical care. This led to a massive attempt to influence the thinking of Congressmen and the general public, in an attempt to tone down the nature of the Clinton proposals.

Agricultural groups

Historically, farm organisations were particularly influential for the agrarian community has been generously represented in the Senate and the House. This influence resulted in the passage of a number of emergency bills in the late 1970s. Much of the campaigning for these laws was conducted by the American Agriculture Movement, which often took a more militant line than the more conservative American Farm Bureau – whilst both often found themselves in disagreement with the NFU.

As the number of family farms declined (the owners having often gone into debt), so agribusinesses, vast farms owned by large corporations, developed in their place. The arrival of business people – familiar with different and more sophisticated techniques of lobbying – has helped to change the image of agriculture. Professional lobbyists are now commonly employed in this field.

Public interest groups

Public interest groups include those which are concerned with the quality of government, consumerism and the environment. Common Cause, 'a national citizens' lobby', has both Democrat and Republican members. It seeks to 'open up' the processes of government, by such means as electoral reform and strict control over the financing of election campaigns. The League of Women Voters is also keen to promote better government, through greater public involvement. There is less disagreement between the various organisations operative in this area than in some other sectors. All are seeking to achieve goals designed to benefit the entire population.

Public interest associations benefit from the fact that everyone is a consumer or is likely to benefit from good government. In other words, there is likely to be a fund of goodwill to many of the causes they take up, though the general public is difficult to organise for it is geographically spread and lacks immediate bargaining power and economic clout. In the run-up to an election, however, their campaigns win enhanced support from the political parties who are anxious to show that they are in touch with the concerns of ordinary people.

Ideological and single-issue groups

Within the ideological sector there is a wide divergence of viewpoints between far Left and far Right. However, members of the groups are likely to share a broad philosophy and outlook, whatever the diversity of their backgrounds. The sizeable and well-known American Civil Liberties Union has been known to defend the rights of the American Nazi Party, a body which it abhors and which would, given power, almost certainly destroy the ACLU. It sometimes co-operates closely with very different organisations such as the National Abortion Rights Action League which is determined to retain the right to abortion and stresses a woman's right to choose.

Such issue groups have mushroomed since the 1960s, and gain public attention by a variety of techniques – ranging from writing to Congressmen to taking action in the courts, from attending demonstrations to participating in other forms of direct action. Generally, they lack the funds available to large interest groups, and their influence often derives from their ability to show that they have the support of many voters.

How groups operate

Groups pursue their goals at various pressure points in the American system of government, partly depending on the objective to be achieved and on the location where relevant decisions are made. Any organisation wishes to concentrate its attention at the level where it can have the greatest influence.

The executive

Lobbying is a proven way of applying pressure on government, and most groups employ full-time persons to perform the task; others may hire a professional lobbyist, as is necessary to represent their interests. Lobbyists are 'persuaders' who inhabit the world of Washington or the states, and they understand the functioning of the political system and often have useful personal contacts. As the seat of the federal government, Washington is the focus of much of their activity. More than 4000 corporations are represented in the capital, and some 3000 associations have an office there.

Some lobbyists have been lawyers, others have moved from working for the Administration into lobbying. Lobbyists are highly skilled, and are selected because they are likely to be able to gain access where others cannot. Any lobbyist wishes to know the key personnel in the various agencies and bureaux of government, for more and more legislation derives from initiatives from within the executive branch. Interest groups have much to offer by way of specialist information, and the group lobbyist and members of the bureaucracy will often seek to develop a sound working relationship. Some writers refer to so-called 'iron triangles' to describe the networks of mutually self-supporting lobbyists, bureaucrats and members of congressional committees, where key decisions of government are made.

Americans speak of the 'revolving door' to describe the easy movement of personnel between the executive and the interest groups. Sometimes, the door – when opened – reveals a murky world of behind-the-scenes influence. In the Reagan–Bush years, there were many scandals involving doubtful ethical behaviour, and Woll and Zimmerman quote[3] as an example the way in which many of Reagan's appointees earned themselves a fortune as lobbyists in the HUD episode.: for calling up old friends at the Department of Housing and Urban Development and obtaining lucrative contracts for clients, they received millions of dollars.

The legislature

Congress is a key target for lobbyists, for the committees in the two chambers have responsibilities for certain subject areas. It is the committees which determine the nature of legislation or indeed prevent it from being passed, so that groups and lobbyists need to be familiar with the relevant Congressmen and the staff who serve them. They discuss legislation with individual Congressmen and provide evidence, written and oral, for committee hearings. Lobbyists are keen to develop close ties, inviting elected representatives to dinners and various entertainments. Abramson[4] has highlighted the bonds which bind together the two sides. Nearly a quarter of ex-representatives move over into lobbying, and members of their families are often similarly involved.

The dismantling of the old 'seniority system' in Congress in the 1970s increased the scope of the lobbyist; new committee chairmen are more vulnerable to group activity. Moreover, party discipline has always been weak. In recent years groups have found it the more easy to have an impact at a time when party labels have lost even more of their never-very-great meaning.

The courts

Some groups carry little weight with the executive or the legislature. When these avenues are closed, they may rely on the courts instead, and hope that they can use their knowledge of the law to gain a favourable interpretation in court rulings. Environmental groups have sometimes used litigation, as have other groups which lack a strong congressional base. One group which gained successes via this route was the National Association for the Advancement of Colored People (NAACP). By using the courts, it was able to bring about pressure for a change in the status of black Americans. In 1954, it won a particularly significant victory in a case which resulted in the judgement that segregation was inherently unequal, and therefore illegal (see p. 30).

Main targets for group activity: a summary

Tier of government	Executive	Legislature	Judiciary
Federal	President, Cabinet, civil servants	House of Representatives, Senate, congressional committees	Supreme Court, other federal courts
State	Governor, departmental heads, officials	Two houses of legislature, committees	State Supreme Court, Courts of Appeal
Local	Mayors, elected and non-elected officials	Councils, school boards, other local boards	Other state courts

Table adapted from 'Access Points' in Alan Grant, The American Political Process, Dartmouth, 1994.

The public

American groups have always placed great emphasis on the use of campaigns directed at the 'man in the street'. By mailing, by advertising, and especially through television, an attempt is made to influence opinion. Propaganda is often targeted towards certain groups such as the voters in a Congressman's home state – in the hope that the electorate will, in turn, pressure their representative to vote as the group wishes when he or she is in Washington. Congressmen are only too aware that their re-election could depend on keeping the electors happy.

Business organisations spend heavily on advertising, often using professional companies to organise a campaign. Many groups once employed indiscriminate mailing, based on names from the phone book. However, with the development of computers, mailing has become a more sophisticated technique, for letters can be personalised and directed at those likely to be sympathetic – members of environmentalist groups, for example.

Direct action

In pursuing their aims, some groups resort to direct action. The anti-abortion associations which are prepared to injure or – at worst – kill those who carry out abortions are but one example. Others are prepared to use less dramatic forms of protest, ranging from demonstrations and strikes to law-breaking in the form of withholding tax or rioting.

Direct action, an attempt to coerce those in authority into a change of viewpoint, can be very effective. It may be militant, but peaceful; sometimes, it may involve ignoring or breaking the criminal law and can easily spill over into violence. What has made its use more commonplace is that extreme behaviour can get publicity and command prime television exposure in news and current affairs programmes.

History confirms that direct action can be effective, and many great social changes have come about because of the willingness of some people to resist what they see as unjust laws. The NAACP engaged in a policy of passive resistance, and Martin Luther King and his followers were ready to break laws they felt to be immoral. This could involve deliberately seeking service at a restaurant which operated a colour bar, or riding on a 'whites only' bus. American blacks took more violent direct action in 1992, when riots broke out in Los Angeles; allegations of police racism provoked the black community into desperate action.

Groups and the electoral system

Pressure groups seek to influence the conduct of government not to assume responsibility for administering policy. They do not contest elections, but wish to influence their outcome. In particular, they may wish to see certain candidates elected and certain ideas advanced. This may involve publishing the voting records of sitting Congressmen in an attempt to show how suitably they fulfil the group's requirements.

The regulation of party funding in the 1971 Federal Election Campaign Act and the Campaign Act of 1974 spawned the growth of the Political Action Committees (PACs), the political arms of pressure groups. These can assist candidates in several ways – by providing research material and publicity, by raising election funds and by providing organisational backup to a candidate who lacks a strong personal political organisation or party machine. For a candidate lacking such party or organisational support and who lacks private funds, PACs can provide invaluable assistance (see opposite).

Of course, not all pressure groups so involve themselves in determining the outcome of election contests. They may wish to reach out to people associated with either party and therefore take a non-partisan approach. The American Telephone and Telegraph Company and Western Electric are examples of groups who prefer to concentrate on educating the voters and parties on their viewpoint.

Political Action Committees

Political Action Committees (PACs) have mushroomed since the 1980s. They represent the political wing of pressure groups and are legally permitted to raise funds to distribute to candidates and parties. Business, labour and trade associations, among others, have PACs to further their political goals. They seek to persuade Congressmen to vote as the group wishes and they offer advice and information to candidates, as well as the financial assistance which is their most important role. Elections are expensive, and candidates need substantial funds from their backers for such things as their advertising campaigns.

Groups have always wanted to influence election results and PACs existed as long ago as back in the 1930s. However, it was in the 1970s that they assumed a much greater significance largely as a result of reforms introduced after Watergate. Now, there are nearly 5000 PACs and the scale of their participation in the political process has dramatically increased.

The case for and against PACs

In favour:
1 They are the modern way to make money available for costly election campaigns. The methods employed are open and preferable to the situation

before they became widespread when the sources of finance were often disguised and unknown to the public. Indeed, it is the very availability of information which has led to criticism of them, criticism which is better directed to the whole system of campaign funding.

2 Such is the cost of campaigning that politicians cannot afford to be unduly beholden to particular PACs. They need a diversity of sources of funding, and this prevents any undue influence – the more so as the $5000 a PAC can donate is the level fixed in the early 1980s.

3 PACs represent a legitimate interest in a pluralist system, and the fact that there are nearly 5000 of them serves to prevent any one of them from gaining excessive influence. Their actions are open to scrutiny, and the media are constantly on the look-out for examples of undue favours being granted.

4 As with groups in general, they offer an outlet through which people can be involved and express their ideas and opinions. On the one hand, they educate the voters, but also they act as a means of communicating their views.

Against:

1 The central allegation against PACs revolves around the idea that money can buy influence and power. A Congressman who has the backing of a PAC is likely to give favours in return, so that they are associated with undue influence. In the words of one writer,[5] PACs are 'a huge coalition of special interest groups dedicated to perverting the political process for private gain'. The fact that some PACs have actually been willing to back rival candidates is seen as evidence of their determination to gain such influence.

2 Most PACs give money primarily to incumbent Congressmen, and this makes it more difficult for a challenger to mount a successful campaign against a person already in office. In as much as this is true, it is seen as undermining the democratic process, for it makes a contest less meaningful and fair.

3 The costs of campaigning in congressional elections has spiralled out of control, a reflection of the easy availability of money collected by PACs. It is not due to the escalating costs of advertising, but more to the fact that Congressmen have used this 'easy money' to equip themselves with needlessly large offices and staffing levels.

4 The usual criticism of pressure groups, the lack of internal democracy, is often mentioned as well. Alan Grant quotes[6] the example of the decision of the AFL/CIO to back Mondale as the Democratic presidential nominee in 1984, even though less than a quarter of union members were asked their preference.

The strength of group activity: prospects for success

The American system of government offers much scope to the lobbyist. It provides many layers of government to target, and the relatively weak party system provides an opportunity for groups to step in and fill the gap. As parties do not have rigid doctrinal platforms, Congressmen are less likely to follow the party line. They have to decide what is best in the national interest and for their geographical area, in the light of the information they receive from all quarters – much of this comes from the interests who seek to persuade them.

It is not easy to generalise about the factors which make group action successful, for there are exceptions to most sweeping generalisations. The party in control may be relevant, for business interests are traditionally catered for by the Republicans who – as in the Reagan era – tend to show greater hostility to organised labour. Yet the Democrats won praise from some manufacturers who were pleased by President Clinton's backing for the North Atlantic Free Trade Area, an issue on which the more conservative party failed to offer him much support. For many years, the Democrats have been viewed as sympathetic to the unions rather than big business, though the bargaining power of organised labour has been reduced under any administration now that membership has so declined.

Size is relevant to influence, for an association able to claim the backing of two million voters is one that cannot be easily ignored; one with 20,000 supporters has less electoral clout. Much, of course, depends on the commitment and organisational skills of those involved, and sometimes an active and persistent small group can be effective.

If a body has nationwide support – such as the AMA, with its local organisation in almost every congressional district – it is likely to be more influential than a group whose support is localised, unless the concern being voiced is a purely local one. Also, as with British groups, resources (especially money and professional expertise) are important. Those groups which can present an impressive case based on soundly researched data are more likely to be listened to. This can be costly.

Sometimes, timing is the key factor. Groups arise because of a growing interest in particular concerns. The environmentalists have been important in recent years, and many associations have sprung up and flourished. In the present mood of social and political conservatism (and particularly with the growing influence of the Religious Right), anti-abortion groups are likely to be listened to with greater respect than those who advance the cause of a woman's right to choose.

Indeed, any group with a liberal agenda is likely to find present circumstances less congenial than in the early 1980s. This applies especially in the area of civil liberties, where women and racial minorities find less support for affirmative action than was previously the case. The President and Congressmen are mindful of election considerations. No cause is likely to be endorsed if it is potentially damaging to their popularity and therefore a threat to their chances of re-election.

The mass media can be very relevant, for favourable attention from broadcasters and journalists can help a group to project its image and address a wider audience. Moreover, if the organisation can convey via the media the impression that its outlook is in the general interest and shared by many people, then those in power or seeking to obtain office will be especially attentive.

The regulation of group activity

The First Amendment to the American Constitution guarantees the right of free speech and to petition for the remedy of grievances. This protection has been used by interest groups over many years as a defence of their activities against the threat of excessive regulation. Some controls were introduced at state level as far back as the early nineteenth century, and within a few decades there was pressure for more to be done. Public anxiety increased because of the widespread influence of big business, in particular the influence wielded by rich corporations who were able to influence Congressmen to gain valuable concessions – especially rights to land where it was hoped to build railroads.

Not until after World War II was anything done by national government to tackle the problems posed by the growth in lobbying. Then, it was felt that there was a need to regularise group activity, whilst recognising its legitimate role in the political process. This was achieved by encouraging lobbyists to disclose details of their aims, membership and funding.

The 1946 Federal Regulation of Lobbying Act required the registration of lobbyists and details of the concern employing them. It was largely unenforced, and frequently the details were either not given or were incomplete. Some groups evaded registration, by arguing that lobbying was not their primary role. An attempt to stiffen the law in 1976 (the Lobby Disclosure Bill) failed, because of powerful opposition from lobbyists who felt that it would needlessly complicate their task and waste their time on pointless form-filling.

However, because of the alarm about some lobbyists' activities in the late 1960s and 1970s (notably about the cost of campaigning and the funding of candidates for elective office), further legislation was devised, in the form of the Federal Election Campaign Act (FECA). The Act, passed in 1971, replaced all earlier statutes. In its present form, thrice amended, it requires candidates and parties to disclose details of their income and expenditure. Individuals and PACs have to declare the costs they incur in providing them with any financial backing. The effect of tightening the control has ironically been to increase the number of PACs and the scale of their contributions.

A further attempt at reform was made by the 103rd Congress. Both houses approved legislation to amend the definition of lobbying so that more individuals would be required to register. Controls also restricted the right of lobbyists to dispense meals and gifts to legislators. Unfortunately there were differences between the proposals before the two chambers and in spite of the President's support, nothing was accomplished.

At the beginning of the twenty-first century, the world of pressure groups is now more open than was formerly the case, and though there may be deals between representatives of interest groups and congressmen, they are today more likely to be exposed. Congressmen are less likely to be in the pay of any one major lobby, and should there be a suspicion of too close an arrangement then there is always another competing group willing to 'blow the whistle'. Because of these considerations, most Congressmen do not recognise a need for more stringent regulation, a reflection of the prevailing American view that the influence of interest groups is generally beneficial to the process of government and in the public interest as well.

The merits and demerits of pressure groups

Most academics and politicians accept that groups have a legitimate role in American government, and recognise that it is inevitable that they will seek opportunities to advance their own interests. Many members of the general public might concede that they offer some advantages, but none the less remain perturbed by their ever-growing influence.

The case against

The names employed to describe the activity of interest groups are themselves a cause for concern to some people. The term 'pressure group' smacks of sinister and harmful behaviour, and when a small number of groups resort to violence or the threat of intimidation to achieve their ends there is understandable alarm. The use of death threats by the anti-abortion lobby can damage the cause, by offending many Americans who themselves are perturbed by the practice of termination. In some respects, the term 'interest group' is no better. It has obvious overtones of self-interest and serves to fuel the fear that such groups are concerned to promote their own advantage rather than the general interest of the community.

Moreover, among these 'interests', some are more powerful than others. They have greater financial resources and can therefore develop highly professional organisations and great expertise. Rivals in the field cannot hope to match the funds and resources of a big corporation. Business and labour are well organised, whereas the voice of consumers was for many years less effectively conveyed. Consumers are now protected by many active individuals and associations, but other interests – the racial minorities, the disabled, the elderly and the unemployed lack the income and bargaining power within the economy to enable them to achieve their goals, unless they can create enough public support as an election approaches. Abramson[7] quotes an analyst who regards Washington as a 'capital so privileged and incestuous in its dealings, that ordinary citizens believe it is no longer accessible to the general public'.

Concern has also been voiced about the unrepresentative character of some group leadership. Some leaders are elected by a small percentage of the membership, others are appointed. Once in their position, they can purvey their own ideas and attitudes, irrespective of whether these reflect the views of those whom they are supposed to represent. One political scientist has noted[8] that

> the system is skewed, loaded and unbalanced in favour of a fraction of a minority [those in the highest social economic and education categories].

Above all, much of the public anxiety is related to fear of behind-the-scenes influence. It is widely suspected that there is something distasteful about lobbying. It may not be illegal, the influence may be legitimate, but there is a suspicion of deals from which the bulk of the public are excluded. There have been enough cases involving corruption and malpractice to make people question the secrecy of lobbying activity, and assume that either side is out to maximise their own advantage.

The case in favour

As for the fears of undue influence, defenders of group activity might point to the fact that, besides the formal legal controls, there are also other interests which can exercise a countervailing pressure. There may not always be equally balanced groups on either side of some particular issue, but whatever the preponderance of views the arguments for and against a question are usually reasonably well aired. For instance, the influence of the energy companies is matched by that of the anti-nuclear groups which wish to halt the development of nuclear energy plants. The desire of management and unions in the northwest woodlands to cut down trees is countered by the complaints of the environmentalists who are active in demanding that the practice is controlled. Again, in the impassioned abortion and gun control debates, the influence of pro-lifers in the former is balanced by those who are pro-choice, just as the influence of the National Rifle Association is matched by that of Handgun Control.

Groups can provide positive benefits to the community and to those in authority. They allow large number of citizens to participate in the political process as members of associations. Some are passive supporters who pay their dues and do little else. Others, usually a small minority, are more deeply committed enthusiasts who try to galvanise the less-active members into giving more positive support.

The presence of many groups ensures that the attitudes and outlook of all groups in society are articulated. It is surely more healthy for all people to have an outlet for their views, however extreme, rather than for them to resort to underground methods. They also convey ideas to and from the elected and appointed officials who make decisions. As intermediaries between the government and the governed, they help to make government accountable. In these respects, rather than being a threat to the democratic process, they actually underpin democracy.

They also provide government with specialist information and expertise, and may help in carrying out policies which law-makers have laid down. They meet Congressmen and officials of the administration at regular intervals, and assist by providing evidence, submitting proposals and attending hearings. This flow of information to the agencies and institutions of government is again an important part of the democratic process. By becoming involved in this way, groups help to modify government decisions and public policy. Some may not like it, but that is what has come to pass.

Apart from the specific arguments quoted above, supporters of group activity often point out to the inevitability of group activity in a pluralist society. This view was developed by David Truman[9] in 1951 and has been widely accepted over the last 50 years. For those who belong to this school of thought, the formation of groups is an obvious method by which people with shared ideas and circumstances cooperate to achieve their goals. They are a natural, desirable and healthy democratic outlet. Any problems in their operation can be controlled by appropriate regulatory machinery.

Recent trends: the changing pressure group landscape

The nature and pattern of group activity has significantly altered in recent years: at the turn of the century, there are far more groups than ever before. We have already noted the proliferation of cause or issue groups which seek to advance particular areas of concern – from abortion to the environment, from gender to the right to bear arms. One reason for this development is the growth of federal welfare and regulatory activities in the 1960s and 1970s. Several groups were formed in response to these initiatives, by groups of people who found their lives affected by the changes. Other factors might be the weakening of political parties and the increasd opportunities for lobbying in Congress.

Lobbying is done also by various 'Think tanks' which seek to convert policy-makers to their approach on a whole series of issues. The Heritage Foundation and the American Enterprise Institute are broadly conservative research bodies which have become an important part of the Washington lobbying network. So too are the state and local governments which now often employ the services of professional lobbyists to influence the federal government – again, via an office in Washington.

There are many more recent groups which compete with the traditional ones in the economic area and in the professions. In medicine, the AMA has long been a leader and it remains very important – but now there are numerous other organisations operating in the medical field. Some are concerned with specialist work such as that of paramedics and nurses, some represent hospitals and clinics, whilst others speak for the insurance companies active in this sector.

For a long while, the lobbying scene in Washington was dominated by three major interests: agriculture, business and labour. These no longer carry the weight that they once did. We have seen that the AFBF and NFU, the large peak organisations, have now lost some of their influence to the product or regional associations. As with agriculture, so with business. The National Association of Manufacturers and the US Chamber of Commerce are still important players, but other organisations have developed and corporations increasingly organise more of their own lobbying. Similarly, the status and impact of unions has been in decline, and whereas their membership peaked at above 30 per cent of the workforce in 1945, today it is nearer to 15 per cent. They remain important in the American economy, but many groups of workers – especially in newer, smaller, high-tech industries – are non-unionised.

The days when Congressmen from the industrial states were desperate to avoid offending the unions or those from the South and Midwest had to show immense sympathy for agrarian interests, have changed. These interests are still important, but the industrial and farming vote are both less crucial than was once the case. Democrats fear being portrayed as too close to labour, and Reagan and Bush were prepared to cut agricultural subsidies in spite of the preferences of the small farmers of Iowa, Kansas and other farm states. Given the large number of groups, it is now less easy for congressional committees to be too close to one particular interest; similarly, an individual Congressman cannot afford to be beholden to one group only. They are open to many influences, and would be unwise to fail to meet delegations from any association, irrespective of their private view.

For the lobbyist, too, things have changed. Not only are there more of them, there are also more targets to influence at national and state level. Nationally, there are more agencies and congressional sub-committees to contact and state governments have become a new focus of attention. Business organisations are particularly active in some states, often employing former state legislators, governors and officials to do their work. Since the days of Reagan's New Federalism, more policies are operated and financed at the state rather than the federal tier, particularly in the welfare field.

Pressure groups in Britain and the United States: a comparison

In Britain and the United States, there is a widespread acceptance of group activity, although America has traditionally been particularly receptive to the operation of lobbying. The two countries have a vast array of groups, both protective and promotional, and although the causes which inspire activity on either side of the Atlantic may differ from time to time, it is striking how many organisations appear on both. In manufacturing industry, agriculture, labour, the professions, and on a variety of matters of civic and social concern, there are similar associations, and on topical issues such as abortion there is the same divide between pro-life and pro-choice bodies.

Such groups perform similar functions and have broadly the same advantages and disadvantages. The arguments surrounding their work overlap, and comments in the press and among the public echoes similar anxieties – about the unrepresentativeness of group leadership, the influence of powerful interests and the secrecy and dangers surrounding lobbying of the legislature. There are, however, some differences in the mode of operation and the strategies adopted, for the reasons given below.

In the US, the federal system means that pressure groups can operate at several levels, and they seek to achieve their aims in local and state governments as well as in Washington. Political power is more diffuse, partly because of the federal structure but also because of the Separation of Powers. For instance, the position of the American courts in pronouncing on the constitutionality of legislation makes them an obvious access point. By contrast, in Britain groups have made less use of the judicial system, though bodies such as the Commission for Racial Equality and the Equal Opportunities Commission make use of legal procedures.

Given the weak party structure and the lack of party discipline in Congress, US groups make Capitol Hill the target of their work. There is much to be gained through contact with individual legislators. By contrast, the greater cohesion of British parliamentary parties means that the powerful groups are keen to gain consultative status in Whitehall, where decisions are made. The unitary system of government concentrates power in government hands, and ministers and civil servants are the people to influence.

Not only are American lobbyists concerned with a wider variety of targets, they also engage in some activities which are unfamiliar on the British scene. UK election campaigns are much more centralised, and the media campaign is run primarily from headquarters. Much of party income goes to the London headquarters, and there are strict controls over what the individual candidate can spend. American elections are more candidate-centred, and there is a significant role for PACs in assisting both financially and organisationally. America makes extensive use of political advertising, and PACs are much involved in putting out their own broadcasts as well as in helping the candidate's team to finance its operations in this field.

CONCLUSION

The United States has a vast array of pressure groups which operate at several access points and have highly significant influence. In recent decades, the extent of lobbying in Washington and the 50 states has increased and the role of Political Action Committees has become a key element in the financing of election campaigns. Group activity provokes much controversy and there have been regular calls for more regulation and control. Debate about groups has centred especially upon the contribution of groups to the democratic process.

In particular, Washington has become a hub of pressure group activity. On any given day, group activists will be involved in many arenas. Some will be testifying for or against proposed legislation in congressional hearings. Others will be arguing in the Supreme Court, perhaps for stricter enforcement of regulations or for the protection of the rights of a section of the American people. Yet others will be meeting with bureaucrats in government departments, perhaps discussing ideas about legislation.

There is an interesting paradox about the participation of Americans in their political system. Many are reluctant to turn out and vote in elections, yet they are willing to involve themselves in pressure group activity. As Schlozman and Tierney[10] have written: 'Recent decades have witnessed an expansion of astonishing proportions in the involvement of private organisations in Washington politics.' They might have referred to the other outlets as well, for many groups are now very active in working the many sub-governments in the American system.

REFERENCES

1 J. Rauch, *Demosclerosis: The Silent Killer of American Government*, Times Books, 1995.
2 P. Woll and S. Zimmerman, *American Government: The Core*, McGraw-Hill, 1992.
3 P. Woll and S. Zimmerman, *American Government: The Core*, McGraw-Hill, 1992.
4 J. Abramson, 'The Business of Persuasion Thrives in Nation's Capitol', *New York Times*, 29 September, 1998.
5 C. W. Griffin, *Cleaning out Congress*, Griffin Associates, 1992.
6 A. Grant, *Contemporary American Politics*, Dartmouth, 1995.
7 J. Abramson, 'The Business of Persuasion Thrives in Nation's Capitol', *New York Times*, 29 September 1998.
8 G. Wasserman, *The Basics of American Politics*, Longman, 1996.
9 D. Truman, *The Governmental Process: Political Interests and Public Opinion*, Alfred A. Knopf, 1958.
10 K. Schlozman, and J. Tierney, *Organised Interests and American Democracy*, Harper and Row, 1986.

USEFUL WEB SITES

Various think tanks and issue groups are listed at **www.policy.com**

Two sites with a broadly ideological perspective are:

www.conservativenet.com Conservative Net.

http://turnleft.com Turn Left.

Individual pressure groups have their own sites dealing with the specific issues of interest to them. Examples are:

www.now.org National Organisation for Women.

www.nrra.org National Rifle Association.

www.sierrraclub.org The Sierra Club.

SAMPLE QUESTIONS

1 Should there be more restrictions on the activity of Political Action Committees?

2 Which 'access points' are most likely to provide opportunities for US pressure groups to achieve their objectives? Does influence vary according to the type of group involved?

3 Discuss the role and value of pressure groups in the American legislative process.

4 'It is possible to over-estimate the effects of pressure group activity. Ultimately, groups cancel each other out'. Discuss.

5 Does lobbying play too large a part in the American political process?

6 Are pressure groups beneficial to American democracy or do they undermine it?

7 'In Britain and America, the producer lobby is far more powerful than that representing consumers'. Is this true and, if so, does it matter?

Conclusion: the condition of American democracy

10

THE MEANING OF DEMOCRACY

The ancient Greeks were the first to give a democratic answer to the question of how to organise a political system. Athenian democracy was practised in a small city-state, and some of its characteristics were:
- The citizens made some political decisions directly, and controlled others.
- There was political and legal equality of all citizens.
- There was widespread political and civil liberty.
- Decisions were taken by majority vote.

Athenian democracy was 'rule by the people'. This was **direct democracy** in action, with people coming together to make decisions whenever necessary. Debates in the assembly were free, open and wide-ranging, each citizen having a single vote. In fifth-century Athens, there was little emphasis on individual rights and liberties.

> **direct democracy**
> Government in which citizens come together in one place to make laws; refers to populistic measures such as the initiative, recall and referendum.

After the Greeks, the notion of democracy went out of fashion, being associated in the eyes of many rulers with factional conflict and violence. Until the early nineteenth century, far from government being rule by the many, it was actually in effect rule by the very few who were not subject to popular control. The majority of people were seen as unfit to rule, and members of the nobility who possessed governing skills did not feel that they should be subject to the whims of the illiterate and ill-informed majority. In *The Federalist*, James Madison echoed the outlook of many of his co-framers of the American Constitution when he wrote:

> Such democracies [as the Greek and Roman] have ever been found incompatible with personal security of the rights of property; and have in general been as short in their lives, as they have been violent in their deaths.

The word 'democracy' is not used in the US Constitution. The framers preferred the term 'republic' to describe the form of government which they wished to create. It lacked the connection with direct democracy – with its possible associations with demagogues, mass rule and the mob. The vision of the Founding Fathers was of a **representative** system, a republic in Plato's sense, by which all those in power obtain and retain their position as a result of winning elections in which all free adults are allowed to take part.

> **representative democracy**
> Government in which the people rule indirectly through elected representatives.

The nineteenth century saw the spread of representative democracy, a system under which a person stands for and speaks on behalf of another. Today, it is widely accepted that this is the only viable form of democracy in a vast country. The mass of people cannot rule, in the sense of making binding decisions. Instead, representatives of the people, freely elected, decide. What is crucial is that there should be effective popular control over the rulers or decision-makers. A system is democratic to the extent that those who have power are subject to the wishes of the electorate. An appropriate definition of a democratic political system is one in which

> public policies are made, on a majority basis, by representatives subject to effective popular control at periodic elections which are conducted on the principle of political equality and under conditions of political freedom.

Abraham Lincoln put it more succinctly: 'government of the people, by the people and for the people'.

THE PAST WORKINGS OF AMERICAN DEMOCRACY: BLEMISHES AND VIRTUES

Democracy is seen as a pre-eminently American value. Yet the United States has not always acknowledged the democratic rights of all its citizens, and some of the developments in the twentieth century have cast doubt upon the genuine attachment to democratic values. For instance, the existence of the right to vote is seen as a major criterion of any democracy. If broad categories of the public are denied the opportunity to express their preference between candidates, then this must be a blot on the landscape. Women obtained the vote in 1920, and in theory all men had the vote from the time the Constitution was created, subject originally to a property qualification. Yet slaves were not allowed to participate in elections, and when slavery ended, ruses were adopted in various southern states to prevent blacks from exercising their democratic rights.

In the absence of an effective universal franchise, there must be doubts about the American commitment to democracy. True, the property qualifications were pitched at a relatively modest level, and by the early nineteenth century some 80 per cent of American men owned sufficient property to qualify. True also that the US was relatively speedy in extending the popular suffrage to include all women. But they were white men and white women, and it was not until the 1960s that the majority of black Americans were able to use their entitlement, if they so wished.

On the score of recognising and respecting minority rights, the Americans again did well in theory. Crucial liberties were granted in the Constitution, most obviously in the first ten amendments which make up the Bill of Rights. These are inviolable, unless there is a further constitutional amendment to change them. Yet, again, there have been blemishes upon the record. Two sets of factors ruin the record of the Americans in protecting and respecting such rights:

1 In the 1920s and in the 1950s, anti-communist hysteria was at a high level. The 1920s was a markedly intolerant decade, in which the liberties of many individuals were infringed, and anyone whose views were mildly progressive was liable to be branded as a 'red'. Similarly, the McCarthy witch-hunt against those portrayed as communists was at a fever pitch in the early 1950s. His techniques of investigation with their emphasis upon smear and innuendo displayed little respect for constitutional niceties. 'Un-American activity' was interpreted very widely, and there was much harassment of individuals and groups. There was in both eras a desperate desire for conformity, and those who did not conform to the American ideal of White Anglo-Saxon Protestants (WASPs) were hounded.

2 The ideal of equality, as proclaimed in Jefferson's resounding cry 'We hold these truths to be self evident, that all men are created equal', is seen as an American contribution to mankind. Certainly, privilege and rank count for less in America than in Western Europe, and an egalitarian fervour is in a way a part of the American Dream – that each person can go out and make a fortune, by using his or her gifts and exhibiting a pioneering spirit. But the position of black Americans until comparatively recently suggested that in practice not everyone benefited from the Jeffersonian dream.

States adopted many differing rules to prevent political and legal equality of white and black from becoming a reality. Segregation and racial discrimination may be particularly associated with the Deep South, but in many northern cities there was much *de facto* segregation well into the 1960s. Even today the opportunities available to many black American are more theoretical than real.

If in several respects, reality has fallen short of the democratic ideal, yet the commitment to democracy for many Americans has always been apparent and to their credit many have always felt uneasy about lapses from that ideal. It would also be fair to point to other areas of political life in which the theory and practice of democracy has been evident:

1 In the Progressive era, the introduction of direct election of senators and the spread of primary elections to defeat the power of the machine bosses were moves which reflected a true concern for democracy.

2 The US has also practised direct democracy as well as the representative form. Devices such as the referendum, the initiative and the recall are practical demonstrations of direct democracy in action, whatever their weaknesses. More unusual is the use of the town meeting in small rural areas of New England. Originally, such meetings were vehicles through which the mainly Puritan religious leaders informed and led other members of the community – a means of seeking a consensus via a guided discussion. They were not opportunities for the expression of majority will on issues of the day and those who declined to agree to the general will were likely to be driven out of the area. However, such meetings have developed into a more acceptable democratic form and in them citizens gather together to make decisions for their community.

AMERICAN DEMOCRACY TODAY

America has long been regarded as a model democracy, but some commentators believe that today the system is not working well. Indeed, Kenneth Dolbeare has written[1] of 'the decay of American democracy' and asks whether the condition is a terminal one. He sees the problem as one compounded by the sheer scale and power of the government in Washington, for this has meant that it is 'increasingly connected only to a steadily shrinking proportion of its affluent citizens'.

Dolbeare discerns several factors which have contributed to the 'decay':
• the decline of political parties;
• the rise of television;
• the dominance of money as a means of access to television and electioneering in general;
• the rise of Political Action Committees;
• near-permanent incumbency in Congress;
• a general abandonment of leadership to the latest opinion poll.

More seriously than any of the above factors, however, he sees the 'thirty-year trend toward abandoning political participation' as the most alarming indication of decay. In particular, this means a continuous decline in voter participation (a point well illustrated by recent presidential elections), particularly a problem for those in the bottom one-third of the social pyramid. He notes the paradox which has emerged:

The growing underclass has rising needs for education, jobs, training, health care etc., but these very services are being held to a minimum or even cut – and yet the voting participation of this same underclass is declining faster than that of any other population group.

Other writers have also noted that at the very time that the Soviet control of Eastern Europe has broken down and given rise to the creation of 'new democracies', the American version of that same system has shown severe signs of fatigue. Paul Taylor is an exponent of this viewpoint:[2]

As democracy flourishes around the globe, it is losing ground in the United States.

The voters

It is convenient to begin our analysis of American democracy with the electorate, the *demos* – the public itself – and to examine political attitudes and participation.

Social disadvantage: an alienated underclass

It is certainly true that there exist dramatic contrasts in lifestyles among the American people, with those in the bottom 40 per cent in need of varying levels of help, some urgently so. Large numbers live below the 'poverty line', and the minority populations are heavily concentrated in this category. Often, people more in the middle of the social pyramid also find life difficult, sometimes only being able to survive comfortably because there are two incomes in the family. Spending cuts have hit the poor disproportionately, and tax cuts in the 1980s especially benefited the rich.

It is the poor who are leaving the electorate, and this lower-class non-voting was an influential factor in the success of the Republicans in the Reagan years. As the Republicans seem to have found a recipe for electoral success, so the Democrats have journeyed to the right and found a new identity. The strategy worked in getting them elected and re-elected to the White House in the 1990s, but the price has been paid by the least well-off who have no reason to see even the Democrats as very sympathetic on issues such as welfare reform. The best that can be said from their point of view is that President Clinton at least defended Medicare and Medicaid (the welfare programmes for health insurance) against Newt Gingrich's designs, in the struggle over the budget in 1995–96. Yet Clinton was also willing to sacrifice the families who found themselves in hardship.

Dolbeare remarks that it is among the least-educated and lower-income groups that 'feelings of discouragement, lack of efficacy, and of never getting what one wants through politics despite one's best efforts, are particularly acute at these levels'. On top of the disadvantages of being poor, the underclass has no political outlet, certainly not one which they deem to be effective.

Turnout

Frances Piven and Richard Cloward have drawn attention[3] to the formidable barriers to voting posed by the various state registration procedures. They were writing before the motor-voting bill became law, and made the point that sometimes the requirements for registration to be completed 30 days before an election hit the less educated especially hard, for the opportunity lapsed before they were 'motivated to take part'. Yet even since 'motor voting' the 1996 and 2000 elections have revealed that many Americans are not inclined to turn out and vote. Figures for presidential elections are poor and the trend has been downward since 1960: in mid-term elections, they are substantially poorer.

If low turnouts reflect an increasing distrust of politicians and a feeling that 'all of them are as bad as each other', then this may seem to be a healthy scepticism. But when large numbers of people feel disenchanted with what they represent and have doubts about their ability and integrity, there is more cause for concern. The rate of support, strong or weak, for political parties has been falling steadily over the years. Many people no longer identify with either party to any significant degree.

The media

The media are able to perform an invaluable role in a democracy. They help by providing information, often in an entertaining way, and give politics a higher profile via news broadcasts than it would otherwise receive. They also expose wrongdoing by those in high places, and the Watergate investigations by Bernstein and Woodward of the *New York Times* were the supreme example of journalistic vigilance. However, such intelligent and public-spirited forms of journalism are a specialised branch of the media, and not representative of much of what is presented in the press. Quality journalists reject the approach of colleagues whose golden rule is to please the news desk, get front-page coverage and stay there every day, reflect the prejudices of readers, defend nationalistic hype and titillate as much as possible.

Bias?

The media may assist by exposing some aspect of the decline of the democratic spirit, but in other ways they can be accomplices to, or at worst a catalyst of, that decline. Former President Clinton often complained about the quality of the American media. He was contemptuous of the treatment he received in parts of the press, and believed that so much of journalism in newspapers and on the main national television channels had been overwhelmingly biased. Because of this, he lessened or even denied access to many journalists, and bypassed many traditional outlets.

Many other politicians share his suspicion of many who work in the media, although complaints of bias are made from both the Democrats and the Republicans. For conservatives, the media are too liberal, and too often take up progressive causes. For liberals, they are unhealthily pro-establishment. For the far Left, the mainstream press, in particular, is a tool of the ruling class, capitalist enterprises which set an agenda favourable to those who control or edit them. Broadly speaking, pro-Republican daily newspapers outnumber pro-Democrat ones by about two to one.

Trivialisation? The emphasis upon personality and appearance

Another of the effects of the media, particularly television, has been to trivialise politics. Journalists prefer to concentrate on personalities, and to express complex issues in a shorthand form which is so abbreviated that all depth is excluded in pursuit of a marketable sound-bite.

Television has changed politics significantly. Marshall McLuhan has pointed out[4] that it is not just another medium through which thoughts and opinions can be transmitted: rather, it has changed the way in which people communicate, and the nature of political discourse. It has placed a new emphasis on looks and personality. An Abraham Lincoln (protruding nose, fleshy lips and sharp chin) might be not be acceptable today, for it is the physical attractiveness, charm and 'likeability' of a candidate which often seem to be more important than experience, knowledge and thinking capacity, and we are witnessing the triumph of propaganda over political distinction.

Laurence Rees has observed[5] that: 'Television as a medium is full of attractive people – often attractive people trying to sell you cars, washing machines or soap powder'. He quotes the example of Adlai Stevenson, an eminent and able intellectual who contested the 1956 presidential election on behalf of the Democrats – the first election in which 'the mass electorate of a democratic country could see regularly on TV the competing nominees for the country's greatest office'. The shape of a man's head, never before a consideration of any political adviser when politicians addressed public meetings or spoke on the radio, suddenly became important. As a result, the one concern that Stevenson's and Eisenhower's teams of advisers shared during the campaign was that when tilting their heads to read their speeches over television, the candidates' hairless scalps were elongated, suggesting giant eggs.

Today, presidents are popularly remembered primarily by their looks more than by their abilities. Once, it was their utterances and the quality of their performance which mattered, but today image is all-important, and as we recall Carter or Reagan we think of how they appeared on television.

Television is primarily a means of entertainment, and the danger is that people who spend much of their time watching the medium judge all who appear on it by the same criteria. Hence the importance of physical appearance and being personable. Dan Quayle, hardly accomplished in other ways, is a personable fellow, of good looks, and the choice of him as George Bush's running mate in 1988 could be seen as an example of someone who passed every screen test yet lacked political acumen. In Ronald Reagan, there was a perfect blending of the worlds of entertainment and politics, and several writers have picked up on this point. Lou Cannon[6] describes the link in this way:

> Over time, the cinematic approach became so woven into the fabric of the Reagan Presidency that subordinates, schooled in economics or stagecraft, routinely used Hollywood terminology to direct Reagan in his daily tasks. One White House aide recalls that Secretary of State, George P. Schultz, huddling with Reagan in the secure vault of the American ambassador's residence in Moscow during the 1988 summit, coached him for his meeting with Mikhail Gorbachev by telling him what to do 'in this scene'.

The emphasis upon broad themes rather than policy

The presentation of policy as well as of the candidate is all-important today. Information-led propaganda is less well suited to television than broad themes. Joseph Goebbels, the Minister of Public Enlightenment in Nazi Germany – and, significantly, an admirer of Hollywood – had a clear understanding of how to communicate his Führer's ideas: constant repetition of short, easily remembered slogans. It was important to create a simple message, ideally seeking to engage the attention of the listener by attuning the propaganda to his or her needs. Above all, it was necessary to move slowly and win people round.

This is a common view among American political consultants, the growing breed of marketing men and spin-doctors who surround any presidential candidate today. They like their candidate to talk not about policy issues, which give too many hostages to fortune, but instead to stick to themes – better to avoid itemising every detail and instead talk in terms of achieving broader goals. When politicians shun this advice they can find themselves encumbered with promises which are difficult to fulfil. George Bush made the unwise promise of 'Read my lips. No new taxes', and when he subsequently found no alternative to an increase it appeared that he had broken his promise. A more general comment on his wish to see 'fair taxation', in which no one suffered an 'unjust burden' might have avoided the pitfall.

Successful politicians in the media age invariably talk in entertainment-oriented themes. This can make political philosophy seem fluid. In the words of Professor Postman:[7] 'You cannot do political philosophy on television. Its

form works against the content. It is television which has enabled the propa-
gandist to put over the candidate's case without recourse to philosophy or
specifics'. As Laurence Rees put it:[8] 'For any politician who lacks conviction but
has charming personal habits and appearance, there has never been a better
time to seek office'.

The tyranny of the pollsters?

Ally the developments we have outlined with the widespread use of polls and
focus groups, and we can see that it is easy for sincere beliefs to be played
down and for a response to popular opinions to become ever more important.
In the past, if politicians wanted to know the public's views on any political
topic, this could be discovered by watching the reaction at public meetings as
opinions were outlined. Today, this is not so, and although polling can be a
useful adjunct in the political process there is a danger that it determines the
ways in which politicians act; it can dictate the message. The candidate might
well find himself or herhself allowing the polls to dictate what he or she
should believe.

Polling has become ever more sophisticated. Focus groups may be asked such
questions as 'Who sounds more decisive?', 'To what social class does the voice
belong?' and others which relate to the style of the utterance and not its
content. The thrust of such questioning is usually much more on the presentation than the content when issues are discussed.

For some people, such polling techniques represent ultimate democracy, but
there are dangers:
1 Persons who respond to pollsters are often responding to information given
   on television, in brief two- or three-minute reports. Depending on what is
   conveyed in those bulletins, and varying according to the precise events of
   the day, that response may change frequently. Politicians listening to the
   popular voice may end up pursuing policies which are inconsistent.
2 More seriously, people might expect leadership from their politicians. At
   various times in history, it has been necessary for individuals to give a lead,
   a point realised by Martin Luther King who – in a sermon in Washington in
   1968 – answered suggestions that he might be following a policy which
   according to the polls could be damaging to his campaign. He observed
   that: 'Ultimately, a genuine leader is not a searcher for consensus, but a
   moulder of consensus'.

Democracy is said to thrive on an atmosphere of reasoned argument and intelligent and rational debate, so that the people are left to make a judgement in
the light of their assessment of the merits of the case. Can this happen today?
Has not television altered the nature of political discourse to such an extent
that the American – and other – people are now in thrall to the medium?

Some people might see no harm in a situation in which fitness for office is increasingly judged in entertainment terms, with politicians responding to the pollster's wishes and providing policies which are built around the views that people express to focus groups. They may even see advantages in present practice. Television may enable people who would never have before become known to make a breakthrough and thereby help to break the hold of political parties on the political process. But if you vote along party lines, you have a better idea of the policies you are supporting. And it is easier to make a politician answerable for a failure to deliver a policy than it is for a failing of personality.

The cost of modern electioneering

Another feature of modern propagandising is its cost. Television has made money a crucial feature of modern electioneering in the US, for candidates need to use television to get their message across and this can prove very expensive. The preoccupation with fundraising has destroyed the ambitions of

Democracy in Britain and the United States: a comparison

In Britain, some of the same anxieties about the health of democracy exist. There is a disaffected underclass which is largely ignorant of and uninterested in political life. Many of its members do not turn out and vote, and turnouts generally are in decline; indeed, in local and European elections, turnout has dropped sharply at the turn of the twenty-first century. There is the same scepticism of politicians, but for many people it is more than a sensible wariness about those who exercise authority. Rather, it is a deep and cynical distrust of those who rule.

In Britain, there is concern about the existence of numerous quangos, power having been handed over to a new lay elite whose members increasingly run a wide range of services. American experience is different, for wherever there is a public office to fill across the Atlantic the tendency is to hold an election. Here, the passion for election does not extend to those who serve on various boards and trusts; neither does it (yet) extend to the second chamber.

In both countries, the media at best provide reflective analysis and commentary on national events, and expose alleged or real corruption, the abuse of power and other forms of public scandal. In so doing, they contribute to the workings of democracy. In other respects, they present a threat to its values. Concentration of ownership in too few hands, the lack of diversity of opinion and intrusive and sometimes shamelessly biased reporting are dangers in the press.

Television can be said to aid democracy by informing voters, via news bulletins, current affairs programmes, and other scheduling which often conveys information in an often entertaining form. But the tendency to trivialise, to concentrate upon personalities and

some talented politicians. Hubert Humphrey back in 1972 observed that the constant need to spend time on the phone soliciting for money was 'making us all beggars. I hate it worse than anything else I have to do'. Governor Askew of Florida claims that he gave up his Senate campaign in 1988 because he was put off by the constant need to seek out sources of funding.

The role of money in American elections has long been controversial, and today's problems centre largely on the sources of money and the unequal distribution of funds available. Spending in presidential and congressional elections is massive, to the extent that Ross Perot could deploy some $60 million of his own finances to pay for advertising shots on television in 1992 – including 30-minute 'infomercials' in which he lectured Americans on the excessive spending which had brought about the budget deficit. Although candidates and political parties are limited in what they can donate at election time, Political Action Committees have stepped in to fill the vacuum. Some PACs give very generous backing to particular candidates, and often use their money to support incumbents and thereby help to frustrate the possibility of change at election time.

personal 'weaknesses' and to express serious issues in a shorthand, sound-bite form has reduced the educative role which at its best the medium can offer.

The basic liberties associated with democratic rule are written into the American Constitution, whereas Britain has traditionally had a negative approach to freedoms. Few of them were guaranteed by law, so that we could do or say something provided that there was no specific law against it. Unlike the situation in other western democracies, there was no bill or rights or document setting out basic entitlements. With the passage of the Human Rights Act in 1998, the European Convention on Human Rights has been incorporated into British law, so that for the first time there is a written record of the liberties and rights of the subject.

Since the 1960s, there has been an expansion of individual rights in Britain and the United States. Positive freedoms have been proclaimed, with legislation and – in the US case – court judgements ensuring that the rights of women and minority groups have been enforced. However, in both countries, the events of 11 September 2001 have led to anti-terrorist legislation which some libertarians see as too all-embracing and out of proportion to the threat which exists.

Finally, on one freedom, that of the right of access to information, the US performance still leaves Britain trailing. America has had a freedom of information act since 1966. Whatever the doubts about the costs of its implementation or its effects on carrying out confidential investigations, most Americans and consumer groups welcome the fact that the legislation is strong and effective, giving Americans a 'right to know'. The more recent British legislation which takes effect in 2002 has been widely criticised for its timidity, even though significant concessions were extracted from ministers during its passage in 1999–2000.

Much of the money which goes on television expenditure is spent on attack advertising. It has been argued by many commentators that one reason for the low turnout referred to earlier in this section is that would-be voters are repelled by the sheer negativity of the election process. In the words of Senator Darnforth (speaking in the Senate, 1990): 'They are sick about modern politics and they are particularly sick about what they see on television'. This view that modern political campaigning induces feelings of cynicism and rejection has now taken root among many commentators.

The threat to civil liberty

After the attacks on New York and Washington, there was widespread debate in the United States and elsewhere about the threats to freedom and security. By their actions, the terrorists involved had destroyed the most basic right of all – the right to life – of nearly 4,000 Americans, and had threatened the 'life, liberty and pursuit of happiness' of many more. Almost every American could agree on the need to ensure greater security of the person, by rooting out terrorists and preventing the danger of further attacks. But critics of the Bush Administration claimed that its package of anti-terrorist measures ('Uniting and Strengthening America By Providing Appropriate Tools Required To Intercept and Obstruct Terrorism' – more usually known as 'the USA PATRIOT Act') – went far beyond what was necessary to achieve these objectives. They detected signs of a serious erosion of accepted freedoms.

Criticism centred mainly on three broad aspects of the Act:

1 The dedication to secrecy

Transparency and accountability are widely seen as basic to American democracy, for only if government is open to public scrutiny can American people judge the effectiveness of their elected representatives and the propriety of their actions. Yet the law enforcement agencies were granted the right to ignore provisions of the Freedom of Information Act, if there was a 'sound legal basis' for so doing. Because of this, it has been difficult to obtain information about the 500 or so detainees held in federal prisons, many of whom are said to have been held on charges unrelated to the events of 11 September.

2 The erosion of basic checks and balances

The doctrine of the Separation of Powers is an essential safeguard against the abuse of power, the idea being that no one branch of government can become unduly influential. The new powers tilt the balance towards the Executive branch and remove from the judicial system some of its power to review the actions of the Administration. For instance, immigration judges now have less opportunity to prevent unlawful detention or deportation of non-citizens, and their review of wire-tapping and surveillance has also been curtailed. Courts exist to ensure that justice is done and basic rights protected. If an innocent person is wrongly harmed, the public is put at risk because the actual terrorist remains at large.

3 The traditional distinction between foreign intelligence gathering and criminal investigation at home has been undermined

Under the new legislation, the FBI can act more like a domestic Central Intelligence Agency (CIA) when seeking a criminal conviction, obtaining a secret warrant from a secret court to gather evidence of crime, without having to present to the court evidence that the person on whom it wishes to spy is involved in crime. Information gathered by domestic law enforcement agencies can now be handed to bodies such as the CIA.

Within a few months of the passage of the legislation, a number of cases occurred which illustrated some of these anxieties. In November 2001, a member of the Green Party USA's committee was surrounded by military personnel as she tried to board a plane in Bangor, Maine, to attend a Chicago meeting on the use of pesticides in war. She was told that because her name had been 'flagged in the computer', the airport was closed to her. Her flight was not refunded and she found that her hotel reservation in Chicago had already been mysteriously cancelled. There were also complaints from some academics opposed to the war in Afghanistan of harassment by university and other authorities.

Such examples and several others inspired the *New York Times*[9] to launch a ferocious attack on the limitations being imposed on personal freedom. In an editorial, it was claimed that:

> Civil liberties are eroding, and there is no evidence that the reason is anything more profound than fear and frustration.
>
> Thousands of detainees being held in secret by the government; wiretaps on prisoners' conversations with their lawyers; public debate about the advisability of using torture to make suspects talk.
>
> Two months into the war against terrorism, the nation is sliding toward the trap that we entered this conflict vowing to avoid. It is time the White House stepped in ... the Justice Department can investigate domestic attacks while respecting the basic rights that we are in this war to preserve.

Detention at Guantanamo Bay

The growing anxiety about the threat to freedom came to a head in early 2002 over the issue of the treatment of terrorist suspects. Instead of establishing prisoner-of-war camps in the Afghan territory it had freed from Taliban control, the US arranged for their transport – in small groups – to a naval base at Guantanamo Bay, in Cuba, instead of to the American mainland. On the mainland, they would have been within the jurisdiction of the American courts, whereas in Cuba their legal status was less clear-cut. The plan was to try them before special military courts, against the decision of which there would be no right of appeal. The Defense Secretary labelled them as 'unlawful combatants' rather than as 'prisoners of war', thus denying them the full protection of the Geneva Convention. But under international law they are not liable to torture nor to inhumane treatment, and civil libertarians around the world have been disturbed by reports concerning the conditions in which they have been held.

Many people would accept that it is understandable for America to wish to glean as much information from the Taliban and Al Qaida detainees. They feel little sympathy for their alleged actions, and recognise that they have been part of a dangerous terrorist conspiracy against Western targets. But they still have rights. If they are not covered by the Geneva 'laws of war', then they are ordinary criminals. As such, if tried in the United States they would be protected by the Sixth Amendment which insists that in 'all criminal prosecutions' in the United States inalienable rights apply, including the right to a jury trial.

Those within America who have criticised aspects of Administration policy and challenge US foreign and defence policy objectives have often been attacked as unpatriotic or anti-American. One writer[10] has written of the 'new McCarthyism' and pointed out that it sits uneasily in a country supposedly noted for its 'freedom of thought and speech, for diversity and dissent'. In his view and that of many other committed civil libertarians, what was being done in the name of preserving the American way of life was actually posing a threat to traditional values, and to accepted ideals of fairness, justice and individual liberty. The case was well expressed in a news release of the American Civil Liberties Union (ACLU):[11]

> Whilst we at ACLU feel as strongly as anyone that the perpetrators of these monstrous crimes [i.e. the September 11th attacks] must be brought to justice, we also feel that America's freedom – the very essence of our national character – must be protected as we respond to the threat of terrorism within our border. Americans can be safe and free. Unfortunately, the government has implemented measures that go light years beyond anything necessary to combat terrorism … if this country proceeds to sacrifice its values and liberty in this manner, justice will be elusive and America's moral victory will be far from assured.

Democracy is sustained by public scepticism, and it is essential that people are allowed to challenge and express dissent. At the same time, a democracy under attack must have the means for its own defence. Getting the balance right between security and liberty is one of the most difficult tasks for any government at a time of national danger.

FUTURE POSSIBILITIES

We have examined some of the problems associated with the operation of democracy in the late twentieth century. Some fears may be over-stated, and different writers and politicians have their own particular misgivings and complaints. There is general agreement among many of them that all is not currently well with the body politic, and that American democracy is today under strain.

As to the future, new forms of democratic involvement have become a possibility with the development of media technology. The scope for the use of e-mail as a means of transmitting opinions and exerting pressure on those in office is enormous. Such technology empowers voters, and provides new means for them to be more actively involved in political dialogue. It opens up the possibility that they will be able to pass information to one another, so that the overall level of knowledge of the American citizenry will be increased. Voters might wish to use these developments to their advantage, and those elected to public office will need to be more conscious of those whose vote placed them there. This does not mean that they have to be subservient to public pressure but certainly their performances will be more effectively monitored.

In the longer term, another possible development is that the computer literate might conduct some form of referendum on the net, giving many people a greater opportunity to participate in the political process than ever before. There may be dangers in 'electronic populism' and 'mobocracy', but for others such as Kevin Kelly[12] 'the Internet revives Thomas Jefferson's 200-year-old dream of thinking individuals self-actualising a democracy'.

In Britain, the system of interactive communications is relatively in its infancy as far as many people are concerned. But as the network of users of information technology is extended over the coming years, British voters too will have more scope to state their problems and express their views to their elected representatives. MPs and Congressmen will need to listen carefully to public demands, but of course they need to remember that those who use the Internet are not representative of the whole electorate. Any elected member must appreciate that it is inevitably a segment of the population which has the facility to play an interactive role in both democracies. They are elected to their respective legislatures to represent the whole constituency, not just those who possess an electronic voice.

REFERENCES

1 K. Dolbeare, *Political Issues in America today: 1990s Revisited*, Manchester University Press, 1999.
2 'Democracy and Why Bother Americans', *International Herald Tribune*, 7 July 1990.
3 F. Piven and R. Cloward, *Why Americans Don't Vote*, Pantheon Books, 1988.
4 M. McLuhan, *Understanding Media*, McGraw-Hill, 1964.
5 L. Rees, *Selling Politics*, BBC Books, 1992.
6 L. Cannon, *President Reagan – the Role of a Lifetime*, Simon and Schuster, 1991.
7 N. Postman, *Amusing Ourselves to Death*, Viking Penguin, 1985.
8 L. Rees, *Selling Politics*, BBC Books, 1992.
9 Editorial, New York Times, 10 November 2001.
10 G. Monbiot, *The Guardian*, 16 October 2001.
11 ACLU Press Release, 14 December 2001.
12 K. Kelly, *Wired* Magazine, quoted in *The Guardian*, 22 February 1995.

SAMPLE QUESTIONS

1 Examine the condition of American democracy today.

2 'A flawed democracy'. Discuss this verdict on the American political system.

3 'Democratic in theory, but less impressive in practice'. Discuss the fairness of this assessment of the operation of the political system on either side of the Atlantic.

Index